Lawrence Shulman
Andrew Safyer
Editors

Supervision in Counseling: Interdisciplinary Issues and Research

Supervision in Counseling: Interdisciplinary Issues and Research has been co-published simultaneously as *The Clinical Supervisor*, Volume 24, Numbers 1/2 2005.

Pre-publication REVIEWS, COMMENTARIES, EVALUATIONS . . .

"Shulman and Safyer have produced A VALUABLE COMPILATION of research and practice issues specific to the evolving art and science of supervision among several allied mental health disciplines. This compendium MAKES AN IMPORTANT CONTRIBUTION for those concerned with insuring the accountability and effectiveness of mental health service delivery. The reader is led to examine what the essential ingredients of productive supervision are among various professional disciplines that often work together on multidisciplinary teams in agencies, clinics, hospitals and schools."

John R. Sougstad, EdS, CSP, LMSW, LMFT
Coordinator of the Certificate Program in School of Social Work
Michigan State University

More pre-publication
REVIEWS, COMMENTARIES, EVALUATIONS . . .

"WELL RESEARCHED AND SCHOLARLY in scope, *Supervision in Counseling*, because of its interdisciplinary focus, makes a unique contribution to the growing professional literature on clinical supervision. This book is A WELCOME AND MUCH NEEDED EVIDENCE-BASED RESOURCE that clinicians involved in any aspect clinical supervision will return to again and again to further their understanding of the supervision process as it affects varied clinical settings. It CONTAINS ESSENTIAL INFORMATION AND GUIDANCE for clinicians on critical aspects of clinical supervision and boldly tackles often neglected yet relevant issues such as culture, personal and professional limitations, knotty ethical dilemmas and legalities. It is rare to read a book these days in which each chapter is so vital, uncompromisingly honest, and chock-full-of pearls. One can only applaud Shulman and Safyer's immense contribution to the field–this book is A MUST HAVE for the library and the desk."

Derek H. Suite, MD, MS
Medical Director &
Supervising Psychiatrist,
Full Circle Health, PLLC

The Haworth Press, Inc.

Supervision in Counseling: Interdisciplinary Issues and Research

Supervision in Counseling: Interdisciplinary Issues and Research has been co-published simultaneously as *The Clinical Supervisor*, Volume 24, Numbers 1/2 2005.

Monographic Separates from *The Clinical Supervisor*™

For additional information on these and other Haworth Press titles, including descriptions, tables of contents, reviews, and prices, use the QuickSearch catalog at http://www.HaworthPress.com.

Supervision in Counseling: Interdisciplinary Issues and Research, edited by Lawrence Shulman, and Andrew Safyer (Vol. 24, No. 1/2, 2005). Supervision in Counseling *presents current interdisciplinary research findings on the core elements of clinical supervision in social work, psychology, counseling and counselor education, nursing, and school psychology.*

Field Instruction in Social Work Settings, edited by Toba Schwaber Kerson, DSW, PhD (Vol. 12, No. 1, 1995). *"Presents a framework for teaching field instruction in various social work settings. For social work field instructors and students." (Reference & Research Book News)*

Psychotherapy Training: Contextual and Developmental Influences in Settings, Stages, and Mind Sets, edited by Thomas H. Peake, PhD, and J. D. Ball, PhD (Vol. 9, No. 1, 1991). *"Explores the neglected important issues of context and developmental stages of the training therapist in modifying technique. . . . Learning to adapt to rapidly changing contexts is the name of the game. Here are a few pointers for survival." (British Journal of Psychiatry)*

Empirical Studies in Field Instruction, edited by Miriam S. Raskin (Vol. 6, No. 3/4, 1989). *"Moves the study of field instruction to a new level . . . Every field education director or coordinator should become familiar with these research reports and consider the questions they raise when planning student replacements." (Journal of Teaching in Social Work)*

Supervision and Training: Models, Dilemmas, and Challenges, edited by Florence W. Kaslow, PhD (Vol. 4, No. 1/2, 1986). *"The volume succeeds admirably in realizing the editor's intention of presenting a multiplicity of variable models, and her summary chapter draws common threads together into a patchwork of issues and themes." (Journal of Family Psychology)*

Clinical Training in Psychotherapy, edited by Tom H. Peake, PhD, and Robert P. Archer (Vol. 2, No. 4, 1985). *The basic resource for all professionals in clinical training; this book highlights relevant research and historical trends in training.*

Family of Origin Applications in Clinical Supervision, edited by Carlton E. Munson, PhD (Vol. 2, No. 2, 1984). *"Unique applications with accompanying rationale and case examples. . . . Adds credibility and direction to the notion of applying family-of-origin concepts in clinical supervision." (Journal of Marital and Family Therapy)*

Supervising Student Internships in Human Services, edited by Carlton E. Munson, PhD (Vol. 2, No. 1, 1984). *Fully demonstrates the supervisor's role as a source of guidance, support, and inspiration for the student intern in human services.*

Supervision in Counseling: Interdisciplinary Issues and Research

Lawrence Shulman
Andrew Safyer
Editors

Supervision in Counseling: Interdisciplinary Issues and Research has been co-published simultaneously as *The Clinical Supervisor*, Volume 24, Numbers 1/2 2005.

The Haworth Press, Inc.
New York • London • Victoria (AU)
www.HaworthPress.com

Supervision in Counseling: Interdisciplinary Issues and Research has been co-published simultaneously as *The Clinical Supervisor*, Volume 24, Numbers 1/2 2005.

Cover design by Kerry E. Mack

Library of Congress Cataloging-in-Publication Data

Supervision in counseling : interdisciplinary issues and research /Lawrence Shulman, Andrew Safyer, editors.

p. cm.

"Co-published simultaneously as The Clinical Supervisor, Volume 24, numbers 1/2 2006."

Includes bibliographical references and index.

ISBN-13: 978-0-7890-3480-9 (hard cover : alk. paper)

ISBN-10: 0-7890-3480-8 (hard cover : alk. paper)

ISBN13: 978-0-7890-3481-6 (soft cover : alk. paper)

ISBN-10: 0-7890-3481-6 (soft cover : alk. paper)

1. Counselors–Supervision of. I. Shulman, Lawrence. II. Safyer, Andrew.

BF637.C6S875 2006

158′.3–dc22 2006019552

Indexing, Abstracting & Website/Internet Coverage

This section provides you with a list of major indexing & abstracting services and other tools for bibliographic access. That is to say, each service began covering this periodical during the year noted in the right column. Most Websites which are listed below have indicated that they will either post, disseminate, compile, archive, cite or alert their own Website users with research-based content from this work. (This list is as current as the copyright date of this publication.)

Abstracting, Website/Indexing Coverage . . . . Year When Coverage Began

- ***Cambridge Scientific Abstracts (A leading publisher of scientific information in print journals, online databases, CD-ROM and via the Internet.) <http://www.csa.com>*** **2006**
- ***EBSCOhost Electronic Journals Service (EJS) <http://ejournals.ebsco.com>*** **2001**
- ***Elsevier Eflow-I*** **2006**
- ***Elsevier Scopus <http://www.info.scopus.com>*** **2005**
- ***Family & Society Studies Worldwide (NISC) <http://www.nisc.com>*** **1996**
- ***Family Index Database <http://www.familyscholar.com>*** **2004**
- ***Google <http://www.google.com>*** **2004**
- ***Google Scholar <http://www.scholar.google.com>*** **2004**
- ***Haworth Document Delivery Center <http://www.HaworthPress.com/journals/dds.asp>*** **2004**
- ***Human Resources Abstracts (HRA)*** **2003**

(continued)

- *Index Guide to College Journals (core list compiled by integrating 48 indexes frequently used to support undergraduate programs in small to medium sized libraries)* **1999**
- *Journal of Social Work Practice "Abstracts Section" <http://www.carfax.co.uk/jsw-ad.htm>* **2000**
- *Links@Ovid (via CrossRef targeted DOI links) <http://www.ovid.com>* **2005**
- *OCLC ArticleFirst <http://www.oclc.org/services/databases/>* **2003**
- *OCLC ContentsFirst <http://www.oclc.org/services/databases/>* . . **2003**
- *Ovid Linksolver (OpenURL Link Solver via CrossRef targeted DOI links) <http://www.linksolver.com>* **2005**
- *Psychological Abstracts (PsycINFO) <http://www.apa.org>* **1983**
- *Scopus (See instead Elsevier Scopus) <http://www.info.scopus.com>* **2005**
- *Social Care Online (formerly CareData) <http://www.elsc.org/uk/caredata/caredata.htm>* **1984**
- *Social Services Abstracts (Cambridge Scientific Abstracts) <http://www.csa.com>* **1990**
- *Social Work Abstracts (NASW) <http://www.silverplatter.com/catalog/swab.htm>* **1989**
- *Social Work Access Network (SWAN) <http://cosw.sc.edu/swan/media.html>* **2005**
- *SocIndex (EBSCO)* **2003**
- *Sociological Abstracts (Cambridge Scientific Abstracts) <http://www.csa.com>* **1991**
- *SwetsWise <http://www.swets.com>* **2001**
- *Ulrich's Periodicals Directory: International Periodicals Information Since 1932 (Bibliographic Access) <http://www.Bowkerlink.com>* **2006**
- *Violence and Abuse Abstracts (Sage)* **1995**

(continued)

Special Bibliographic Notes related to special journal issues (separates) and indexing/abstracting:

- indexing/abstracting services in this list will also cover material in any "separate" that is co-published simultaneously with Haworth's special thematic journal issue or DocuSerial. Indexing/abstracting usually covers material at the article/chapter level.
- monographic co-editions are intended for either non-subscribers or libraries which intend to purchase a second copy for their circulating collections.
- monographic co-editions are reported to all jobbers/wholesalers/approval plans. The source journal is listed as the "series" to assist the prevention of duplicate purchasing in the same manner utilized for books-in-series.
- to facilitate user/access services all indexing/abstracting services are encouraged to utilize the co-indexing entry note indicated at the bottom of the first page of each article/chapter/contribution.
- this is intended to assist a library user of any reference tool (whether print, electronic, online, or CD-ROM) to locate the monographic version if the library has purchased this version but not a subscription to the source journal.
- individual articles/chapters in any Haworth publication are also available through the Haworth Document Delivery Service (HDDS).

Supervision in Counseling: Interdisciplinary Issues and Research

CONTENTS

ABOUT THE EDITORS

Lawrence Shulman, MSW, EdD, has been a social work practice educator for over thirty years. He has done extensive research on the core helping skills in social work practice, supervision, and child welfare. He has published numerous articles and monographs on direct practice and is the author or co-editor of seven books. These include: *The Skills of Helping Individuals, Families, Groups and Committees*, 4th Edition, 1999, F. E. Peacock, Publisher and *Teaching the Helping Skills–A Field Instructor's Guide*, 2nd Edition, 1993, Council on Social Work Education.

Dr. Shulman was the author of the entry on consultation and supervision in the most recent edition of the Social Work Encyclopedia (National Association of Social Workers Press). He has also authored a book entitled *Interactional Supervision*, published in 1993 by the National Association of Social Workers Press. Dr. Shulman also co-authored a book on supervision and management for school principals.

Andrew Safyer, MSW, PhD, has been a clinical researcher and practitioner for twenty-five years. He obtained his doctorate in social work and psychology from the University of Michigan. His clinical practice and supervisory experience has primarily focused on psychotherapy with individuals and families. Dr. Safyer has also authored a range of articles and chapters in the clinical and mental health arena. His research area is high risk early adolescents and their families and has been engaged in testing the usefulness of an array of prevention programs with the aim of facilitating healthy development. His present interests also include leadership development and succession planning as it pertains to nonprofit organizations.

ALL HAWORTH BOOKS AND JOURNALS
ARE PRINTED ON CERTIFIED
ACID-FREE PAPER

Introduction

Lawrence Shulman
Andrew Safyer

In the fall of 2004 an interdisciplinary group of leaders in the field of clinical supervision research came together at the University at Buffalo for a two-day meeting to plan for the first international and interdisciplinary conference to be held in June of 2005. The conference was funded by a grant from the National Institute of Drug Abuse (NIDA) and was designed to bring together practitioners, educators and researchers to critically examine the current state of knowledge in this area and to make suggestions regarding future research directions. Increasingly, National Institute of Health (NIH) funding agencies have recognized that clinical supervision is a critical element in the transfer of research findings to practice in all fields of helping. While millions were spent on the development of new knowledge if it did not reach the field as best practices they would have little impact on the delivery of services.

Another rationale for the conference was the existence of a form of tunnel vision within disciplines and settings with little opportunity for cross-disciplinary communications that could identify research finding on the core elements of all effective clinical supervision as well as those that focused on the variant elements introduced by discipline (social work, psychology, school counseling, etc.) or setting. Researchers tended to present at their own conferences rather than having an opportunity to engage in discourse across disciplines. This new conference was designed to be a forum where that could happen. It would also be an op-

[Haworth co-indexing entry note]: "Introduction." Shulman, Lawrence, and Andrew Safyer. Co-published simultaneously in *The Clinical Supervisor* (The Haworth Press, Inc.) Vol. 24, No. 1/2, 2005, pp. 1-2; and: *Supervision in Counseling: Interdisciplinary Issues and Research* (ed: Lawrence Shulman, and Andrew Safyer) The Haworth Press, Inc., 2005, pp. 1-2. Single or multiple copies of this article are available for a fee from The Haworth Document Delivery Service [1-800-HAWORTH, 9:00 a.m. - 5:00 p.m. (EST). E-mail address: docdelivery@haworthpress.com].

Available online at http://cs.haworthpress.com

doi:10.1300/J001v24n01_01

portunity to establish networks that crossed discipline so that research collaborations could be developed and implemented.

In order to start that process for the planning committee itself the two-day committee meeting included presentations by a number of members who looked to update recent findings in their own disciplines and to make suggestions regarding future research directions. In this collection, five of these presentations are included, including Marion Bogo's review of clinical supervision research in social work and a second article focusing on field practicum supervision; L. DiAnne Borders' five-year review of clinical supervision in counseling and counselor education; Rodney Goodyear's five-year review of scholarship in psychology; and Janice Jones's review of clinical supervision in nursing. While not covering all fields and disciplines these make a good starting point for updating what we know from the research about this complex process.

The work also contains three presentations from the 2005 conference. In one, Tony D. Crespi and Jennifer M.B. Dube examine challenges, considerations, ethical and legal issues in school psychology. This adds another discipline addressed in this issue to five: social work, psychology, counseling and counselor education, nursing and school psychology.

Finally, two 2005 conference plenary addresses are included. In the first, Janine M. Bernard provides a history that helps to trace the evolution of clinical supervision across disciplines. In the second, Lawrence Shulman addresses a core element of clinical supervision; the development of the supervisor-supervisee working alliance and the parallel process in supervision.

With a successful first conference in 2005, with 225 attendees and over 50 presentations, the new conference was launched. The NIDA agency is again providing funding with plans to continue to support at least three more conferences. At the time of this writing, abstracts and registrations for the 2nd International and Interdisciplinary Conference on Clinical Supervision, to be held in the first week of June of 2006, are being received daily. For more information on the conference, and future conferences, the reader can go to *www.socialwork.buffalo.edu/csconference*. As co-editors of this book we see an important link between the conferences as an opportunity to present state-of-the-art research on clinical supervision and this publication as a medium for dissemination of findings. This volume is an example of that partnership in action.

Tracing the Development of Clinical Supervision

Janine M. Bernard

SUMMARY. Major developments in clinical supervision over the last twenty-five years are reviewed and contrasted with supervision as it was understood and practiced early in its development. Recent areas of growth are divided into those that attend to the infrastructure of supervision (organizational matters, ethical and legal issues, and evaluation), variables that affect the supervision relationship (individual differences, relationship processes), and the enactment of supervision itself (models of supervision, modalities for conducting supervision). Commentary is included on all major developments. doi:10.1300/J001v24n01_02 *[Article copies available for a fee from The Haworth Document Delivery Service: 1-800-HAWORTH. E-mail address: <docdelivery@haworthpress.com> Website: <http://www.HaworthPress.com> © 2005 by The Haworth Press, Inc. All rights reserved.]*

KEYWORDS. Clinical supervision, infrastructure of supervision, history models organization

---

Janine M. Bernard, PhD, is Professor and Chair, Counseling and Human Services, Syracuse University, 259 Huntington Hall, Syracuse, NY 13244 (E-mail: Bernard@syr.edu).

This article is based upon a plenary presentation at the First International and Interdisciplinary Conference on Clinical Supervision, June 2005, Amherst, NY.

[Haworth co-indexing entry note]: "Tracing the Development of Clinical Supervision." Bernard, Janine M. Co-published simultaneously in *The Clinical Supervisor* (The Haworth Press, Inc.) Vol. 24, No. 1/2, 2005, pp. 3-21; and: *Supervision in Counseling: Interdisciplinary Issues and Research* (ed: Lawrence Shulman, and Andrew Safyer) The Haworth Press, Inc., 2005, pp. 3-21. Single or multiple copies of this article are available for a fee from The Haworth Document Delivery Service [1-800-HAWORTH, 9:00 a.m. - 5:00 p.m. (EST). E-mail address: docdelivery@haworthpress.com].

Available online at http://cs.haworthpress.com

doi:10.1300/J001v24n01_02

I'd like to begin with an appeal for empathy. I'm sure many of you have been in the situation of looking at a title you chose for a paper or a presentation and saying to yourself, "What was I thinking?" Deciding to trace the development of supervision at this point in its evolution is a little like reviewing the growth of Websites over the last 15 years. Well, not that bad, but you certainly understand my dilemma. And, of course, my qualms are exacerbated by both the fact that my audience consists of many of the people responsible for the development of clinical supervision over the last few decades, and that this conference itself continues the push toward development. And as a last disclaimer, although I attempt to keep an eye to the development of supervision in other disciplines, I am certainly most grounded in counseling and psychology. So, with your permission, I would like to alter the title of this address to something like Highlighting Particular Developments of Clinical Supervision.

Exactly 25 years ago, George Leddick and I published an article in *Counselor Education and Supervision* entitled "The History of Supervision: A Critical Review" (Leddick & Bernard, 1980). And until I started to prepare for this plenary, I don't think I had gone back to read that article. But I thought doing so would be fun to see where we were then, where we've come since then, and comment, to the extent I am able, on some of the key developments of clinical supervision.

In 1980, it was still relatively simple to review everything that was in the professional literature on the topic of clinical supervision, especially if you ignored social work, which at the time we did. [For an exemplary review of the history of social work supervision, I recommend Munson (1993).] So, let me begin with a brief review of where we were then and use that as the springboard for where we've come since then.

Leddick and I asserted that supervision as we knew it in 1980 had begun in earnest in the mid to late 1920s within the practice of psychoanalysis. (This timing, I have since learned, is not that different from the inception of supervision as a topic within social work.) By the late 1950s, Eckstein and Wallerstein had published their classic text (Eckstein & Wallerstein, 1958) in which they described the process of supervision using the analogy of a chess game, that is, having an opening, a mid-game, and an end game. Eckstein and Wallerstein described the opening phase of supervision as a period of assessment where both supervisor and supervisee were sizing up the other in terms of strengths and vulnerabilities. The mid-game was characterized as a time of interpersonal conflict that included attacking, defending, probing, or avoiding. This stage of obvious conflict was also viewed as the working stage of supervision. (While we presently view harmful or conflictual supervision as an anomaly of supervision, Eckstein and Wallerstein apparently saw conflict as normative, most likely because they were focused on supervision relationships that were relatively long-term.) Finally, these authors viewed the end game of supervision as characterized by the more silent supervisor who supports a more independent supervisee. With this last stage, Ekstein and Wallerstein reflect what Stoltenberg (1981) later referred to as the conditionally autonomous supervisee working within an environment that is low on structure, high on influence, and predicated on supervisor competence as a therapist.

While psychodynamic theory was *directly* addressing supervision as early as the 1950's, client-centered theorists and behavioral theorists were addressing supervision more *indirectly*. By that I mean that Rogers (1957), Krumboltz (1966), and Lazarus (1968), to name a few, had not truly articulated a supervision process separate from their therapies. Modeling was the intervention of choice as these masters apprenticed new therapists. Because each of these therapies was predicated on assumptions different from other therapies, supervision practices that grew out of them seemingly had few functional similarities.

By the late 1960s and early 1970s, Truax and Carkhuff (1967) were making inroads into client-centered thinking and attempts were made to codify empathy. The work of Ivey and his associates (Hackney, 1971; Ivey, 1971; Ivey, Normington, Miller, Morrill, & Haase, 1968) to break down process behaviors led eventually to "training" as we now know it and instruction was firmly added to modeling for skills development. In hindsight, it could be speculated that as important as training models were to the development of psychotherapy competence, they may have stalled supervision development because of their focus on microskills and their relative inattention to what we would refer to as the supervisory relationship. Having said this, it is important to acknowledge the contribution of Mueller and Kell in 1972. These authors had sensibilities that were quite integrative. They addressed trainee vulnerability and defensiveness in a way that reflected psychodynamic thinking; they proposed that supervisors offer facilitative conditions to address supervisee defensiveness; and they spoke of supervisee goals for learning that reflected comfort with behavioral terminology. Still, at this point in the history of psychology and counseling, supervision was clearly embedded within theories of psychotherapy.

While Norm Kagan's work has been occasionally elevated to a model or demoted to a technique, it seems to me that when Interpersonal Process Recall was introduced as something around which supervision could be organized (Kagan, 1976; Kagan & Krathwohl, 1967), the hold of psychotherapy theory to dictate supervision was relaxed, never to reclaim total dominance. Or perhaps we were all getting to the same point in our thinking about the supervision process and Kagan was riding the same wave as the rest of us. Certainly Simon's classic description of the origins of live supervision in the late 1960s must be viewed in this context (Simon, 1982). Whatever the impetus, by the late 1970s and early 1980s, models were being developed that specifically addressed supervision. Stoltenberg's (1981) developmental model and my Discrimination Model (Bernard, 1979) are such examples. Hess's 1980 edited text in psychotherapy supervision (Hess, 1980) simultaneously redefined supervision, it seems to me, by including discourse on legal issues in clinical supervision, and racial, ethnic, and social class considerations in supervision. While Hess's text still emphasized psychotherapy models of supervision, it also gave considerable emphasis to relationship variables. Especially for psychology and counseling, I don't think it's an overstatement to say that the Hess text became a template for books that followed, continuing to the present (e.g., Bernard & Goodyear, 2004; Bradley & Ladany, 2000; Falender & Shafranske, 2004; Munson, 2002).

I'd like to end this trip down memory lane by underscoring some omissions that Leddick and I noted in our 1980 review:

- While supervisor roles were being discussed, there was very little discussion of technique or competencies;
- Any specific focus on differences between supervisors and supervisees was lacking (e.g., learning styles, personalities, theoretical differences);
- Reference to systematic evaluation of supervisees were minimal (I should note that the exception to this was the work of Kadushin who included a chapter on evaluation in the 1976 edition of his text on supervision in social work [Kadushin, 1976].);
- Reference to delivering feedback in a manner that was developmentally appropriate or that took into account supervisee characteristics was lacking;
- There was no discussion of training supervisors;

- There was no discussion of evaluating supervisors;
- Finally, there was no discussion drawing from educational specialists to help us conceptualize supervision.

In summary, then, and with full knowledge that I am most assuredly missing some essential contributions, in 1980 we were just beginning to break away from a view of clinical supervision that was organized around psychotherapy theory. Because of the previous dominance of psychodynamic influences within supervision literature, we were still focused primarily on intrapersonal differences between supervisor and supervisee and viewed relationship variables mostly within those limits. At that time, we simply were not entertaining the notion, for example, that a concrete sequential supervisee might find the direction of an abstract random supervisor to be frustrating. Those kinds of individual differences as the focus of supervision were simply below our radar in 1980. With the exception of marriage and family therapy, which developed standards for supervisors in the early 1970s (Falvey, 2002), we were not doing much at the time to professionalize supervision. Ethical codes specific to supervision were non-existent. And implications of the Tarasoff case (*Tarasoff vs. California Board of Regents*, 1974) were just beginning to infiltrate our awareness. To underscore the fact that this was a different time, may I add that in 1980 attachments were feelings between people, not manuscripts that arrived on your desktop. For that matter, your desktop was the top of your desk in 1980 (something seen by some and not by others). It was a fundamentally different time. Or was it? Perhaps looking at some developments over the past 25 years will help us decide.

I have arrived at the more difficult, if not impossible, aspect of the task I gave myself, which is to recognize some of the most striking developments in supervision over the last 25 years. In the first edition of our text (Bernard & Goodyear, 1992) Rod Goodyear and I commented that, in 1992, clinical supervision was still in its adolescence growing energetically and randomly as adolescents do. Between 1992 and 2004 (i.e., the first and third editions of our text) the field simply exploded, as reflected in part by the number of filing cabinet drawers I now devote to supervision reprints. Suffice to say that the interest in clinical supervision has been vigorous over the last quarter century producing a good amount of research, new approaches to the various tasks of supervision, and significant contributions that I would place under the heading of professionalizing supervision. For my remaining time, I would like to offer a conceptual map of the contributing factors that make up clinical supervision as I understand it (see Figure 1), and offer some comments about some of the main thrusts since 1980.

While preparing for a workshop a couple of years ago, I developed this figure in an attempt to deconstruct some of the contributing elements to supervision. While I believe most of us think of the "doing" of supervision when we refer to the term, my figure is an attempt to underscore the importance of a structure to support the activity of supervision, as well as to highlight relationship dynamics in their various forms as also influencing the central activity of delivering supervision. Using Figure 1 as an outline, I'd like to try to track and comment upon (a) advances we have made in professionalizing supervision, specifically in the areas of organizing supervision and in our understanding of the ethical and legal parameters of supervision; (b) the ever growing and deepening literature around individual differences and relationship processes that influence supervision; (c) advances in our thinking regarding models of supervision; and (d) advances in modalities used by supervisors. But first, I'd like to offer a metaphor that may help you to understand the contributing elements of supervision as I do.

If conducting supervision is anything like conducting music, the infrastructure is the stuff without which the performance appears unchoreographed. The infrastructure gives each musician the same sheet

FIGURE 1. Supervision Survey

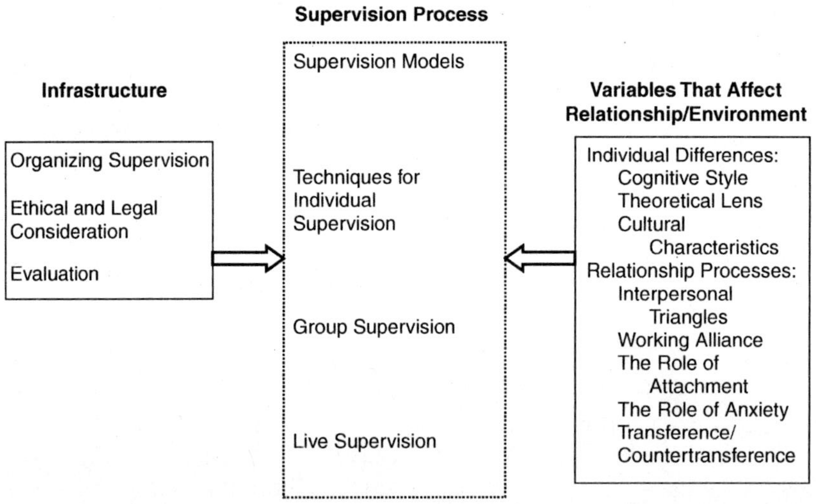

of music; it provides instruments to play and an adequate sound system; it organizes sections if it's a symphony or lowers the lights if it's jazz. In other words, infrastructure enhances the talent of the musicians rather than frustrating that talent. Occasionally, brilliance can break through an inadequate infrastructure, but most musicians will be pulled down by potent inadequacies.

Individual differences and relationship processes determine the quality of the music. Are all the musicians in sync? Have they taken the time to tune their instruments? Are they all on the same page? Do they come to the performance with a feel for the music? Or are they mechanical in their approach? Are they experienced at this process and comfortable performing? Or are they in disharmony with themselves or with the task at hand? In short, most of the intangibles that distinguish a good performance from a bad one fall in this category.

The process of supervision is the type of music we will be hearing. It may be a sweet symphony or a dark and heavy dirge; it may be the predictability of a Souza march or the unpredictability of jazz. In supervision we call the type of music models or modalities. Despite the genre of music, however, it is strongly influenced by infrastructure and relationship variables. In other words, the performance will be as good as the attention that has been paid to these seemingly extraneous conditions. Or conversely, if attention has not been paid to them, the performance will be compromised by a microphone that fails, an instrument that hasn't been tuned, or a musician with her head in another place. Furthermore, in leaving the performance, these annoying disturbances can come to define the experience of the audience (and most likely the musicians) more than the selections played.

With this metaphor in mind, I'd like to begin the update by addressing the task of organizing supervision.

ORGANIZING SUPERVISION

When I teach supervision, I always begin here. I do this for two reasons: (1) it provides some tools to help my students organize themselves before they meet their first supervisee; (2) it gets an admittedly dry subject out of the way first. This second reason is part of my rationale for addressing this topic early.

While the practice of supervision has always been organized, more or less, the professions weren't talking much about it 25 years ago. And, to be honest, unlike topics such as ethical issues in supervision and models of supervision, there is still relative silence about organizing the delivery of supervision. In Bernard and Goodyear (2004), we remarked that the personality profiles of clinical supervisors may lean in the direction of relationship variables rather than infrastructure variables. Still, the last 25 years have pushed us in this direction, albeit kicking and screaming for some.

Again, I want to note that social work supervision was tuned into infrastructure early on (Kadushin, 1976). Perhaps this is because social work supervision grew out of a pragmatic concern for what was occurring in the field. Social work supervision and fieldwork supervision were almost synonymous before 1980 and are still more symbiotic, it seems to me, than supervision as it is discussed and studied in the other mental health professions. For the rest of us, supervision has been more focused on paradigms, techniques, and relationship than structure.

The impetus for the change that has occurred, I believe, has come primarily from two places. The first of these is the use of technology in supervision. At this point, I'm not talking about newer technologies, but the movement toward using direct samples in supervision that were introduced by persons like Kagan (1976) in the form of IPR and Haley and Minuchin (Simon, 1982) in the form of live supervision. While gaining traction in the 1970s, using videotape, audiotape, and live supervision capability took off in the 1980s. In what I believe is the first comprehensive book in family therapy supervision, Liddle, Breunlin, and Schwartz (1988) devoted several chapters to what they called the pragmatics of supervision which included the types of infrastructure needed to use technology well. In summary, our increasing interest in complicating the process of supervision by the use of technological aids simultaneously required increased attentiveness to organizational matters. The more technology is central to supervision, the less spontaneous it can be.

The second driving force for tightening up infrastructure is a combination of accreditation, certification, and regulatory mandates that dictate life within academe. I trust that any of us in accredited training programs or accredited internship sites can attest to the amount of organization that is required to meet standards. We must insure that supervision is conducted by persons with particular credentials and in particular ways. We must conduct particular evaluations and use these to inform future practice. And all of this must be documented. To a lesser extent, these kinds of practices are replicated for individual needing to document post-graduate supervision, at least until one attains certification or licensure. While this represents what might be viewed as the annoying, intrusive part of accreditation and regulation, some good things have emerged as well. More supervisors use contracts to inform their supervisees of what to expect in supervision. Professional disclosure statements are fairly commonplace. In general, the context for supervision has tightened up, providing perhaps more quality control. I concede that these practices can potentially hinder creativity or at least spontaneity within supervision. Whether we have arrived at an optimal place in this matter is an unknown. While some studies have indicated that disorganized supervision is dissatisfying (Magnuson, Wilcoxon, & Norem, 2000), in general this is an area that has not attracted the researcher.

ETHICS AND LEGAL PARAMETERS

I'm sure it surprises no one, that there have been significant developments in the ethical and legal area since 1980. While AAMFT (American Association for Marriage and Family Therapy) formalized standards for training of clinical supervisors as early as 1971 and AMHCA (American Mental Health Counseling Association) did so in 1989 (Falvey, 2002), ACES (Association for Counselor Educators and Supervisors) was, I believe, the first mental health professional group to develop ethical guidelines specifically for supervisors (Supervision Interest Network, 1993). While other professions have increased in their sensitivity to supervision in their ethical codes, occasionally devoting a section to supervision, I believe counseling is still unique in having separate ethical standards for supervisors.

Interestingly, the 1993 ACES guidelines were not late relative to the attention given to supervision ethics in the mental health literature. While the 1980s gave us a few key contributions in the area of ethics and supervision (e.g., Bernard, 1987; Cormier & Bernard, 1982; Kitchener, 1988; Whiston & Emerson, 1989), it was the 1990s that represented a heightened interest in all aspects of ethical and unethical behavior. Certainly the ethical transgression of choice was that of the dual relationship, equally known as a boundary violation. We studied incidence and type of violations and filled the literature with admonitions. Pearson and Piazza (1997) classified dual relationships for us ranging from the benign, through the potentially harmful, on to the insidious, and ending with the truly sleazy. It seems that we exhausted the topic (and perhaps ourselves) in the 1990s because there hasn't been a whole lot of additional work since 2000. Yet, unlike other areas in the development of supervision, it's difficult to say if we've made much progress in our ethical behavior. The study reported by Lamb, Catanzaro, and Moorman (2003) found that 40% of those psychologists who had engaged in sexual relationships with students or supervisees were either ambivalent about their behavior or did not view their involvement as harmful to the other individual. So, it's possible that the additional attention paid to this topic in the '90s has not translated to a heightened professional superego.

As a different outcome of our collective focus on boundary violations, I became aware over the past couple of years that sensitivity to dual relationships was putting too much distance between me and my students. As a result of my understanding of the evolution of professional ethical sensibilities, I was seeing a potential troublesome encounter around every corner. I found myself pining over my early years as a counselor educator when doctoral students became friends before we hooded them. Last summer, I was fortunate to spend some quality time with a colleague of many years from another institution (now retired). I realized that she had not fallen victim to the same brand of timidity that I had, and had rich relationships with former students based on both professional and personal experiences they had shared while these persons were still students. Since that time, I have enjoyed breaking some of my over-zealous rules about boundaries and am inching back to some degree of normalcy. Therefore, as I reflected on this development in the area of clinical supervision, I considered that the results are dubious for both transgressors and nontransgressors. Still, without evidence to the contrary, I will assert that it is good that we've come this far (wherever that is) and that we have some interesting empirical work and thoughtful commentary to help us navigate ethical waters within supervision.

It wasn't until I was preparing this plenary that I realized the extent to which legal topics predated ethical topics in the supervision literature. Slovenko's (1980) chapter on legal issues in psychotherapy supervision was certainly my first education in the area. While Slovenko leaned heavily on opinions gleaned from therapy and translated these to supervision, the Tarasoff (1974) case had caught the attention of therapists and supervisors alike. Tarasoff was (and still is) for supervision what Miranda is for law enforcement. The word itself gets one's mental wheels turning. Since then, relatively few cases have emerged in the courts that address supervisors directly or even indirectly. (Falvey [2002] identified 12 such cases.) Still, in light of our generalized litigious nature as a country, legal implications of supervision are here to stay.

EVALUATION

I would posit that some of the ways that supervision has been formalized have been key to establishing a clearer context for evaluation. While there certainly has been progress in the area of evaluation, I want to highlight one development that is situated in the area of evaluation but has ethical and legal implications, and that is our relatively new focus on the supervisees with problematic behaviors (e.g., Forrest, Elman, Gizara, & Vacha-Haase, 1999). (While the mental health professions have drifted toward the use of the term "impaired supervisee," Falender, Collins, and Schafranske [2005] admonished that use of the term is only advisable within the parameters of the Americans With Disabilities Act.) We've always had problematic supervisees and they've always worried us, but the last 5 to 10 years have found us more deliberate in our confrontation of the problem. It makes sense that the professionalization of supervision has made us more transparent and, therefore, more vulnerable when supervisees with serious issues are sanctioned to become members of the mental health delivery system. And this is as it should be. I acknowledge that, for supervisors, supervisees with significant problematic behaviors are sure sleep busters; yet, the thoughtful work of persons like Forrest and her colleagues has been both challenging and consoling in the way that one is always in a more peaceful space after one has confronted one's demons. Certainly, my circle of close colleagues have put new energy into early identification of troubled trainees and we come to the task of confronting the problem of these supervisees with knowledge of potential pitfalls that our predecessors were lacking.

INDIVIDUAL DIFFERENCES AND RELATIONAL THEMES

I would now like to move to the opposite wing of my figure and address topics that fall under the umbrella of relationship variables. While the development of our understanding of individual differences and our ongoing investigations of the interpersonal dynamics within supervision both fall under this umbrella, they need to be separated because their histories are so different. Let me begin with individual differences.

Individual Differences. If I may, I'd like to stereotype the thinking 25 years ago in order to draw a contrast to our thinking today. In general (though there were certainly exceptions including both Gardner's [1980] and Bodsky's [1980] contributions), individual differences were viewed as differences in intrapsychic health across supervisees. Supervision, then, more closely mirrored therapy by identifying a deficit in the supervisee and attempting to rectify the deficit through supervision. Theoretical differences were also acknowledged and the solution here was to screen supervisees for theoretical fit or, if that wasn't possible, to ignore differences in theory because the supervisor always won anyway! My point is that individual differences were primarily conceptualized as the supervisee's problem. The profile of the supervisor was seemingly unquestioned. Like the Wizard of Oz, the supervisor hid behind, and was sometimes puffed up by, his (sic) authority.

Perhaps in this area more than any other, we have enjoyed a true paradigm shift in the past quarter century. While some individual differences are still perceived as a "problem," they are more often viewed as differences to be accessed, honored and accommodated, but not to be eliminated. Constantine (2005) reviewed the major contributions that have assisted supervisors in addressing cultural differences within supervision. She also noted the gap between our present accomplishments and any right we may eventually have in claiming multicultural competence within supervision. Our interest in cultural differences and their effect on therapy and supervision has been a hallmark of the last 25 years and shows no sign of waning. To date, it's interesting to note that our efforts within supervision have been found to be too timid . . . or too arrogant . . . certainly too ignorant . . . and often (sadly) irrelevant. We've had some false starts to be sure but with the kind of research suggested by Constantine, the next 25 years will certainly help us find more productive avenues to accessing and engaging culture within supervision.

Other individual differences have also attracted increasing attention since 1980, including some that reflect personality and others that reflect cognitive style, cognitive complexity and so forth. It seems to me that our focus in these areas is a statement that supervision has reached a point where there is an agreed upon base upon which to function (whether that's theoretical, practical, or professional) and we are now able to pay attention to mediator and moderator effects, thus indicating a turning point in our collective research agenda. Because of the endless possibilities in this regard, as well as our modest gains thus far, this is an area that will most certainly continue to draw our attention.

Relationship Processes. Interestingly, this is perhaps the one area in which "where we were then," and "where we are now" is not all that different. It's not that we haven't refined our understandings of concepts like the working alliance, power, resistance, attachment, parallel process, countertransference and so on within supervision because we have (haven't we?). But when it comes to the relationship between supervisor and supervisee, we were in our element from the beginning and we are drawn back to the relationship womb whenever we get tired of evaluation forms, supervision contracts, and the videorecorder that just stopped working. The literature on relationship processes within supervision was rich in 1980; it's richer still today.

What is new in the more current literature is its fusion with the individual differences literature . . . and that really is very different from where we were in 1980. A nice example of this is the new text by Ladany, Friedlander, and Nelson (2005) where the authors study interpersonal conflicts and crises drawing from an awareness of individual differences as well as old standbys like countertransference.

In summary, the broad area of relationship variables is the hardest area to comment on because of its vastness, its breadth, and the relative youth of supervision literature in general. Relationship factors continue to be where the action is, literally. Everything else revolves around it. That was true 25 years ago and it's true today.

MODEL DEVELOPMENT

As I stated earlier, in 1980, psychotherapy-derived models of supervision were still dominant. We were truly at a crossroad in this regard. In the early '80s, the field of supervision would turn its attention to developmental models (Stoltenberg, 1981; Loganbill, Hardy, & Delworth, 1982; Littrell, Lee-Borden, & Lorenz, 1979) and what Bernard and Goodyear (2004) refer to as social role models and Falender and Shafranske (2005) refer to as process-based models. My comments will focus on developmental models and then quickly move ahead to the present.

The developmental framework for working with supervisees captured the imagination and the trust of the professions in the early 1980s. The premise that we are engaged in a process that stimulates progress along some developmental continuum was and is too affirming to discard. And, even while developmental models have been criticized for their lack of empirical support (e.g., Fisher, 1989; Holloway, 1987), the basic assumptions proposed by Stoltenberg, Delworth, Littrell, and others are fundamentally embedded in our consciousness as supervisors. Better research is still needed surely. We'll get better at figuring out how to measure developmental milestones and the conditions related to these. Because if the developmental proposition is fundamentally flawed, then supervision is reduced to case management and gatekeeping. I prefer to maintain my faith in the developmental paradigm even if its principal contribution remains intuitive. To that extent, it's comforting to remember that it is in good company!

Since the explosion of the early 1980s, model development in supervision has been relatively low-key. In the last 25 years, the professions have been more engaged in model refinement, model exploration, and limited model testing (Castle, 2004). Constructivist theory has found its way into supervision (e.g., Bob, 1999), including solution-focused approaches (Rita, 1998; Triantafillou, 1997). Time-honored psychotherapies, such as psychoanalysis and cognitive-behaviorism, continue to refine their approaches to supervision. But all in all, model building has not driven the last 15 or so years of supervision discourse. What is sometimes referred to as a new model, such as feminist supervision, is really the infusion of an ideology into supervision, and therefore a transformation of existent models rather than model development per se. Similarly, the application of models to new contexts, populations, or for particular purposes has been a lively and enlightening aspect of the literature over the last 25 years.

MODALITIES/TECHNIQUES

In 1980, we had individual supervision, group supervision, and live supervision. We had the audiotape and the videotape. We had telephones. We did not have the Internet. The question is what are we doing now that we weren't doing then?

A review of the modality literature of the last five years (Smith, 2005) identified sixteen articles, nine devoted to e-technology, four discussing peer supervision, and five articles related to creative expression. I found this to accurately reflect my own thoughts about where we are in the world of modality and techniques. While individual supervision and live supervision have received modest attention of late (i.e., in relation to each as a modality), group supervision is receiving renewed attention. The need for peer supervision in work contexts that do not provide other forms of supervision is one reason for the renewal. Economy is obviously another. But I also think group supervision had been neglected in the past, especially in light of its potential (c.f., Proctor, 2000).

The Internet has also opened up new possibilities for the process of supervision. We are still somewhat caught between those who are instinctively attracted to cyberspace and those who are afraid of it on this issue. For those who prefer to live in cyberspace, the question becomes whether their major contribution is conquering geography while delivering traditional forms of supervision. (That alone has the potential of being an enormous contribution.) My guess is that, indeed, the Internet has the power to change some of the fundamentals of supervision. To date, research in this area is minimal.

Those who are cautious of the Internet and its use for supervision focus more on quite reasonable fears about confidentiality issues and the demise of the supervisory relationship if e-supervision or other forms of Internet-enhanced supervision take over. For the present, we need both of these camps to keep us honest. Certainly the next quarter century will affirm one if not both.

And finally, while much of supervision was organized around the intrapsychic in 1980, an increasing amount of supervision now seems to be addressing the right brain. Constructivism has contributed to this interest by encouraging us to consider the variety of ways by which we can understand our experience. Developmental thinkers have stressed the importance of reflectivity for therapists. One outcome has been increased interest in art (Bowman, 2003), metaphor (Sommer & Cox, 2003), sand tray work (Fall & Sutton, 2004), and play (Drisko, 2000) as useful tools broadening and deepening the supervision experience.

CONCLUSION

As I look back at the last 25 years of development in clinical supervision, I believe we have moved from "fledgling" to "robust." The numbers of books and articles on clinical supervision have increased exponentially; more voices have emerged; the discipline has been significantly enhanced by inquiry and thoughtful commentary. Simultaneously, supervision has emerged as a distinct professional activity, separate from psychotherapy, with its own ethical codes, and regulatory bodies. Yet, despite this growth and increased sophistication, despite the Internet, despite increased requirements for documentation to avoid vulnerability in an increasingly cynical environment, the core of supervision remains something Ekstein and Wallerstein (1958) understood over 45 years ago. Supervision is fundamentally a generative enterprise that enhances the supervisor only through the enhancement of the supervisee.

Everything else we can say about supervision must somehow inform this fundamental contract. Some of the growth over the last 25 years can become a distracter to this enterprise; some of our newly acquired insights, especially about the supervisory relationship, have hopefully enhanced it. But at the end of the day, supervision was, is, and will be defined by the realization of our supervisees that they understand the therapeutic process and themselves at least a tad better than when they entered supervision, and our own realization that we have been players in the professional development of another. It is as simple and as profound as this.

REFERENCES

American With Disabilities Act of 1990, 42 U.S.C.A.§ 12101 *et seq.* (West, 1993).

Bernard, J.M. (1987). Ethical and legal considerations for supervisors. In L.D. Borders, & G.R. Leddick, *Handbook of counseling supervision.* Alexandria, VA: Association for Counselor Education and Supervision, 52-57.

Bernard, J.M., & Goodyear, R.K. (1992). *Fundamentals of clinical supervision.* Boston, MA: Allyn and Bacon.

Bernard, J.M., & Goodyear, R.K. (2004). *Fundamentals of clinical supervision* (3rd ed.). Boston, MA: Allyn and Bacon.

Bernard, J.M. (1979). Supervisor training: A discrimination model. *Counselor Education and Supervision, 19* (1), 60-68.

Bob, S.R. (1999). Narrative approaches to supervision and case formulation. *Psychotherapy, 36*, 146-153.

Bowman, D.R. (2003). Do art tasks enhance the clinical supervision of counselors-in-training? Unpublished doctoral dissertation, Virginia Polytechnic Institute and State University.

Bradley, L., & Ladany, N. (2000). (Eds.) *Counselor supervision: Principles, process, and practice* (3rd ed.). Philadelphia, PA: Brunner-Routledge.

Brodsky, A.M. (1980). Sex role issues in the supervision of therapy. In A.K. Hess (Ed.). *Psychotherapy supervision: Theory, research, and practice.* New York: John Wiley and Sons, 509-522.

Castle, K.S. (2004). Supervision models: A review of the literature of 1999-2003. Unpublished manuscript, Syracuse University.

Constantine, M. (2005). *Multicultural supervision for practice with underserved populations.* Presentation at the International Interdisciplinary Conference of Clinical Supervision, Buffalo, NY.

Cormier, L.S., & Bernard, J.M. (1982). Ethical and legal responsibilities of clinical supervisors. *The Personnel and Guidance Journal, 60* (8), 486-491.

Drisko, J. W. (2000). Play in clinical learning, supervision and field advising. *The Clinical Supervisor, 19*, 153-165.

Ekstein, R., & Wallerstein, R. S. (1958). *The teaching and learning of psychotherapy*. New York: International Universities Press, Inc.

Falender, C.A., Collings, C., & Shafranske, E.P. (2005). *Impairment in psychology training*. Presentation at the International Interdisciplinary Conference of Clinical Supervision, Buffalo, NY.

Falender, C.A., & Shafranske, E.P. (2004). *Clinical supervision: A competency-based approach*. Washington, DC: American Psychological Association.

Fall, M., & Sutton, J.M., Jr. (2004). *Clinical supervision: A handbook for practitioners*. Boston, MA: Allyn and Bacon.

Falvey, J.E. (2002). *Managing clinical supervision: Ethical practice and legal risk management*. Pacific Grove, CA: Brooks/Cole.

Fisher, B. (1989). Differences between supervision of beginning and advanced therapists: Hogan's hypothesis empirically revisited. *The Clinical Supervisor, 7*(1), 57-74.

Forrest, L., Elman, N., Gizara, S., & Vacha-Haase, T. (1999). Trainee impairment: A review of identification, remediation, dismissal, and legal issues. *Counseling Psychologist, 27* (5), 627-686.

Gardner, L.H. (1980). Racial, ethnic, and social class considerations in psychotherapy supervision. In A.K. Hess (Ed.). *Psychotherapy supervision: Theory, research, and practice*. New York: John Wiley and Sons, 474-508.

Hackney, H.L. (1971). Development of a prepracticum counseling skills model. *Counselor Education and Supervision, 11*, 102-109.

Hess, A.K. (Ed.). (1980). *Psychotherapy supervision: Theory, research, and practice*. New York: John Wiley and Sons.

Holloway, E.L. (1987). Developmental models of supervision: Is it supervision? *Professional Psychology: Research and Practice, 18*, 209-216.

Ivey, A.E. (1971). *Microcounseling: Innovations in interviewing training*. Springfield, IL: Charles C. Thomas.

Ivey, A.E., Normington, C.J., Miller, D., Morrill, W.H., & Haase, R.F. (1968). Microcounseling and attending behavior: An approach to prepracticum counselor training. *Journal of Counseling Psychology, 15* (5), Part 2.

Kadushin, A. (1976). *Supervision in social work*. New York: Columbia University Press.

Kagan, N. (l976). *Influencing human interaction*. Mason, MI: Mason Media, Inc. or Washington, DC: American Association for Counseling and Development.

Kagan, N., & Krathwohl, D.R. (1967). *Studies in human interaction: Interpersonal process recall stimulated by videotape*. East Lansing, MI: Michigan State University.

Kitchener, K.S. (1988). Dual role relationships: What makes them so problematic? *Journal of Counseling and Development, 67*, 217-221.

Krumboltz, J.D. (1966) Behavioral goals for counseling. *Journal of Counselng Psychology, 13*, 153-159.

Ladany, N., Friedlander, M.L., Nelson, M.L. (2005). *Critical events in psychotherapy supervision: An interpersonal approach*. Washington, DC: American Psychological Association.

Lamb, D.H., Catanzaro, S.J., & Moorman, A.S. (2003). Psychologists reflect on their sexual relationships with clients, supervisees, and students: Occurrence, impact, rationales and collegial intervention. *Professional Psychology: Research & Practice, 34*, 102-107.

Lazarus, A.A. (1968). The content of behavior therapy training. Paper presented at the meeting of the Association for the Advancement of the Behavioral Therapies, San Francisco.

Leddick, G.R. & Bernard, J.M. (1980). The history of supervision: A critical review. *Counselor Education and Supervision, 19* (3), 186-196.

Liddle, H., Breunlin, D., & Schwartz, R. (Eds.). (1988). *Handbook of family therapy training and supervision.* New York: Guilford.

Littrell, J.M., Lee-Borden, N., & Lorenz, J.A. (1979). A developmental framework for counseling supervision. *Counselor Education and Supervision, 19*, 119-136.

Loganbill, C., Hardy, E., & Delworth, U. (1982). Supervision: A conceptual model. *The Counseling Psychologist, 10*, 3-42.

Magnuson, S., Wilcoxon, S.A., & Norem, K. (2000). A profile of lousy supervision: Experienced counselors' perspectives. *Counselor Education and Supervision, 39*, 189-202.

Mueller, W.J., & Kell, B.L. (1972). *Coping with conflict: Supervising counseling and psychotherapists.* New York: Appleton-Century-Crofts.

Munson, C. E. (1993). *Clinical social work supervision* (2nd ed.). New York: The Haworth Press, Inc.

Munson, C.E. (2002). *Handbook of clinical social work supervision* (3rd ed.). New York: The Haworth Press, Inc.

Pearson, B., & Piazza, N. (1997). Classification of dual relationships in the helping professions. *Counselor Education and Supervision, 37* (2), 89-99.

Proctor, B. (2000). *Group supervision: A guide to creative practice.* London: Sage Publications.

Rita, E. S. (1998). Solution-focused supervision. *Clinical Supervisor, 17*(2), 1998, 127-139.

Rogers, C.R. (1957). The necessary and sufficient conditions of therapeutic personality change. *Journal of Consulting Psychology, 21*, 95-103.

Simon, R. (1982). Beyond the one-way mirror. *Family Therapy Networker, 26*(5), 19, 28-29, 58-59.

Slovenko, R. (1980). Legal issues in psychotherapy supervision. In A.K. Hess (Ed.). *Psychotherapy supervision: Theory, research and practice.* New York: John Wiley & Sons, 453-473.

Smith, L.C. (2005). Supervision modalities: Recent contributions in the professional literature. Unpublished paper. Syracuse University.

Sommer, C.A., & Cox, J.A. (2003). Using Greek mythology as a metaphor to enhance supervision. *Counselor Education and Supervision, 42*, 326-335.

Stoltenberg, C. (1981) Approaching supervision from a developmental perspective: The counselor-complexity model. *Journal of Counseling Psychologists, 28*, 59-65.

Supervision Interest Network, Association for Counselor Education and Supervision. (1993, Summer). ACES ethical guidelines for counseling supervisors. *ACES Spectrum, 53*(4), 5-8.

Tarasoff v. Regents of the University of California. 118 Cal. Rptr. 129, 529 P 2d 533 (1974).

Triantafillou, N. (1997). A solution-focused approach to mental health supervision. *Journal of Systemic Therapies, 16*, 305-328.
Truax, C.B., & Carkhuff, R.R. (1967). *Toward effective counseling and psychotherapy: Training and practice*. Chicago: Aldine.
Whiston, S.C., & Emerson, S. (1989). Ethical implications for supervisors in counseling of trainees. *Counselor Education and Supervision, 28*, 318-325.

doi:10.1300/J001v24n01_02

The Clinical Supervisor-Practitioner Working Alliance: A Parallel Process

Lawrence Shulman

SUMMARY. The focus of my presentation this morning is the core dynamics and skills of the supervisor-practitioner working alliance, or what I will refer to as the working relationship. I will present a model that suggests that the use of certain communication, relationship and problem-solving skills by the supervisor can influence the development of a positive working relationship with the supervisee, and that this working relationship is the medium through which the supervisor influences the practitioner. I stress the words "influence" because a central assumption of this approach is that both supervision and direct practice are interactional in nature. The supervisor and the supervisee each play a part in the process. The outcome of supervision is the result of how well each contributes to the process. This morning's presentation focuses on the supervisor's role. One of the discussions is the concept of the "parallel process." While the role of the supervisor and the purpose of supervision are quite different from counseling and therapy, nevertheless there

Lawrence Shulman, MSW, EdD, is affiliated with the School of Social Work, University at Buffalo, NY.

This article is based upon a plenary presentation at the First International and Interdisciplinary Conference on Clinical Supervision, June 2005, University at Buffalo, Amherst, NY.

[Haworth co-indexing entry note]: "The Clinical Supervisor-Practitioner Working Alliance: A Parallel Process." Shulman, Lawrence. Co-published simultaneously in *The Clinical Supervisor* (The Haworth Press, Inc.) Vol. 24, No. 1/2, 2005, pp. 23-47; and: *Supervision in Counseling: Interdisciplinary Issues and Research* (ed: Lawrence Shulman, and Andrew Safyer) The Haworth Press, Inc., 2005, pp. 23-47. Single or multiple copies of this article are available for a fee from The Haworth Document Delivery Service [1-800-HAWORTH, 9:00 a.m. - 5:00 p.m. (EST). E-mail address: docdelivery@haworthpress.com].

Available online at http://cs.haworthpress.com

doi:10.1300/J001v24n01_03

are striking parallels in the dynamics and skills. There is a suggestion that "more is caught than taught" and that our supervisees watch us very closely. Whether we like it or not, whether we are aware of it or not, our supervisees learn more about practice from the way we work with them than from what we say about their actual practice. Supervision is not therapy. In fact, supervisors who are seduced into a therapeutic relationship with their supervisees actually model poor practice since they lose sight of the true purpose of clinical supervision and their role in the process. doi:10.1300/J001v24n01_03 *[Article copies available for a fee from The Haworth Document Delivery Service: 1-800-HAWORTH. E-mail address: <docdelivery@haworthpress.com> Website: <http://www.HaworthPress.com>*

KEYWORDS. Clinical supervision, parallel process, supervising, supervisors role, supervision outcome

INTRODUCTION

The focus of my presentation this morning is the core dynamics and skills of the supervisor-practitioner working alliance, or what I will refer to as the working relationship. I will present a model that suggests that the use of certain communication, relationship and problem-solving skills by the supervisor can influence the development of a positive working relationship with the supervisee, and that this working relationship is the medium through which the supervisor influences the practitioner. I stress the words "influence" because a central assumption of this approach is that both supervision and direct practice are interactional in nature. The supervisor and the supervisee each play a part in the process. The outcome of supervision is the result of how well each contributes to the process. This morning's presentation focuses on the supervisor's role.

Another theme of the presentation is the concept of the "parallel process." While the role of the supervisor and the purpose of supervision are quite different from counseling and therapy, nevertheless there are striking parallels in the dynamics and skills. I will be suggesting that "more is caught than taught" and that our supervisees watch us very closely. Whether we like it or not, whether we are aware of it or not, our supervisees learn more about practice from the way we work with them than from what we say about their actual practice. I want to emphasize that supervision is not therapy. In fact, supervisors who are seduced into a therapeutic relationship with their supervisees actually model poor practice since they lose sight of the true purpose of clinical supervision and their role in the process.

UNDERLYING ASSUMPTIONS

There are a number of assumptions underlying this morning's presentation. First, I believe there is a core to the supervision process that is central to all helping relationships. This core consists of the dynamics and skills that make up the "constant" elements of any form of helping. The working relationship, often referred to as the therapeutic alliance in practice, is the medium through which help is offered. The development of this relationship begins in the first session and continues to evolve throughout the counseling or supervision process. My definition of the term "working relationship" has emerged from my research on practice and supervision. The variables I have used to define the working relationship between practitioner and client, supervisor and practitioner, and doctor and patient include *rapport*, *trust*, and *caring*. For example, in one of my child welfare studies (Shulman, 1978, 1991, 1993) parents were asked to respond to my questionnaires or in an interview, and rate the following statements:

- "I get along with my counselor" (*rapport*).
- "I can say anything on my mind." "I can risk my failures as well as my successes" (*trust*).
- "My counselor cares as much about me as she/he cares about my children." "My counselor is trying to help me, not just investigate me" (*caring*).

In a simultaneous and parallel study (Shulman, 1991) discussed in more detail later in this presentation, the same elements were examined in practitioner/supervisor relationships. For example, one of the *caring* questions was adapted as follows: "My supervisor cares as much about me as she or he cares about my clients." One *trust* question was phrased: "I can tell my supervisor anything on my mind."

Second, there are "variant" elements of the helping process introduced by many factors. For example, in our direct practice, variables such as age, the nature of the problem, whether the client is voluntary, mandatory or semi-voluntary, and the modality of practice–individual, family or group–all may affect interactions between the person offering help and the person seeking it. In a like manner, there are variant elements that affect supervision such as the degree of authority of the supervisor and the age and experience of the supervisee.

Third, important variations are introduced by the discipline of the supervisor and the practitioner, and the setting in which the practice takes place. The work of a school psychologist in an elementary school, a nurse practitioner in a hospital, a psychotherapist in private practice or a social worker in a family counseling clinic may all appear to differ in certain ways. Their supervision may be varied as well; however, the core dynamics and skills are the same.

Finally, as I stated in the introduction, a parallel process is inherent in the supervisory relationship, meaning the way in which the clinical supervisor interacts with the supervisee models what the supervisor believes is at the core of any helping relationship. In addition, the parallel process may work at several levels as the supervisee may "act out" during the supervision process the problem he or she is experiencing in practice. A defensive supervisee, at times, may be indirectly (and unconsciously) saying to the supervisor: "Show me how to deal with a defensive client by dealing effectively with me."

During the balance of this presentation, I would like to do the following: explore the four central assumptions I've outlined above, both in direct practice and in clinical supervision; describe and illustrate the core dynamics and skills in the beginning or engagement phase of direct practice; discuss how these dynamics and skills also relate to the beginning phase in clinical supervision, highlighting the similarities in both processes and share some of my research findings in this area. I'd like to conclude with an illustration of the model with examples from clinical supervision.

THE PHASES OF WORK

The helping process in either practice or supervision is complex. Building on the work of a friend and mentor, William Schwartz (Schwartz, 1961), I have found it helpful to consider these processes against the backdrop of time.[1] Every counseling or supervisory relationship can be understood as having a preliminary, beginning, middle and ending/transition phase. Each phase, both in practice and supervision, has unique dynamics and requires some unique skills on the part of the practitioner or supervisor. For example, in the beginning or "contracting" phase, both client and supervisee must make a "first decision" as to whether or not to engage meaningfully with the helping professional. The purpose of the work and the role of the helper must be explicitly defined and the supervisee/client must see a connection to the work. Issues of authority must also be addressed, for example, evaluation in the supervisory relationship or the mandated nature of a client's participation.

The middle, or work phase, is when the work is actually accomplished. In this phase the supervisor and the practitioner must be alert to the "illusion of work," referring to the ability of both client and supervisee to appear actively involved when in fact they are dealing with surface issues or "near problems." The skill of making a "demand for work," a facilitative confrontation challenging the illusion can lead the client or supervisee to make the "second decision," that being to deal with the more difficult and often emotionally powerful issues.

Finally, the ending and transition phase anticipates the work coming to a close and the client or staff member leaving counseling or the agency, or a supervisor leaving his or her position. This phase is often marked by what is commonly referred to as "door knob therapy," when the client or staff member raises the most important issues as the work is coming to an end. This can be considered making the "third decision."

The model I have discussed will be used here to describe the life of the work in practice and clinical supervision over time, as well as a means to better understand each individual session or conference. For example, there is a preparatory, beginning, middle and ending/transition phase for each supervisory session. Let me illustrate this framework and explore the four assumptions listed earlier by considering the preliminary and beginning phases first in practice and then in supervision. I believe this will help to illustrate the parallel process most clearly.

THE PRELIMINARY AND BEGINNING PHASES IN PRACTICE

In the preliminary phase, the practitioner prepares for a first session by using a skill called "tuning in" (Shulman, 1994, 2005, 2006). Practitioners put themselves into the shoes of their new clients and develop a preliminary empathy about what their client may be thinking and feeling about the engagement. It is equally important for practitioners to tune in to their own thoughts and feelings in preparing for the encounter. This preliminary empathy can help the practitioner connect to what the client may be feeling and thinking but expressing only through indirect communications. Thus, the practitioner can be a better receiver of these communications and develop strategies for "responding directly to indirect communications."

For example, a question on the mind of the new client or patient is: "Who is this counselor and what kind of person will he or she be?" This concern can be viewed as part of a general "authority theme." While the question is important, issues of authority are usually considered taboo, and like other taboo subjects clients will tend to raise them in an indirect manner.

We professionals are not immune from this concern about directness with persons in position of authority. I assume, for example, that all of you have experienced at one time or another, a boring presentation or workshop. Now tell me, have any of you came back from a break, raised your hand and told the presenter: "This is really boring"? I'm not surprised that none of you are raising your hands right now. When I do have workshop participants raising their hands in response to that question they usually went to Berkeley University in the '70s. You have communicated that you were bored to the speaker, but you did it indirectly. What were some of the ways you let the presenter know you were bored?

- Coming late, leaving early or not showing up–what I call voting with your feet.
- Falling asleep or your eyes glazing over.
- Reading a newspaper, staring out the window or looking at your watch.
- Encouraging what I call the "deviant member." This is the person who confronts the instructor, asks the challenging questions or even changes the discussion to an irrelevant but more interesting area of conversation. I say you encourage him or her because during the break a number of you say: "Keep it up. I will hold your coat." This person is speaking for you.

Why are we so indirect? Politeness is one reason, but also we have all learned to be cautious when dealing with people in authority especially in new encounters. Even when a teacher or supervisor invites honest feedback we witnessed them, at times, responding defensively or responding to even a gentle negative comment by cutting the participant down.

To your clients and to your supervisees you are the symbol of authority. In the beginning phase, they will be cautious. This may continue until they feel safe and sense a solid working relationship has been established. If the authority theme is not addressed early in the relationship, authority issues can remain below the surface, growing in power, and ultimately may haunt the engagement, blocking effective work.

Let me share a common illustration from direct practice. You are supervising a student intern or a new counselor who has just graduated from school. The intern is young and unmarried with no children. In a first interview with a family the mother asks the young practitioner the dreaded question: "Are you married?" or "And how many children do you have?" There are other versions of this question, often asked indirectly, such as: "Have you walked the walk and talked the talk?" The client is asking if the practitioner has been addicted and participated in a recovery group. Other variations include: "You're white; I'm African-American–how could you understand me and my family?" Or similarly, "You're straight; I'm gay." The authority theme issues in the practitioner-client relationship will often emerge indirectly since the issues deal with taboo areas. For my purposes this morning, I'd like to use the parenting question to illustrate the importance of the skill of "tuning in."

It is not uncommon for the new practitioner or student to feel defensive in response to such questions. Unless the supervisee has been helped by the supervisor to tune in to the underlying question, the response will often come from the feeling of being challenged as incompetent. The result may be defensive responses, including:

- "I may not have children but I have taken a number of courses on child behavior theory."
- "A doctor does not have to have an illness in order to be able to cure it."
- "We are here to talk about you, not me!" (The classic response often taught in skill training programs.)
- "I came from a big family."
- "Why do you ask?" (Responding to a question with another question.)

If we tune in to the underlying meaning of that question we can infer that what the client is asking may be one or a combination of the following:

- "How can you understand what it is like for me?"
- "How can you help me?"

- "Can I trust you or will you be like other professionals I have dealt with who have criticized me?"

It is easy in retrospect to see how defensive responses to reasonable questions may negatively impact the development of the working relationship rather than enhance it.

If we understand the mother's question about the practitioner's parenting status, what would be an example of a direct and non-defensive response? I have termed this skill "responding directly to an indirect cue." I'd like to share one version of a response. Before doing so, I want to set out three criteria I believe should be met when responding directly to any authority theme question or actually, to any client comment.

First, the response must convey a sense of genuiness–that is the practitioner must feel or come close to feeling what it's like for the client. All too often students are trained to use mechanical responses, such as reflection, without connecting to the emotions the client is experiencing. For example the client may say: "I am angry at the staff at my child's school!" and the practitioner would echo: "You are angry at the staff at your child's school." This hollow, mechanical response might rightly cause a client to think: "Dummy, I just told you I was angry!"

Another version is the common "I hear you saying . . . " repeating the client's comment but without real feeling. In one video taped interview, one of 120 hours of individual and group direct practice examined in another of my studies (Shulman, 1981), after a practitioner responded: "What I hear you saying is . . . ," the client said, with strong emphasis: "You heard me say that?" The counselor's comment wasn't even close to what the client was feeling because the counselor was using the words without feeling the emotions. In my research studies I have found that clients were most often aware of whether their counselors were really connecting to them. This was also true for supervisees and their supervisors.

The second condition is that the client must be able to hear the genuine empathy expressed by the counselor. For some of our clients who are not ready to engage, to face their problems, or perhaps are addicted and in the "pre-contemplation stage,"[2] or are angry if they have been mandated into counseling, they simply are not able to hear empathy at that moment. Genuine empathy can have an impact only if it is heard and accepted by the client.

Finally, I believe it is important that the practitioner find her or his own voice and express personal artistry guided by evidenced-based science. It is what I have referred to as the integration of our personal and professional selves. One of the tasks in the supervisory process is to help supervisees find their own voice and to feel safe in expressing their artistry in a professional manner.

If these conditions are met (the practitioner is genuine, the client is able to hear and appreciate the empathy, and the words used reflect the artistry of the practitioner), consider the potential impact if the counselor's response to the parenting question were the following:

> I'm not married and I don't have any children. Why do you ask? Are you concerned that I may not understand what it's like for you? I'm concerned about that as well. For me to help I'm going to have to understand, and in order for me to understand, you are going to have to tell me.

Would this response or one like it, have a more positive impact on the development of the working relationship (*rapport*, *trust*, and *caring*) than would a version of "We are here to talk about you, not me?" My research has indicated that the core skills contained in the response I offered above, when used in early sessions, tended to enhance the working relationship which again is the medium for providing help.

Let's break down the four elements of the response and identify the skills, all of which I will argue in the second part of this paper, are the same skills used by the supervisors in implementing their functional role.

First, "I'm not married and I don't have any children." The practitioner is being honest. Honesty does not mean we must answer every question. I have worked with teenagers who have asked questions I would not answer. I still could be honest by saying: "I don't feel comfortable answering that question." My central point is that I believe we have tried everything else in the helping professions; why not give honesty a chance?

Second, "Why do you ask? Are you concerned that I may not understand what it's like for you?" This is an example of articulating the client's feelings one "half-step" ahead of the client. Reflection, a simple repetition of what the client has just said, keeps the practitioner behind the client. I don't believe the question, "Why do you ask?" offers enough help for the client. If the client could honestly answer that question the subject would not be taboo. This intervention is a complex one in that it also displays the practitioner's interest and concern in what the client thinks and feels; it validates the concern; and it encourages discussion in a taboo area.

I'm aware that some models of practice would argue for "open ended questions," not "leading the client," etc. The fear is that we may be wrong and end up putting words into the client's mouth. My practice and my research have taught me that we make more mistakes of omission, failing to say something, than mistakes of commission, saying the wrong thing. What if the client denied it was a problem, perhaps saying: "You seem like a nice person. I'm sure you would understand"? While encouraging direct responses to indirect cues, I think it is important to respect the client's defenses, especially in early encounters. Therefore, I would not insist on my interpretation that this was an issue; however, I would give the client a "second chance" if they demurred. For example, I could say: "It wouldn't surprise me if you have met other professionals who have not understood." By giving the client a second chance I also make clear that I'm really ready to discuss the authority theme. If the client refuses my second offer I could say: "OK, but it is important to me to understand how you are feeling. If you ever feel I'm not I would like you to let me know."

Third, "Because I was concerned about that as well." This is an example of the skill of sharing the practitioner's feelings, something I was taught never to do. My professional training required that I separate my personal and professional selves. My practice and research have taught me that I actually have to integrate my personal and professional selves, rather than separating myself from the process. In my view, this is a life-long professional learning task. Of course, as with answering clients' questions, sharing every feeling obviously is not appropriate. Even if the practitioner felt like responding to the parenting question by saying: "You're absolutely right! What is my supervisor doing sending me out to work with you and your family. I've never even changed a diaper or heated a bottle," I don't believe the client wants to hear this. These are concerns and feelings that should be shared with the practitioner's supervisor. In a questionnaire response to a question in my practice research one client said the following about her practitioner: "I really like her! She's not like a social worker she is more like a real person." I think all helping professions need to be concerned if the perception that we are not real persons is widely held by our clients.

I realize the use of this skill raises all kinds of questions about counter-transference, the expressing of inappropriate affect, etc. This is the reason I argue that the personal needs to be integrated with the professional. This is not an argument for simply acting out. In my research studies in the areas of practice mentioned earlier, the skill of sharing feelings–being a real person–had the strongest positive impact in developing the working relationship of all of the skills studied. In fact, where there were differences between practitioner and client, for example differences of race, gender, ethnicity, class, sexual orientation, etc., the practitioner's honesty was even more important. It is ironic that this is the very skill I was cautioned against using during my professional training.

I believe we borrowed this artificial dichotomy between personal and professional from the medical profession. However, my observation and research has indicated that making this separation does not work for doctors either. In my study of medical practice (Shulman and Buchan, 1982), patients were well aware of their doctor's attitudes toward them (positive, neutral, or negative), and the doctor's attitude was a strong predictor of patient comprehension, rapport, willingness to refer friends and family members, and even compliance as measured in self-reports one week after seeing the doctor.

Finally, "If I'm going to help you I have to really understand and for me to do that you are going to have to tell me." This is a complex comment with a number of elements. It credits the client's life experience since the client is the expert on their own life. It starts the contracting process with the client, including an explanation that the helping process is not something the practitioner will do to the client, but rather is something they will do together. The practitioner's role is not to be the expert on life, even though there is some knowledge that can be shared, but rather to listen to and to understand what the world looks like to the client. I liked what one respondent in one of my early studies wrote in the comment section of her questionnaire: "My worker is very young but I think I can educate her!"

Let me summarize these practice skills that emerged in the example above, and then make the transition to supervision in the next section. I will argue that the same dynamics, processes and skills can be seen in the supervisory working relationship, keeping in mind that the functional role of the supervisor is different from that of the therapist, and that the purpose of supervision is not therapy. The skills contained in the example response were:

- Honesty with appropriate self-disclosure.
- Articulating the client's feelings a half step ahead of the client.
- Demonstrating interest and concern in the client's feelings.
- Validating the client's concerns and feelings.

- Sharing the counselor's own feelings (integrating personal and professional).
- Validating the client's life experiences.
- Contracting to work *with* the client not *on* the client.

Of course the question of the practitioner's parenting experience is not always raised so politely. One of my students described his first meeting in a hospital with a group of mothers, all of whom had a child with a serious chronic illness. Taking over from a departing social worker, my student tuned into a number of potential themes and rehearsed with his supervisor direct responses to certain issues should they arise. These included issues related to his gender, his status as a non-parent, the fact that the mothers may know more about the illness then he did, and left over anger at the social worker who left in the middle of the year. By tuning in and rehearsing he believed he was ready for everything–except what happened.

> Before he could start, one client confronted him in an angry voice and said: "I want you to know what we think of this dammed hospital. We have doctors who don't listen to us, nurses who push us around, and we keep getting young social workers like you who don't even have kids." I asked the student what he felt like saying at that moment. He responded that he felt like saying: "I may be in the wrong room!" I asked him what he did say and he revealed that he had responded spontaneously and said: "I may not have kids but I have a mother just like you!"
>
> There was a momentary stunned silence in the group with him thinking, as he later reported, "Oh, oh! Can I tell my supervisor about this?" The client was probably thinking "What kind of social worker is this?" In her initial comment she had related to him as a stereotype. In his response, he was anything but stereotypical. The group members quickly changed the subject and initiated a superficial discussion that was an example of an "illusion of work."

In my class discussion of this example I told the student he had made a "beautiful mistake." He was a bit shocked by that comment. I went on to point out that at least he was honest and spontaneous. I thought a worse mistake might be to say what I was taught to say in situations like this, which was: "Thank you for sharing that" or "Do you want to go with that feeling." I also argued that developing practice skill involved shortening the distance between when one makes a mistake and when one catches the mistake. It is crucial that supervisors and educators help young practitioners to be willing to risk, to make mistakes and to learn from them. We need to help practitioners understand that they can learn from "active" mistakes as opposed to "passive" mistakes.

In the class, the student then tuned into the underlying issues associated with the anger and he began the next group session as follows:

> Mrs. X, I want to comment about last week. It was my first time leading a group and as a result I didn't understand the pain and disappointment that was under your comment. You have met many helping professionals who simply didn't understand what it was like to have a child who is sick and never seems to get better. When you saw me you thought: "Here comes another one."

There was silence in the room after his comment. The student was prepared for what might be inside of the silence. The group members may have been having different reactions including: "he thought about us during the week; this discussion is going to get real; he is trying to understand," and most important, they may be experiencing the pain to which he referred. The angry mother began to cry and pointed out she was the only one in the group who did not have a partner to share the load. A member next to her said she was married–"big deal." She went on to describe a husband who worked all the time and avoided discussing the child.

The student began to understand the first woman's anger represented "fight" and the husband's working all the time represented "flight" (Bion, 1961). Both were maladaptive ways of coping with the pain. The angry mother in the first session was really saying: "Do you want to see how I push people away when I need them the most?" The additional insight the student gained from this incident was how often the process in his work closely connected to the content of the work. This was an important start in understanding and rejecting another false dichotomy–process versus content.

THE PRELIMINARY PHASE IN SUPERVISION

As with direct practice, there are constant and variant elements that can affect the supervisory relationship, including among others:

- The amount of authority and accountability carried by the supervisor.
- Whether the supervisor is promoted from within the staff group or is hired externally.
- The education and experience of the supervisee.
- Clinical supervision may be a very structured and intense process for students and new and inexperienced supervisees or case consultation for those practitioners with substantial experience and skill.

Just as in the beginning of the practice relationship, issues related to the authority theme may be raised, often indirectly. For example, in workshops I have led common issues faced by new supervisors promoted from within include:

- Having to supervise former peers, two of whom applied for the same job;
- Coming into the coffee room on your first day as supervisor and having everyone become silent–and you fear they were talking about you;
- Dealing with active and passive resistance;
- Having to supervise friends and former colleagues.

Another common issue raised in my workshops by new supervisors brought in from the outside is what I refer to as "the hired gun syndrome." Direct and indirect questions emerge from staff asking "Which side the new supervisor will be on? Will he or she be with the administration or with the staff members?" Supervisors describe this as feeling "caught in the middle." With experience, they learn they cannot do their job unless they are with both staff and administration at the same time.[3]

Just as the authority theme may be raised indirectly in the practice relationship, as I discussed earlier, it may also be raised in the supervisor-practitioner context. One common example is the practitioner who says to the new supervisor: "Well I'm glad you're here now because our last supervisor was a real jerk." This can occur in an individual session or a staff meeting. It usually puts the new supervisor on the spot, uncomfortable talking about their predecessor.

With some tuning in one can begin to understand that staff members may not be talking about the last supervisor. This is often an indirect way of asking: "And what kind of supervisor are you going to be?" Rather than changing the subject out of discomfort, the new supervisor could respond directly by saying: "It sounds as though you feel you did not get along with your last supervisor. What kind of problems did you perceive?" Attention needs to be drawn to the word "perceive" since it does not represent an endorsement of the problems, just of the practitioner's perception. The new supervisor is not asking the worker to complain about the previous supervisor since the conversation will immediately move to the current relationship.

Depending upon the response the new supervisor has opened up an opportunity for a discussion about his or her own approach to supervision–which is often the real underlying question. For example, if the practitioners complain about lack of availability the new supervisor could respond as follows:

> I want you to know I see it as my job to be available for you not only when we schedule conferences but in between as well, if you need a quick consultation. I also realize that with the pressures I have to deal with and other demands on my time I may not always be able to respond right away. If you ever feel that is becoming a pattern–an ongoing problem–I want you to let me know.

The key here is that the new supervisor lets the practitioner know that he or she is aware that the concern is not about the previous supervisor, but rather about what king of supervisor the new person will be. The supervisor is also extending an invitation for honest feedback from the front-line practitioners.

If staff concerns relate to the way the previous supervisor handled job management issues, the new supervisor might seize the opportunity to clarify his or her expectations and management approach. For example, the new supervisor might say:

> Maybe this is a good time for me to let you all know my views about these issues. Occasional lateness, for example, is a problem we all may have but if lateness becomes a pattern then I see it as my job to meet with you and to discuss it.

In both examples the supervisor has brought to the surface the underlying concerns and questions about the way she or he will work with her supervisees, and has demonstrated willingness to be direct about what are often experienced as taboo issues. Most important, the supervisor is modeling exactly what is expected of the practitioner when a client starts to raise concerns about the "last counselor" when actually referring to the new one.

Just as in practice, unless these underlying issues related to the authority theme are addressed in a direct manner they may fester under the surface, increasing in their power, and block the development of a sound supervisory relationship. Taboo subjects that are surfaced directly in the work tend to lose their power. Responding directly speeds up the process. Even more difficult for the new supervisor from the outside is when practitioners talk about how wonderful the last supervisor was. In one example a new supervisor described in a workshop I presented how, seemingly out of nowhere during a meeting, staff began to reminisce about the great food at a barbecue the last supervisor held in her backyard just before she left. The supervisor reported thinking: "And I don't even cook!" In retrospect she realized there was more to this than just food. At her next staff meeting she raised the issue directly: "I was thinking about your reminiscing about Jane last week. You really sound as though you miss her. What was it that made her such a good supervisor? I'm not Jane, but I would like to be helpful as well." Once again, this opened up a discussion of staff expectations of the supervisor and the supervisor's expectations of staff. It also demonstrated the supervisor's understanding and lack of threat about feelings and issues associated with the loss of the last supervisor. It modeled how practitioners can handle the same issue with clients when they speak about their former "terrific" counselors.

In the workshop in which the above example was shared, a participant who was a Catholic nun raised her hand and said: "Now I know what was going on at the hospital where I just took over as mother superior, replacing someone who had been there for over 25 years." She continued, "I was in place only three weeks when it became apparent that I had replaced Mary Mother of God!" When the laughter died down she reflected that in her own anxiety about replacing a beloved predecessor she had ignored addressing the serious issues of loss experienced by her staff. She indicated she was going to re-open the discussion the next week since for nurses dealing with patients and their families, losses of any kind were important issues to be addressed.

RESEARCH FINDINGS

In one of my major studies of child welfare in the Canadian Province of British Columbia, I had six levels of participants, including 5 Executive Directors (macro areas of the Province); 10 Regional Managers; 10 regional Family and Children Service Coordinators; 68 Front-line District Supervisors; 171 front-line social workers; 51 family support workers; 305 Families; and over 449 children (Shulman, 1991).[4] Mailed questionnaires were developed and tested for reliability and validity and then administered to both staff and clients over a period of two years. When possible, data was obtained directly from clients through personal interviews.

While the study was an effort to develop a holistic model of child welfare practice incorporating variables that took into account the context of the practice and supervision/management, demographic variables, skills variables, etc., for the purpose of this presentation, I will address only the findings related to supervision with an emphasis on skill use and the parallel process.

For each of the six levels of the study, we examined the association between the use of the skills described above and the development of a working relationship (rapport, trust, and caring) as well as satisfaction (the client with the worker; the worker with the supervisor, etc.) and their perception of helpfulness. Where appropriate, we also examined "hard" measures such as time spent in foster care, rate of return to biological families, etc. While much of the data consisted of perceptions (for example, the use of certain skills by practitioners as perceived by their clients), we built in a number of validity checks such as asking the supervisor to also rate the social worker's level of skill. We then compared that to the rating given by the same social worker's clients. We also adopted the position that the only variable that counted was the *perception* of skill use by the client or worker. Somewhat like the example of a tree falling in the forest making no sound unless someone is present to hear it, a skill such as empathy has no impact unless the client perceives it.

A scale of supervisor skill was developed that incorporated three of the supervisory skills that had been identified as important in an earlier study (Shulman, Robinson, and Luckyj, 1981) and through a general review of the literature. The core skills selected for the study and their wording on the questionnaires were as follows:

- Articulates the supervisee's feelings ("My supervisor can sense my feelings without my having to put them into words").
- Communicates the supervisee's views to administration ("My supervisor effectively communicates my views about policies and procedures to the next level of the agency").

- Encourages negative feedback ("When I am upset about something my supervisor says or does, he/she encourages me to talk about it").

Staff on each level was asked to rate their supervisors or managers working a level above using a Likert scale. Thus, 10 managers rated the 5 executives; 62 supervisors rated their 10 managers; and 151 workers rated their 68 supervisors.

The findings, briefly summarized here, indicated the following:

- 40% of the managers "agreed" or "strongly agreed" that their administrators (the Executive Directors) were able to articulate their feelings.
- Only 21% of the supervisors "agreed" (none "strongly agreed") that their mangers demonstrated this skill.
- On the practitioner level, 26.5% "agreed" or "strongly agreed" that this skill was evidenced by their supervisors.

All three levels of administration scored lower on the use of this skill than their workers did when rated by their clients. In interviews with staff groups to discuss the findings, it was clear that one of the issues may be the perception by supervisors that empathic responses to supervisees might be construed as too close to "therapy" and thus they were less likely to use the skill. It was not always clear to staff that empathy when used in pursuit of their supervisory function was not therapy but rather supportive and effective supervision.

In contrast to the empathy findings, when asked about communicating views to higher levels of administration:

- 70% of the managers "agreed" or "strongly agreed" that their Executive Directors effectively communicated their views to administration.
- On the supervisor-manager level, 72.3% "agreed" or "strongly agreed" that their mangers evidenced this skill.
- Only 53.7% of the front-line workers "agreed" or "strongly agreed" that their supervisors were as effective.

The findings for the third skill, encourages negative feedback, indicated that:

- 77.8% of the managers "agreed" or "strongly agreed" that their executives evidenced this skill.
- Only 46.8% of the supervisors felt this way about their managers.
- 50% of the workers reported that they "agreed" or "strongly agreed" that their supervisors demonstrated this skill.

The supervisee's perceptions of the supervisory relationship and supervisor helpfulness were also examined along with other variables. For the purpose of this presentation, I will report the correlation between supervisory skills, as defined by the average score on the three skill variables above, and four of the dependant measures. Supervisory skill demonstrated moderate to strong correlations with the social worker's trust in the supervisor ($r = .75$), rapport ($r = .82$), helpfulness ($r = .76$), and positive morale ($r = .47$). These findings paralleled the analysis of the same or similar variables in the social worker-client level of the study.

The full study explored other variables such as the impact of job manageability, job stress, and availability of support and the impact of these variables on supervisor skill use. Supervisor skill use, in particular the empathic skill, also associated positively with worker perception of the supervisor's helpfulness, the worker's morale and the worker's ability to manage the job. The availability of peer support for the supervisor was associated at high levels with the supervisor's perception of the availability of emotional support for him or her, the ability of the supervisor to manage his/her job, lower job stress, and higher job manageability.

While it is important to keep in mind that these study results need to be considered in light of the limitations of the study, as described in the full report, they nevertheless suggest that the core assumptions of the model presented here are supported. There is a parallel process involved, meaning that effective supervision at all levels can increase the possibility of effective practice.

ILLUSTRATIONS FROM CLINICAL SUPERVISION

The first example illustrates supervision of a child welfare worker's visit to a young, Native Canadian mother who had just moved to Vancouver, British Columbia, and was living in a single-room occupancy hotel with three young children. She was twenty-one years old and had fled the reservation because of fear of sexual abuse of her children. The worker visited because of calls to the agency's hot-line reporting neglect of the children. The counselor reported the details of her interaction with the client during supervision. The supervisor made use of "memory work" in that she asked the worker to describe the interview in some detail. While analysis of a brief written recording of the process of the interaction is valuable, it is not always available. The worker began by indicating she was concerned about the safety of the children. A portion of the supervision session follows:

> *Counselor:* I explained to her that we had received a telephone call on the 800 line that raised concerns about her children not being cared for. As I talked with her, the two-year-old came over near her feet and she firmly asked her to move away and play with her toys. She came back again and this time the mother was quite angry. Finally, she grabbed the child and shook her angrily telling her to leave her alone.
>
> *Supervisor:* What did you say to her?
>
> *Counselor:* I asked her if she could find another way to tell her child to leave her alone. Oh, yes, I also told her about our parent effectiveness-training program.
>
> *Supervisor:* How did she respond?
>
> *Counselor:* She got very silent and I could see she was angry.
>
> *Supervisor:* You know she probably felt you were being critical of her and that shut her down. Couldn't you find a gentler way to talk to her about her behavior?
>
> *Counselor:* Well I guess I could have, but you weren't really there so you don't know how bad it was.

In thinking about the supervision interview just described, ask yourself this question: With whom was the supervisor emotionally identified? That is, whose feeling was the supervisor experiencing? Clearly, she was tuned in to the mother. Now ask yourself, who was emotionally with the counselor? You can all sense that at that moment the answer is no one.

Pick up the conversation right at the point the counselor had described the client's angry response to the child. The supervisor's response was to ask the counselor to consider the mother's feelings. Consider this alternative response:

Supervisor: How did it make you feel when the mother got so angry?

Counselor: I was upset that she was treating the child that way.

Supervisor: You must have also been angry at her for that behavior.

Counselor: I was angry. It's just a little child. She shouldn't be so angry with her.

Supervisor: Were you also worried about what she might do if she got angry when you are not around?

Counselor: Sure I was. I don't want her hurting that child.

Supervisor: I can understand your reaction. Most people would be upset witnessing that kind of behavior. I agree that you also have to be concerned about the safety of the child. My sense is that at that moment you were understandably emotionally identified with the child. Who was with the mother?

Counselor: (pause) I guess no one.

Supervisor: I think the hard part of the work is to find a way to be with the mother and the child at the same time. To address issues of safety for the child, but at the same time to address the concerns of the mother. Let's take a moment and think about what it must be like for the mother . . . (the supervisor and the counselor tune in to what it might be like to be a young mother, with three young children, recently moving off the reserve in a rural area and moving into single room occupancy housing with no family or other sources of support).

Counselor: OK, I can understand how tough it must be for her. I'm not sure what I could say at that moment.

Supervisor: Let me take a crack at it. What if you said to the mother: "Is this what it's like for you all of the time? Do you never get a chance to be alone without the kids? You must be feeling lonely and overwhelmed."

Counselor: I can see how that would make a better connection with the mother. She might not feel as threatened by me. But what about the safety issue?

Supervisor: You need to address that as well in an honest, direct and supportive way. You can tell her you are worried about her and the child. You can suggest that you can help with some of the resources available–particularly from the Native community (for example, Native housekeepers, respite care, legal help).

Counselor: I blew it, didn't I?

Supervisor: Don't be so hard on yourself. You reacted from your gut but you just weren't clear about needing to be with both clients at the same time. Let's work on how you can go back and start again with that Mom.

At this point in the conference, the counselor role played out how to take responsibility for not hearing the mom in the first interview and asking to start over again. The parallel is obvious. In the first example, the supervisor is asking the counselor to tune into and to empathize with the young mother while at exactly the same time she is not tuning into the counselor. She is actually demonstrating the opposite of what she would like the practitioner to do with the client. In the second example, the supervisor teaches by modeling the skills of being with the counselor and the client at the same time. To emphasize the parallels, if the first supervisor realized she had been criticizing the worker she could have returned later in the day and also said: "Can we start over? I was so concerned about the child's mother I forgot to connect with how you must have been feelings."

Of course, another question we could ask at this moment is who is with the supervisor? As reported earlier, my research has indicated that a supervisor's ability to provide needed support for a front-line practitioner somewhat depends on the supervisor's ability to find that same support from either their own supervisor or peers. This was brought home to me dramatically in a workshop I presented for a conference of social workers in pediatric oncology settings. Dealing on a daily basis with children and families where terminal cancer is not uncommon clearly would create tremendous stress on a practitioner and other staff as well.

A recently graduated social worker reported in the workshop an example in which a young mother was informed by the oncologist that her seven-year-old child had a terminal cancer and most likely had less than a year to live. The doctor sent the woman to see the social worker without dealing with the mother's emotional turmoil. When she entered the social worker's office, she appeared to be stunned and in a protective shell. The worker asked the mother why the doctor had sent her to see a social worker and she replied: "He just told me my baby is going to die." At this point the shell broke and the woman began to sob. The social worker was deeply moved, took her hand and cried with her.

In my view, no words would have helped at the moment. I believe what the mother needed was someone to "be with" her at this most painful and difficult moment. There are many ways to convey our capacity for empathy, and for each professional it may vary as our personal self dictates how it will be done. Remaining respectful and silent, facial expression, touch where appropriate and even tears send important messages to the mother. There would be time before the interview ended to discuss how she would get home, how she would share this with the family, and how she would take care of herself so she could take care of her daughter. All of these issues are important; however, at this moment I don't think the mother would have heard a word.

The worker continued by sharing with the workshop participants that her supervisor walked by her open door, saw her crying with the mother and called her out into the hall. The supervisor told her to pull herself together, saying she had "lost it." In my view, the worker had "found it." I asked the worker what she learned from the experience and she said: "I learned to keep my door shut!"

I told her I didn't think that was good enough because eventually, in a position such as hers, she might find herself burning out. If she cut off her feelings and tried to treat her work as a 9 to 5 job, she could easily burn out. If she continued to allow herself to feel deeply the pain of her clients, and if she did not get support from her supervisor, that also could be the start of burning out.

When I inquired whether or not there was a support group for all of the staff on her service–counselors, doctors, nurses, etc., she replied that they met once a week for a staff meeting, but never actually discussed their own feelings and their stress. The meeting, led by the oncologist, focused on the patients and their cancer. I suggested that the doctor's avoidance of the mother's feelings and the supervisor's seemingly harsh comment were probably indirect signals that something was missing in the service. My profession, social work, is rooted in a history of both helping individuals and working for social change. I have termed this the "two client" idea. I suggested to the worker that the hospital and the oncology service were her "second clients." We discussed a strategy by which she could raise, in a professional manner, the issue of a support group for staff who had to deal with the pain of children dying and grieving families. The social worker role-played how she could start this conversation at the next staff meeting. The example opened up a discussion for all of the workshop participants on the importance of having their needs met if they were to meet those of the children and their families.

CONCLUSIONS

I believe we have an important research and teaching agenda in the area of clinical supervision. We must advance our research efforts to explore the common core in practice and supervision. We need to better understand the variations on the themes or the "variant elements" of effective supervision. How are we the same as clinical supervisors and how are we different as social workers, counselors, psychologists, nurses, etc.? We need to more closely understand the way in which the clinical supervisor's interaction with the practitioner (the process) either reinforces effective practice concepts (the content) or models the exact opposite.

I would like to leave you with a final story. I consulted with four men who established in Vancouver, British Columbia some of the first North American groups for men who batter. One described his last meeting with the group of men when he told them he had a consultant named Larry Shulman who told him he would learn from mistakes, improve his group leadership, and then make more sophisticated mistakes. He went on to ask the men how he had done. One man replied: "Don't worry Jim. You're not making sophisticated mistakes yet." I wish all of you and the practitioners you supervise many sophisticated mistakes.

NOTES

1. I have most recently described this practice framework in a book entitled: *The Skills of Helping Individuals, Families, Groups and Communities, 5th edition* (2006) and for supervision in a book entitled *Interactional Supervision (1993).*

2. This is the first stage in a change model developed by Prochaska and DiClemente (1982) first employed in considering the change process for addicted persons.

3. The issue of caught in the middle is discussed in detail in my book "Interactional Supervision" (1993).

4. This study followed an earlier project examining supervision skills in social work, nursing and residential treatment settings from across Canada (Shulman, Robinson & Luckyj, 1981). There were 109 supervisors and 671 practitioners in that sample.

REFERENCES

Gitterman, A., & Shulman, L. (2005). *Mutual aid groups, vulnerable and resilient populations and the life cycle* (3rd ed.). New York: Columbia University Press.

Prochaska, J.O., & DiClemente, C.C. (1982). Transtheoretical therapy: Toward a more integrative model of change. *Psychotherapy: Theory, Research and Practice, 19*, 314-323.

Schwartz, W. (1961). The social worker in the group. In *New perspectives on services to groups: Theory, organization and practice* (pp. 7-34). New York: National Association of Social Workers.

Shulman, L. (1978). A study of practice skills. *Social Work, 23*, 281-290.

Shulman, L. (1981). *Identifying, measuring, and teaching helping skills.* New York: Council on Social Work Education and the Canadian Association of Schools of Social Work.

Shulman, L. (1991). *Interactional social work practice: Toward an empirical theory.* Itasca, IL: Peacock.

Shulman, L. (1993). *Interactional supervision.* Silver Spring, MD: National Association of Social Workers.

Shulman, L., & Buchan, W. (1982). *The impact of the family physicians communication, relationship, and technical skills on patient compliance, satisfaction, reassurance, comprehension, and improvement.* Vancouver: University of British Columbia.

Shulman, L. (2006). *The skills of helping individuals, families, groups and communities* (5th ed). Belmont, CA: Thomson Brooks/Cole.

doi:10.1300/J001v24n01_03

Clinical Supervision in Social Work: A Review of the Research Literature

Marion Bogo
Kathryn McKnight

SUMMARY. In social work, supervision is valued as a crucial activity for professional learning and development. Over time, an extensive body of literature has developed that is largely theoretical and practice-oriented. The development of an empirical body of knowledge for supervision has been slow with most approaches supported solely by anecdotal accounts. An extensive review of the empirical studies on supervision conducted in the past decade was undertaken. Two separate streams of inquiry were found; one focused on supervision of professional staff and one focused on field education of students. This body of research is reviewed in two companion papers. Recent studies of supervision of staff are largely descriptive and exploratory yielding limited knowledge for evidence-based supervision. Organizational and professional issues related to the dearth of studies are discussed. doi:10.1300/J001v24n01_04 *[Article copies available for a fee from The Haworth Document Delivery Service: 1-800-HAWORTH. E-mail address: <docdelivery@haworthpress.com> Website: <http://www.HaworthPress.com> © 2005 by The Haworth Press, Inc. All rights reserved.]*

KEYWORDS. Social work supervision, clinical supervision, research on supervision

---

Marion Bogo is Professor, and Kathryn McKnight is Doctoral Candidate, Faculty of Social Work, University of Toronto.

[Haworth co-indexing entry note]: "Clinical Supervision and Field Instruction in Social Work." Bogo, Marion, and Kathryn McKnight. Co-published simultaneously in *The Clinical Supervisor* (The Haworth Press, Inc.) Vol. 24, No. 1/2, 2005, pp. 49-67; and: *Supervision in Counseling: Interdisciplinary Issues and Research* (ed: Lawrence Shulman, and Andrew Safyer) The Haworth Press, Inc., 2005, pp. 49-67. Single or multiple copies of this article are available for a fee from The Haworth Document Delivery Service [1-800-HAWORTH, 9:00 a.m. - 5:00 p.m. (EST). E-mail address: docdelivery@haworthpress.com].

Available online at http://cs.haworthpress.com

doi:10.1300/J001v24n01_04

This volume brings together the current state-of-the-art in research on clinical supervision in social work. A review of recent empirical literature was conducted, examined, and appraised. The following papers present supervision concepts supported in these studies, summarize general themes, and identify challenges for researchers and supervisors that emerged from this review.

Historically in social work the term supervision encompasses a range of functions, including professional development of staff and administrative activities such as managing staff to achieve efficient service delivery. Schools of social work developed in the early part of the twentieth century and since their inception included academic courses and an agency or community-based field work component. Originally field work took place in an agency where students were required to receive supervision from a member of the American Association of Social Workers (Raskin, 2005). In 1935, further interpretation of this requirement included that supervision has an educational focus. With the establishment of the Council on Social Work Education in the mid-fifties, educational terms began to be used when referring to field work, including the need to train field supervisors as field instructors (Raskin, 2005). However, the original terminology of supervision, reflecting its agency-based context, often remained, and it is still not uncommon to see the terms supervisor and supervision used to apply to both the educational development of staff and of students. Increasingly, however, two distinct bodies of knowledge and research about professional development have evolved: one that refers to supervision of staff in agencies, and the other that refers to professional education of social work students in the field practicum. While some concepts, processes, and techniques may be generic and used interchangeably in both sectors, the difference in context, purpose, and role of supervision of staff and of field education of students support the division of this body of literature into two domains.

Supervision in social work is primarily conceived of as an administrative function that aims to provide accountability in relation to the agency mandate. That is, supervision of workers is provided to ensure that services to clients are offered in an effective and efficient manner. When educational and supportive functions are provided, they are in the service of this broader goal. Put more crassly, workers are hired by an agency to do a job and supervisors oversee that the job is done well.

Defining supervision in this manner renders it an inappropriate term to describe the educational preparation of students for social work practice. Students enroll in universities, pay fees, and expect to be taught to become competent social workers. One component of their educational program takes place in the field practicum where field instruction, also referred to as field education, provides opportunities for teaching and learning about social work practice. Primary learning experiences are those that involve students in delivering an agency service to clients or community members. Since these services are offered within an organizational context, field instructors are accountable to the agency and the clients for the service provided and hence some aspect of overseeing the work of students must be present. The primary role, however, is that of educator with the goal of student development and learning social work practice.

Given these definitions of supervision and field instruction, this review of recent research in social work is presented in two papers. The first paper addresses clinical supervision of staff, and the second paper addresses field instruction of students. In the world of agency practice some social workers still use the term supervision to refer to both staff and students. While this is rarely the case in contemporary literature, this review found some studies on field education in which researchers still refer to "student supervision." In the review article on field education, the term student supervision is used only when the author reviewed uses this term. Most researchers maintain a distinction between the two topics and address either supervision of staff or field instruction of students. Conclusions are not made nor are generalizations drawn across these two domains of scholarly and practice activity.

DEFINITION

An enduring feature in the conceptualization and definition of supervision in social work reflects its organizational purpose: to offer the agency's service to the client in an efficient and effective manner (Kadushin & Harkness, 2002). It is a primary vehicle through which agency accountability is achieved. Supervisors, often located at mid-level in the organization's hierarchy, oversee the work of front-line staff as they carry out the mandate and purpose of an organization. The importance of education and support of workers has also been well recognized as a crucial aspect of supervision that contributes to effective prac- tice. Three interrelated functions are reflected in frequently cited definitions of supervision: administrative, educational, and supportive (Kadushin & Harkness, 2002; Munson, 2002; Shulman, 1993). Administrative supervision refers to case assignment, and monitoring of assessment, intervention planning, and ongoing work to assist social workers to implement agency policy and procedures and work within the structure of the agency (Shulman, 1993). The supervisor evaluates the worker's performance and participates in decisions about the supervisee's career advancement and salary increases (Gibelman & Schervish, 1997). In this capacity, the supervisor is accountable to the public to ensure that competent practice and effective service is delivered. The second function, educational supervision, aims to develop the professional capacity of supervisees through enhancing their knowledge and skills including developing greater self-awareness (Barker, 1995; Munson, 2002). Education includes direct teaching about all aspects of social work such as practice with the client, the team, the professional environment, and the relevant political and social systems (American Board of Examiners in Clinical Social Work, 2004). The third function, supportive supervision, involves helping the worker handle stress, through providing encouragement, reassurance, and appropriate autonomy (Kadushin & Harkness, 2002). It is concerned with enhancing staff morale and job satisfaction of social workers.

In their review of the social work labor force engaged in supervision, Gibelman and Schervish (1997) contrasted this broad definition of social work supervision with clinical supervision. They defined clinical supervision as not necessarily agency-based or concerned with practice in an agency context. Rather, clinical supervision focuses on the dynamics of the client situation and the social worker's interventions. Hence it is more likely to include only educational and supportive features. Their definition of clinical supervision differs from Munson's (2002) who viewed it as organizationally based and interactive, and consistent with emerging definitions of clinical social work practice. Munson (2002) located clinical supervision within an organization and emphasized that the clinical supervisor is assigned or designated to assist in and direct a supervisee's practice through the supervisory functions of teaching, administration, and helping. Supervision is agency-based, hierarchical, and includes an evaluative component. Workers are accountable to the supervisor for their practice with clients. Munson (2002) used the term consultation to refer to a social worker voluntarily contracting for professional input and guidance outside of an agency framework. Consistent with Munson's (2002) definitions, the recent Position Statement on Clinical Supervision of the American Board of Examiners in Clinical Social Work (2004) drew the distinction between an agency employed supervisor in an organization that confers authority and accountability on the role and a consultant who is not given authority as a supervisor, rather provides education and expert opinions. Consistent use of terms by the academic and practice community is strongly recommended to facilitate study and communication about these roles.

MODALITIES

Similar to the primacy accorded to the client and worker relationship as the vehicle for social work practice, the one-to-one supervisee and supervisor dyad is the most widely used model of supervision (Kadushin & Harkness, 2002). Group supervision is another modality used and consists of one supervisor leading a group of supervisees. Group supervision is used both as the exclusive method of accomplishing the goals of supervision and also as a supplement to the individual conference. Group supervision is recommended as an efficient use of time and as a vehicle where social workers can learn from each other (Kadushin & Harkness, 2002). It is believed that the experience of sharing common challenges can normalize reactions to stressful work environments and practice experiences, and alleviate isolation through connection and support between workers (Barretta-Herman, 1993). Another use of a group modality for continuing professional development is that of the peer group. In this approach, all participants occupy similar positions in the agency hierarchy. With the absence of a supervisor in an authority role, power and control issues are not present and, it is proposed, a mutual aid model can flourish (Brashears, 1995). This form of peer consultation at times is incorrectly referred to as peer supervision despite the absence in the group of any person with the authority inherent in the supervisory role.

Little is known about the prevalence of various types of supervision models in social work. Unfortunately, in the only study found on this topic individual supervision and group supervision were collapsed into one category and compared with peer supervision (actually peer consultation) and supervision by a non-social worker. Berger and Mizrahi (2001) examined supervisory models used in a national sample of hospitals in 1992, 1994, and 1996. They found that both individual and group models decreased over time, but remained the most frequent models of supervision. Peer supervision (consultation) increased from time one to time two but dropped off in time three, lower than its rate at time one. Peer supervision (consultation) was the second most frequent model used in hospitals. The use of non-social work supervision increased over all three times tested.

REVIEW OF RESEARCH ON CLINICAL SUPERVISION IN SOCIAL WORK

Following the request of the editors of *The Clinical Supervisor* journal in June, 2004, peer-reviewed journal articles that reported on research conducted on social work supervision in the past five years were sought. A search was conducted using the Social Work Abstracts database for the keywords "social work" and "clinical supervision" and "supervision." Only eight studies were located from 1999 to the present, half of which were conducted outside the United States. Due to the small numbers of studies found, the search period was expanded to include all studies conducted over a ten year period, since 1994. This search yielded 22 peer-reviewed journal articles that were reports of studies. Since context significantly affects social work supervision, a decision was made to review studies conducted in the United States (note). This resulted in a review of 13 articles that reported on 11 studies (one study yielded three papers).

Characteristics of Supervisors

Drawing on the NASW annual membership database for 1988, 1991, and 1995, Gibelman and Schervish (1995) examined the characteristics of members who reported supervision as their primary function. They found a significantly higher proportion of males as compared to females reported their primary function as administration/management, supervision, or teaching. The great majority of supervisors (91.4%) held an MSW as their highest degree. The degree of diversity among supervisors was higher than the general membership. This was particularly true of African-American members, who constitute 5.3% of the overall members and 9.2% of supervisors.

Organizational Context of Supervision

As noted in the definition of social work supervision, its organizational base is a dominant feature and affects functions, scope, and processes. Anecdotal evidence over the past decade suggests that changes to organizations employing social workers have had a profound impact on the nature and availability of supervision. In their study of the NASW database, Gibelman and Schervish (1997) found that the availability of supervision varies between sectors. It is relatively scarce in the for-profit sector, over-represented in the not-for-profit and state government sectors, and somewhat under-represented in local government. Social workers in the for-profit sector independently contract for external supervision or receive very little supervision at all. Supervision is more frequently carried out by NASW members in the court/justice system, residential facilities, and social service agencies than in other types of settings.

When employed in public schools or hospitals, social workers are likely to be supervised by non-social workers or not supervised at all (Gibelman & Schervish, 1997). The researchers concluded that the prevalence of managed care in health, mental health, and social services has led to cost containment measures such as eliminating middle-management supervisory positions. Similarly, Berger and Mizrahi (2001) in a national study on the use of various models of supervision in hospitals between 1992, 1994, and 1996 found a decrease in supervision. As noted earlier, traditional models of supervision (individual and group) decreased significantly as did peer supervision (consultation). While the overall numbers of social workers reporting supervision by non-social workers was small, there was a significant increase over each of the years in the study. The researchers concluded that as hospital resources decline, social workers will no longer be able to rely on traditional models of supervision to provide professional development. They suggested that social workers will seek clinical supervision (consultation) outside the organization and use peer models as alternatives.

Organizational policies can also affect supervision, and two studies examined the impact of policy and program changes: one study is of supervisors in long term care and the other is in child welfare. In a qualitative study of 20 case manager supervisors in long term care services, the researchers explored their perceptions about effective supervision (Bowers, Esmond, & Canales, 1999). The case managers pointed out how increasing needs of clients in the long term care support system, longer waiting lists, larger caseloads, and more demands for accountability resulted in supervisors becoming "more of a business-minded person than a social worker" (Bowers et al., 1999, p. 36). Contextual factors required programs to serve more clients with fewer resources and fewer service providers. These supervisors reported that as a result they focused more on workers filing forms on time than on quality of outcomes, and the majority described themselves as becoming less client-centered over time.

The second study that examines the affect of context on supervision investigated how the introduction of a new child welfare policy, kinship foster care, required supervisors to develop a new practice model while simultaneously training child welfare caseworkers to carry out this approach (Gleeson & Philbin, 1996). This small exploratory study of eight supervisors and three program directors found these supervisors invested an enormous amount of time in training caseworkers in the administrative and clinical aspects of practice. Training took place mainly in individual supervision in response to concerns brought by caseworkers. Many contextual factors made model development and training difficult; these factors included the complexity of the child welfare system (policies and procedures at Federal, state, and local levels), the complexity of the cases, a lack of trained caseworkers and trainers in kinship care, and lack of clarity and consensus in the agency about the goals and purpose of kinship foster care.

Organizational climate in the public child welfare system was also found to affect supervision, in this instance the job satisfaction of supervisors. In a study of 70 child welfare supervisors, Silver, Poulin, and Manning (1997) found fairly high job satisfaction associated with organizations where supervisors perceived greater levels of trust among the professional personnel. Additional factors that influenced job satisfaction were time in their current position, with longer periods associated with greater emotional exhaustion and diminished satisfaction; race, with higher levels of satisfaction in non-minority supervisors compared to minority supervisors; and collaboration, with higher satisfaction associated with more time devoted to collaborating with other professionals.

In summary, this group of studies supports the enduring conceptualization of social work supervision as an organizational function; its forms and functions emanate from the organization's mandate. The organizational culture and political imperatives shape the nature of supervision provided and supervisors' job satisfaction. Specifically, in the past ten years cost containment in a range of health and social services has resulted in fewer supervisory positions and less use of traditional social work supervision in hospitals. This may account for the dearth of studies on supervision. The few studies reflected that supervisors must focus on whatever is the "order of the day": for example, help supervisees complete administrative requirements for funding, or develop and teach workers a new model of care.

Diversity and Cultural Competence

Social work practice literature has increasingly focused on the ways in which diverse characteristics of clients and social workers such as race, gender, ethnicity, class, sexual orientation, religion, and ability affect a range of relationship factors between client and worker including power dynamics, the nature of services offered, and client outcomes (e.g., Garcia & Soest, 2000; Gutierrez, Parsons, & Cox, 1998; Lum, 2000, 2005). Surprisingly, ethnicity and race were studied in only two projects, both of which examined links between organizational factors, ethnicity, and supervisors. MacEachron (1994) compared the level of professionalization and satisfaction of two groups of child welfare supervisors in Arizona. One group consisted of 36 supervisors in tribal child welfare agencies, and the other consisted of 49 state supervisors employed in state child welfare offices. The researcher used a mailed survey to assess the difference in the two groups with reference to supervisors' credentials (whether they held social work degrees), child welfare experience, the number of staff supervised and span of control. Differences were not found between the two groups on any of these measures or on their level of job satisfaction. Differences were found in the tasks of each group with state supervisors providing only traditional supervision and tribal supervisors carrying a client caseload and having agency and community responsibilities in addition to traditional supervisory tasks. Differences were also found on perceived training needs with tribal supervisors wanting training in more task domains than state supervisors. The researcher concluded that whether a service organization is culturally affiliated or not is an important component in understanding ethnic-sensitive administrative practice.

The second study on ethnicity reported the findings of a dissertation study that used questionnaires to survey professional and paraprofessional staff in services for Mexican-American people in Texas. Three hundred and twenty three respondents completed a survey instrument about their perception of their supervisors' adequacy of knowledge about Mexican-American culture and issues affecting service delivery, approach to supervision, and use of parallel process. Findings indicated that Hispanic supervisors were perceived as more adequately equipped with culturally laden knowledge and hence more likely to transmit ethnic-sensitive knowledge to supervisees in comparison with non-Hispanic supervisors (Ramierez, 2001). There was no difference between Hispanic and non-Hispanic supervisors in respondents' perceptions of supervisors' application of conventional approaches to supervision and use of parallel process.

While not exclusively focused on culture or diversity, recall two studies reviewed above that reported on race and supervision. Gibelman and Schervish (1995) found a greater percentage of African-American supervisors than African-American members in their NASW survey. Silver and colleagues (1997) found higher levels of job satisfaction in non-minority public child welfare supervisors when compared with minority supervisors. Neither study provided additional data to interpret the meaning of these findings.

With few studies on diversity and cultural competence beyond the surveys reported here, there are not enough data to draw conclusions about the ways in which a range of social identity characteristics are evident in practice and play out in power dynamics in supervision. A strong recommendation is that future studies must include salient features of this crucial dimension of social work. Research methodologies should be used, which will provide a deeper understanding of processes and dynamics.

Towards an Evidence-Based Supervisory Practice

Consistent with the movement to develop evidence-based research for social work practice, supervisors are motivated to learn and use knowledge about effective supervisory practices and techniques which will ultimately improve client outcomes. Two groups of studies are presented. The first group examines global aspects of the supervisory relationship as supervisees and in some cases supervisors perceive it, and the second group links supervision process and client outcome.

In Hensley's (2002) doctoral study of social workers' views of cure and their own experiences in personal therapy and supervision, a key theme that emerged was the influential nature of the supervisory relationship. This qualitative study of 20 social workers revealed that they gained in many ways from their supervision: skills, often related to theory; professional growth and support; role modeling of professional and personal qualities; and mutuality through an interactive supervisory relationship.

Another study used a mixed method design to develop and test a competency based method for supervisees to give feedback to supervisors in Child Protection Services (Drake & Washeck, 1998). Focus groups of supervisees and of supervisors developed an evaluative instrument including supervisory competencies identified in the literature such as availability, knowledge, tasks, communication, and professionalism (integrity and flexibility). When administered, mean scores varied substantially, with supervisees rating more experienced supervisors in a more negative light than newer supervisors. The researchers speculated that some supervisors may withdraw and become less accessible over time. This finding is similar to Silver and colleagues' (1997) finding reviewed earlier that job satisfaction diminished for public child welfare supervisors with greater length of time on the job and increased emotional exhaustion.

When supervisors and supervisees have similar expectations and perspectives about practice and supervision, they perceive that they work together effectively. Similarity of client-centeredness in case management was identified as a factor that could enhance the supervisory relationship or make it difficult (Bowers et al., 1999). The degree of responsibility and the presence of support are two factors that were examined by York (1996) using Hersey and Blanchard's (1988) situational leadership theory. This theory proposes that the leader alter his or her emphasis on relationship behavior or task behavior according to the task readiness of the followers. The theory postulates that the need for emotional support wanes over time as workers develop confidence. York (1996) used a questionnaire to survey a random sample of NASW members in a range of sectors and found strong agreement with the idea that supervisees with high task maturity should be delegated more responsibility than those with either moderate or low task maturity. However, the respondents did not agree that support should vary based on task maturity. The researcher concluded that social workers value an emphasis upon support regardless of their task readiness (York, 1996).

As noted earlier, supervisory practice lacks a well developed empirical base despite decades of theoretical and practice explication. The studies reviewed thus far begin to contribute to evidence-based supervisory practice. A limited number of components in the supervisory relationship are identified. Supervisors are prized who (a) are available, (b) are knowledgeable about tasks and skills and can relate these techniques to theory, (c) hold practice perspectives and expectations about service delivery similar to the supervisee's, (d) provide support and encourage professional growth, (e) delegate responsibility to supervisees who can do the task, (f) serve as a professional role model, and (g) communicate in a mutual and interactive supervisory style. All studies reviewed used self-assessment measures of perception of supervisory helpfulness and hence, while these dimensions appear important to the workers, there is no evidence they affect client or worker outcomes. Future studies should examine the impact of these components on client outcomes. As well, supervisee outcomes such as increased professional development and performance, improved job satisfaction, and organization retention warrant study.

The second group of studies that aims to build an evidence-based approach to supervision links supervision process and client outcome. Following a review of research on supervision conducted between 1955 and 1985, Harkness and Poertner (1989) concluded that despite the emphasis on accountability in definitions of social work supervision, the focus of the literature was primarily on training workers. They argued for a focus on client outcomes that would articulate the behaviors and associations across "a three link chain" (Harkness & Hensley, 1991, p. 506): the supervisor, the social worker, and the client. They credited Shulman (1982) with a proposal that supervisory help should be evaluated in terms of client outcomes rather than staff perceptions.

In a dissertation research project, Harkness (Harkness, 1995, 1997; Harkness & Hensley, 1991) studied these relationships using a small sample of one experienced supervisor, four staff members, and 161 clients in a community mental health centre. Staff members received eight weeks of supervision with a mixed focus (administration, training, and clinical consultation) followed by eight weeks of supervision with a client focus (client concerns and outcomes, and worker interventions). Two client outcomes were measured: scores on a depression scale and scores on a client satisfaction scale. Client outcomes were compared with those of the clients of two additional staff members who received only mixed focus supervision from the same supervisor. When the two types of supervision were compared on reduction of client depression, there was no difference. When compared on client satisfaction, there was an increase on clients' perception of goal attainment, worker's helpfulness, and sense of partnership (Harkness & Hensley, 1991). In further analyses of this data set, Harkness (1995, 1997) found some associations between supervisory skills, supervisory relationship, and practice. The researcher concluded that this study lent modest and conditional support to a concept of helping as the product of interaction across supervisory and client systems. While the use of a small sample is a significant limitation to this work, the researcher demonstrated the importance of designing studies that capture both dynamics of supervision and of practice, exploring links across the two systems, and examining a range of process and outcome measures.

Barriers to Research

The dearth of empirical studies on supervision in the past decade may reflect the declining prevalence of supervision as documented in two studies reviewed earlier in this paper (Berger & Mizrahi, 2001;

Gibelman & Schervish, 1997). If agencies are cutting back on supervision, they may no longer accord it a high priority for study and model development. If this is the case, the development of the empirical base for supervision will need to be initiated by interested and committed individual scholars or professional associations who value its contribution and believe there is much to be gained from systematic study of the area.

The small exploratory and survey studies conducted in the past ten years provide some insights about supervision but reveal an absence of a vibrant community of supervision researchers who build on each others' work as they systematically move forward with their own programs of research. In order to develop evidence-based supervision models, well-designed and large scale studies are required, with substantial resources. It is not readily apparent where a researcher interested in funding for a project on supervision would seek support. Social work researchers have successfully conducted funded projects that contribute substantially to understanding phenomena in high risk populations such as children living in poverty, those diagnosed with HIV-AIDS, the homeless and so on. A recent review of a decade of empirically-supported intervention studies conducted by social workers reflects their success in conducting research with the seriously mentally ill, child and youth behavioral issues and maltreatment, substance abuse, domestic violence, aging and health issues (Reid & Fortune, 2003).

Supervision researchers may wish to consider joining projects aimed at testing specific practice models or programs in fields such as child maltreatment, domestic violence, and adolescent delinquency. In these projects, attention is given to educating staff to carry out specific interventions and best practices to a standard of competence. Such projects might provide researchers interested in advancing the empirical base of supervision with the opportunity to examine the effects of various supervisory approaches and techniques on such variables as workers' adherence to program and model guidelines and client outcome.

CRITIQUE AND FUTURE DIRECTIONS

While there is a theoretical, clinical, and anecdotal literature on social work supervision, as noted throughout this paper, in the past decade there has been a dearth of empirically-based knowledge to support claims made about the importance of supervision or of the effectiveness of various approaches. The studies reviewed reflect single projects on specific topics rather than programs of research with the aim of theory building or developing models of supervisory practice. Single project studies reflect supervision in one sector, for example child welfare (Gleeson & Philbin, 1996; Silver et al., 1997) or hospitals (Berger & Mizrahi, 2001). The extent to which social work supervision is a generic process useful in all fields of specialization or whether it is field specific has yet to be addressed. Systematic development of the discipline of social work supervision is clearly called for in the future.

The majority of the studies reviewed for this paper used small samples, limiting the generalizability of their findings; only two studies used data drawn from national samples (Berger & Mizrahi, 2001; Gibelman & Schervish, 1997). Most of the studies used samples of convenience with only a minority utilizing a random sampling method. In a number of studies the sample was not clearly identified; for example, it was unclear whether the workers had social work degrees or degrees from another discipline. This is important data as one study in child welfare included workers with no formal social work education. Other than studies specifically addressing ethnic (Ramierez, 2001) or native status (MacEachron, 1994), few studies provided data about a range of personal and social identity characteristics that are considered crucial in contemporary social work practice. Only one study included both supervisors and supervisees providing the opportunity to examine processes in the dyad (Harkness & Hensley, 1991). This study was the only one that also included client outcomes. Only one study (Bowers et al., 1999) reported whether approval from an institutional research ethics review board had been received.

Of the twelve studies examined, eight used quantitative methodology, mainly survey research, three used qualitative methodology, and one study used a mixed method approach. Of the eight quantitative studies, more than half did not report the validity or reliability of the scales used in their study. In the six studies that did report, five reported only the validity measure and only one reported both the reliability and validity of the instrument (Silver et al., 1997). Five of the studies reported how instruments were developed and two of these studies did not indicate any validity measures. The four studies that used qualitative methods, while exploratory and small in scale, were well done. The research questions were clear and transparent, and the method used to answer the questions was adequately defined. For all studies, purposeful sampling techniques were employed. Most used in-depth interviews of one to two hours and one study also used a focus group. Only one study identified that open-ended questions were used (Gleeson & Philbin, 1996); the other studies did not identify whether interview guides, open-ended questions or the like were used. Some studies identified the method for recording the data (i.e., tape recording, transcription) and analyzing it. In both quantitative and qualitative studies, data were generally collected retrospectively in cross-sectional surveys. Only one study compared two approaches to supervision (Harkness & Hensley, 1991).

Future research in clinical supervision should aim to include large samples from multiple sites representing a range of geographical locations and service sectors. Comparability of results between studies would be enhanced with the development of reliable and valid instruments that could replace the current reliance on unique self-administered questionnaires. As more studies use the same instruments, findings can be compared and pooled.

There is a need for studies of the effectiveness of a range of supervisory models. Such studies must clearly define their theoretical principles and related supervisory processes and skills. Longitudinal and comparative research on these models would assist in establishing both the superiority of specific models and the common factors across approaches. Finally, a range of relevant outcome measures must be developed. As noted throughout this review, a primary purpose of social work supervision is to ensure accountability to the agency that clients are receiving effective service. While it is a useful beginning point to know about supervisees' and supervisors' experiences and perceptions of important supervision processes, if the research is to contribute to the ultimate goal of improved client service, then better outcome measures must be a part of future studies. Numerous standardized measures for assessing client outcomes and changes in client functioning exist and can be used in these studies based on the goal of the service. For example, there are instruments to measure a range of mental health problems, family and couple processes, child development, and risk factors associated with child maltreatment. Many situations social workers confront are affected by systemic, structural, and organizational barriers. As a result measuring change solely in relation to client outcome may be limited and evident only after many years. Therefore it would be useful to include organizational and administrative outcomes that might be influenced by effective supervision. For example, it is important to learn about the impact of supervision on wait lists, improved worker retention, changes to caseload volume, and changes to duration of service contact. Furthermore, in the interests of developing continuing education programs targeted to professional development needs, a more refined understanding of professional competence and methods to assess competence would be useful. The crucial question in this instance is whether supervision has an impact on professional competence.

CONCLUSIONS

Supervision of practice is a long-standing tradition in social work that has in the past decade received less attention in the professional literature. The dearth in literature may be a result of the diminishing role of supervision due to organizational changes such as cost-cutting measures in agencies, lack of reimbursement coverage through managed care, and down-sizing and re-organization in hospitals. A theoretical and clinical literature was developed by many scholars and practitioners especially since the mid-seventies. The contributions of Kadushin (Kadushin, 1976, 1986, 1992; Kadushin & Harkness, 2002), Munson (Munson, 1983, 1993, 2002), and Shulman (Shulman, 1982, 1993), all of whom conducted studies on aspects of supervision, are to be commended for providing the foundation for understanding the practice of social work supervision. Through the leadership of Munson as founding editor of the journal, *The Clinical Supervisor*, social work supervisors and researchers were able to disseminate innovations, observations, and empirical findings.

In the past decade, the volume of empirical work on supervision in social work has diminished with the majority of social work journals publishing little on this topic. From the current review, it is apparent that those studies that were conducted were modest in scope. One might conclude that supervision in social work is no longer viewed as an important topic of study, despite practitioners' numerous anecdotal accounts of its importance in their professional development.

Recently, under the leadership of Lawrence Shulman and Andrew Safyer, co-editors of the journal, *The Clinical Supervisor*, support for the first annual interdisciplinary conference on supervision has been obtained from the National Institute on Drug Administration and The Haworth Press, Inc. Annual meetings will provide a much needed vehicle for reinvigorating intellectual stimulation and exchange about current issues in supervision and for dissemination of innovations and research findings on clinical supervision. It is hoped that this initiative will encourage new investigators to locate their work in the area of supervision and provide a scholarly community for academic and practice researchers already engaged in this field.

NOTE

The journals searched were those represented in the Social Work Abstracts database: *The Clinical Supervisor, Social Work in Health, Health and Social Work, Journal of Ethnic Diversity in Social Work, Social Work Research, Research on Social Work Practice, Child Welfare, International Journal of Social Work, Canadian Social Work Review, Affilia, Child & Adolescent Social Work Journal, Child and Family Social Work, Arete, Atlantis, Journal of Gerontological Social Work, Social Work, Clinical Social Work Journal, Journal of Social Work Practice, Families in Society*, and *Child Abuse Review*. Since so few studies were found, the research assistant manually reviewed key social work journals, especially in the fields of child welfare and social work in health. No additional studies were found. It is still quite possible that articles on supervision were missed and are not included in this review.

The thirteen articles reviewed were published in the following journals: *The Clinical Supervisor* (8), *Administration in Social Work* (2), *Child Welfare* (1), *Social Work* (1), *Social Work in Health Care* (1).

Several articles within the search parameters reported on studies conducted outside the United States; five studies were from Israel, two studies were from Australia, one study was from Great Britain, and one was from Hong Kong. As noted earlier, the organizational context of supervision is central to the definition and practice of social work supervision. Moreover, the organizational context reflects national and local policies, funding arrangements, and hence supervisory practices. Therefore, it was decided to focus on studies conducted in the United States. We also noted that the Social Work Abstracts database does not reflect a comprehensive inventory of the literature from any country other than United States, and therefore conclusions about the amount of research on supervision conducted in those countries during the search period cannot accurately be made.

REFERENCES

American Board of Examiners in Clinical Social Work. (2004). Clinical supervision: A practice specialty of clinical social work. A position statement of the American Board of Examiners in Clinical Social Work.

Barker, R. L. (1995). Social work supervision, *Social work dictionary*. Washington, DC: NASW Press.

Barretta-Herman, A. (1993). On the development of a model of supervision for licensed social work practitioners. *The Clinical Supervisor, 11*(2), 55-64.

Berger, C., & Mizrahi, T. (2001). An evolving paradigm of supervision within the changing health care environment. *Social Work in Health Care, 32*(4), 1-18.

Bowers, B., Esmond, S., & Canales, M. (1999). Approaches to case management supervision. *Administration in Social Work, 23*(1), 29-49.

Brashears, F. (1995). Supervision as social work practice: A reconceptualization. *Social Work, 40*(5), 692-699.

Drake, B., & Washeck, J. (1998). A competency-based method for providing worker feedback to CPS supervisors. *Administration in Social Work, 23*(3), 55-74.

Garcia, B., & Soest, D. V. (2000). Facilitating learning on diversity: Challenges to the professor. *Journal of Ethnic and Cultural Diversity in Social Work, 9*(1/2), 21-39.
Gibelman, M., & Schervish, P. H. (1995). Pay equity in social work: Not! *Social Work, 40*(5), 622-629.
Gibelman, M., & Schervish, P. H. (1997). Supervision in social work: Characteristics and trends in a changing environment. *The Clinical Supervisor, 16*(2), 1-15.
Gleeson, J. P., & Philbin, C. M. (1996). Preparing caseworkers for practice in kinship foster care: The supervisor's dilemma. *The Clinical Supervisor, 14*(1), 19-34.
Gutierrez, L. M., Parsons, R. J., & Cox, E. O. (1998). *Empowerment in social work practice.* Pacific Grove, CA: Brooks/Cole.
Harkness, D. (1995). The art of helping in supervised practice: Skills, relationships, and outcomes. *The Clinical Supervisor, 13*(1), 63-76.
Harkness, D. (1997). Testing interactional social work theory: A panel analysis of supervised practice and outcomes. *The Clinical Supervisor, 15*(1), 33-50.
Harkness, D., & Hensley, H. (1991). Changing the focus of social work supervision: Effects on client satisfaction and generalized contentment. *Social Work, 36*(3), 506-512.
Harkness, D., & Poertner, J. (1989). Research and social work supervision: A conceptual review. *Social Work, 34*(2), 115-118.
Hensley, P. H. (2002). The value of supervision. *The Clinical Supervisor, 21*(1), 97-110.
Hersey, P., & Blanchard, K. H. (1988). *Management of organizational behavior.* Englewood Cliffs, NJ: Prentice-Hall.
Kadushin, A. (1976). *Supervision in social work.* New York, NY: Columbia University Press.
Kadushin, A. (1986). *Supervision in social work* (2nd ed.). New York, NY: Columbia University Press.
Kadushin, A. (1992). *Supervision in social work* (3rd ed.). New York, NY: Columbia University Press.
Kadushin, A., & Harkness, D. (2002). *Supervision in social work* (4th ed.). New York, NY: Columbia University Press.
Lum, D. (2000). *Social work practice and people of color: A process-stage approach* (4th ed.). Belmont, CA: Wadsworth.
Lum, D. L. (2005). *Cultural competence, practice stages, and client systems.* Belmont, CA: Thomson Brooks/Cole.
MacEachron, A. E. (1994). Supervision in tribal and state child welfare agencies: Professionalization, responsibilities, training needs, and satisfaction. *Child Welfare, 73*(2), 117-128.
Munson, C. E. (1983). *An introduction to clincial social work supervision.* Binghamton, NY: The Haworth Press, Inc.
Munson, C. E. (1993). *Clinical social work supervision* (2nd ed.). Binghamton, NY: The Haworth Press, Inc.
Munson, C. E. (2002). *Handbook of clinical social work supervision* (3rd ed.). Binghamton, NY: The Haworth Press, Inc.
Ramierez, N. (2001). Supervisors' personal-professional attributes and approaches to supervision in organizations providing clinical services to Mexican-American persons. *The Clinical Supervisor, 20*(2), 117-131.

Raskin, M. (2005). Time-line for the development of CSWE field standards. Presented to the Field Education Council, CSWE-Annual Program Meeting. New York.

Reid, W. J., & Fortune, A. E. (2003). Empirical foundations for practice guidelines in current social work knowledge. In A. Rosen & E. K. Proctor (Eds.), *Developing practice guidelines for social work intervention: Issues, methods, and research agenda* (pp. 59-79). New York: Columbia University Press.

Shulman, L. (1982). *Skills of supervision and staff management.* Itasca, IL: Peacock.

Shulman, L. (1993). *Interactional supervision.* Washington, DC: NASW Press.

Silver, P. T., Poulin, J. E., & Manning, R. C. (1997). Surviving the bureaucracy: The predictors of job satisfaction for the public agency supervisor. *The Clinical Supervisor, 15*(1), 1-20.

York, R. O. (1996). Adherence to situational leadership theory among social workers. *The Clinical Supervisor, 14*(2), 5-24.

doi:10.1300/J001v24n01_04

Snapshot of Clinical Supervision in Counseling and Counselor Education: A Five-Year Review

L. DiAnne Borders

SUMMARY. Clinical supervision articles in journals published by the American Counseling Association and in two international counseling journals over the last five years include both conceptual pieces and empirical studies. These articles are reviewed and discussed in light of themes, trends, and implications for the practice of clinical supervision as well as supervisor training. doi:10.1300/J001v24n01_05 *[Article copies available for a fee from The Haworth Document Delivery Service: 1-800-HAWORTH. E-mail address: <docdelivery@haworthpress.com> Website: <http://www.HaworthPress.com> © 2005 by The Haworth Press, Inc. All rights reserved.]*

KEYWORDS. Supervision approaches, ethical and legal issues in clinical supervision, multicultural supervision, substance abuse counselors, supervisory relationships, supervisor evaluation, group supervision, supervision research

---

L. DiAnne Borders, PhD, is Burlington Industries Excellence Professor and Chair, Department of Counseling and Educational Development, University of North Carolina at Greensboro, PO Box 26170, Greensboro, NC 27402-6170 (E-mail: borders@uncg.edu).

Earlier versions of this article were presented both at the Clinical Supervision Planning Committee meeting in October 2004 and at the First International Interdisciplinary Clinical Supervision Conference in Amherst, NY, June 2005. The author thanks Catharina Chang and Jack Culbreth for their helpful feedback.

[Haworth co-indexing entry note]: "Snapshot of Clinical Supervision in Counseling and Counselor Education: A Five-Year Review." Borders, L. DiAnne. Co-published simultaneously in *The Clinical Supervisor* (The Haworth Press, Inc.) Vol. 24, No. 1/2, 2005, pp. 69-113; and: *Supervision in Counseling: Interdisciplinary Issues and Research* (ed: Lawrence Shulman, and Andrew Safyer) The Haworth Press, Inc., 2005, pp. 69-113. Single or multiple copies of this article are available for a fee from The Haworth Document Delivery Service [1-800-HAWORTH, 9:00 a.m. - 5:00 p.m. (EST). E-mail address: docdelivery@haworthpress.com].

Available online at http://cs.haworthpress.com

doi:10.1300/J001v24n01_05

Similar to other helping fields, supervised clinical work is a pivotal experience in the development of professional counselors. Indeed, the field has given much attention to developing counseling supervision as a unique profession. Some 20-plus years ago, working groups within the Association for Counselor Education and Supervision (ACES) created standards for counseling supervisors (Dye & Borders, 1990), a curriculum guide for supervisor training (Borders et al., 1991), and ethical guidelines specific to the practice of supervision (Hart, Borders, Nance, & Paradise, 1995). Working collaboratively with the National Board for Certified Counselors (NBCC), the Approved Clinical Supervisor (ACS) credential was created in 1998. One challenge in creating these documents was the expanse of the field. Professional counselors see clients from across the lifespan, and provide services in schools, mental health agencies, college counseling centers, career counseling centers, hospice, cancer patient support services, inpatient and emergency services, rehabilitation settings, substance abuse agencies, older adult services, facilities for at risk youth and domestic violence clients, outdoor/experiential settings, and private practice, among many others. Professional counselors also provide couples and family counseling, play therapy for children, assessments, psycho-educational and therapeutic groups, in-home counseling, and a range of other preventive and remedial services.

Professional counselors are licensed at the master's-level. Their training, accredited by the Council for Accreditation of Counseling and Related Programs (CACREP), includes a minimum of 100 hours of practicum and 600 hours of internship in a field placement. Of the 600 internship hours, at least 240 must involve direct contact with clients. Weekly individual and group supervision of these experiences is required, including direct observation methods (e.g., live observation, review of audio taped or videotaped sessions). Following graduation from a 48- to 60-hour master's program, 1200 or more post-degree clinical hours are required (the number varies somewhat by state). Increasingly, counselor licensure regulations include requirements related to the practice of post-degree supervision (e.g., direct observation) and the preparation of the supervisor (e.g., specified hours of training specific to counseling supervision; Borders & Cashwell, 1992; Sutton, 1997). Master's-level practitioners also are eligible for the National Certified Counselor (NCC) credential through NBCC, and may work toward several specialty credentials through NBCC (e.g., school counseling, substance abuse counseling).

At the doctoral level, instruction in supervision theory and skills and supervised practice of supervision are required for programs accredited by CACREP. Doctoral graduates may pursue practice in a range of settings, leadership positions within agencies, or academic posts as counselor educators. Doctoral graduates, then, often provide supervision as part of their regular work. In fact, ongoing supervision across one's professional counseling career is encouraged, with the type and frequency of supervision evolving over time. This brief overview of the profession suggests the broad scope of the field, and thus the challenges in addressing supervision needs of counseling students, licensure applicants, and seasoned practitioners. These challenges and related issues are addressed in the literature reviewed here.

Conducting a review of supervision literature in counseling and counselor education also presents challenges. Counselors publish in a variety of journals, including those specific to the counseling field (e.g., *Journal of Counseling and Development*, *Counselor Education and Supervision*), as well as those based in other related fields (e.g., *Journal of Counseling Psychology*, *Addiction: Theory and Research*) and those that are interdisciplinary (e.g., *The Clinical Supervisor*). Similarly, authors from other fields, particularly counseling psychology, sometimes publish in counseling journals. Nevertheless, it can be assumed that articles in counseling-specific journals, regardless of author, reflect the philosophical stance of the counseling field. Thus, for the purposes of this review, I have focused on journals published by the American Counseling Association (ACA), the umbrella organization over divisions with a specialized focus (e.g., school counselors, substance abuse counselors, family counselors). Counseling increasingly has become globalized, both in terms of practice and training (NBCC site). Accordingly, I also have included supervision articles that appeared in two international counseling journals during the last five years, *International Journal for the Advancement of Counselling* and *British Journal of Guidance and Counselling*; no supervision-related articles were found in the *Canadian Journal of Counselling*). Nevertheless, it should be noted that articles published by counseling professionals in non-ACA journals are not included here. In addition, books (e.g., Bernard & Goodyear, 2004; Borders & Brown, 2005) and book chapters (e.g., Borders, 2001) published by counseling professionals during this time, as well as multimedia materials (e.g., Baltimore & Crutchfield, 2003; Borders & Benshoff, 1999), also are not reviewed. Following guidelines for this collection, the primary focus here is on articles published within the last five years, roughly late 1999-early 2005. Numbers of supervision articles published in each journal during the review period are provided in Table 1. Numbers by supervision topic and type of article are provided in Table 2.

The counseling supervision literature during the last five years has addressed a variety of topics, using a variety of research methods. Similar to previous decades of supervision literature, recent publications have been more applied than theoretical. Counseling journal editors typically have required researchers to emphasize implications of their findings for practice. This applied emphasis is appropriate to the field, given that the majority of ACA members are master's-level practitioners, and the majority of doctoral-level counseling professionals (those who are publishing) primarily are involved full-time or part-time in the

TABLE 1. Clinical Supervision Publications in Counseling Journals (ACA and International), 1999-2004

Journal	Quantitative Studies	Qualitative Studies	Conceptual	Total # of Supervision Articles
Journal of Counseling and Development (JCD)	4		4	8
Counselor Education and Supervision (CE&S)	16	2	13	31
Counseling and Values (C&V)			2	2
Journal of College Counseling (JCC)			1	1
Journal of Humanistic Counseling, Education & Development (JHCED)		1	2	3
Journal of Mental Health Counseling (JMHC)			5	5
Journal of Multicultural Counseling and Development (JMCD)	2	1	5	8
Journal of Specialists in Group Work (JSGW)		2		2
Measurement and Evaluation in Counseling and Development (MECD)	1			1
Professional School Counseling (PSC)	2	1	3	6
Journal of Addictions and Offender Counseling	1			1
The Family Journal			5	5
Rehabilitation Counseling Bulletin (RCB)	2		1	3
British Journal of Guidance Counselling	2	1		3
International Journal for the Advancement of Counselling	1		4	5

Note: There were no supervision publications in *Adultspan, Career Development Quarterly* (*CDQ*), or *Journal of Employment Counseling* (ACA journals) nor the *Canadian Journal of Counselling* during the review period. "Quantitative" includes experimental studies, descriptive studies, *ex post facto* studies, and surveys.

TABLE 2. Clinical Supervision Publications in Counseling Journals, Categories/Topics by Type of Article, 1999-2004

Topics	Conceptual	Quantitative	Qualitative	Total
Supervisory Relationship	2	5		7
Attachment theory	1	1		2
Counter-transference	2			2
Working alliance		6		6
Multicultural Supervision	8	6	1	15
Age	1	1		2
Gender	1	3	1	5
Language (bilingual)	1			1
Physical disability			1	1
Race/ethnicity	2	2	1	5
Racial identity development			1	1
Religion	1		1	2
Sexual orientation		1	1	2
Socioeconomic status	1		1	2
White supervisors	1			1
Counseling Specialties	6	9	2	17
Career counselors	1	1		2
Family/couple counselors	5			5
Mental health counselors	1			1
Rehabilitation counselors	1	2		3
School counselors	4	5	2	11
Substance abuse counselors		2		2
Supervisors	3	11	1	15
Supervisor competence			1	1
Supervisor feedback and evaluation		3		3
Supervisor self-disclosure		3		3
Supervisor style		7		7
Supervisor training	3	3		6
Supervisees	3	4		7
Anxiety	3	1		4
Case conceptualization		1		1
Satisfaction with supervision		6		6
Self-efficacy	1	3		4
Self-evaluation		1		1
Supervision Approaches/Strategies (Individual supervision)	11		1	12
Developmental Models	5	1		6
Discrimination Model	6	1		7
Group Supervision		2	4	6
Technology in Supervision	1	2		3

TABLE 2 (continued)

Topics	Conceptual	Quantitative	Qualitative	Total
Ethical and Legal Issues	6	1		7
Spirituality in Supervision	3			3
Client Issues	2			2
Eating disorders	1			1
Suicide	1			1
Supervising Counselor Licensure Applicants	2			2

Note. "Quantitative" includes experimental studies, descriptive studies, *ex post facto* studies, and surveys.

teaching and supervision of future practitioners. In addition, counseling interns typically are supervised by both university faculty members (or supervised doctoral students) and on-site master's-level practitioners, who typically have limited to no supervision training. The recent supervision literature, then, also includes a number of "how to" articles, including applications of theory, descriptions of models or supervision strategies, guidelines for ethical supervision practice, identification of key issues, and discussions of dynamics affecting the supervisor enterprise (e.g., multicultural, group process). To write a review of the counseling supervision literature without including these conceptual pieces would be a disservice to the field. Indeed, these articles represent the field's commitment to enhancing the practice of clinical supervision not only in program-based (i.e., in-house, at the university) training clinics for counseling students, but also for interns and practitioners in the wide variety of settings where they work. Thus, although the primary focus of this paper is a review of recent empirical publications on supervision within the counseling field, I will begin with an overview of conceptual articles published during the past five years.

THE CONCEPTUAL LITERATURE

Supervision Approaches

A number of conceptual articles involved descriptions of supervision approaches or strategies. Some writers adapted counseling approaches to supervision, such as solution-focused (Presbury, Echterling, & McKee, 1999), strength-based (Edwards & Chen, 1999), and systemic (Montgomery, Hendricks, & Bradley, 2001) perspectives. These articles typically were built on similar works published earlier, and were primarily instructive (i.e., how to). Others drew on diverse psychological theories to explain aspects of supervision, such as attachment (Neswald-McCalip, 2001), goal-setting (Curtis, 2000), and self-efficacy (Barnes, 2004), illustrated by case examples. Barnes' (2004) discussion of self-efficacy theory is a particularly strong piece, as she explored the theory in some depth and provided a critical review of a relatively large body of empirical literature specific to counselor training and supervision. Cognitive theories were explored by two authors. Granello (2000) described the use of Bloom's Taxonomy to increase counselors' cognitive complexity, an outcome goal of most developmental models of supervision (see Blocher, 1983, in particular). Granello included an instructive table of sample skills and questions appropriate to each level of Bloom's Taxonomy. Fitch and Marshall (2002) provided an overview of cognitive restructuring techniques to address counseling students' anxiety and self-defeating thoughts.

A few authors described a particular technique (e.g., use of transcripts, Arthur & Gfroerer, 2002; bug-in-the-eye approach, Miller, Miller, & Evans, 2002). Sommer and Cox (2003) proposed the use of Greek myths as metaphors for counselor development during supervision. Žorga, Dekleva, and Kobolt (2001) offered suggestions for effective peer supervision groups. Champe and Kleist (2003) provided a review of research on the effectiveness of a supervisory intervention, focusing on live supervision approaches. Such reviews are rare, likely due to the relative lack of studies investigating the effectiveness of supervisory interventions.

Other writers focused on particular counseling specialties. McMahon and Patton (2000) urged clinical supervision for career counselors. Foster and McAdams (1999) presented a model to guide supervision of counseling students who experience client suicide. Specific activities in ongoing supervision (e.g., case review, opportunities to talk to counselors who have had similar experiences) are recommended, and counselor training programs are urged to have specific written procedures in place for responding to such situations. DeLucia-Waack (1999) described a group supervision model, based in parallel process, for female counselors leading eating disorders groups. Counselors' counter-transference issues related to body image, food, and weight are the focus of supervision. It is expected that the group leaders will discuss personal reactions to group members and group topics, how personal issues affect group process, and the relationship between co-leaders during group supervision sessions. As needed, group leaders are referred to individual counseling to address personal issues that continue to interfere with their work.

Not surprisingly, increased attention to spiritual issues in the counseling field was reflected in recent supervision literature. Bishop, Avila-Juarbe, and Thumme (2003) called for the infusion of spirituality into the supervision process, viewing spirituality as another aspect of client diversity, and outlined potential research questions for exploring this area. Polanski (2003) provided an instructive discussion regarding ways spiritual and religious issues might be addressed in supervision. Polanski used Bernard's (1997) discrimination model as a framework for describing relevant intervention skills (e.g., assessment of client's spiritual and religious beliefs, using words and images consistent with these beliefs), conceptualization skills (e.g., relevance of client's beliefs to presenting issue), and personalization skills (e.g., how the counselor's beliefs may impact the counseling process). Included are issues beyond stated beliefs, including whether religion is a source of strength or guilt, how religious traditions influence one's ideas and images of God (e.g., God as parent), and how oppression of some individuals (e.g., women, gay and lesbian persons) in some religious institutions can play a role in client's issues. Finally, Frame (2001) illustrated the use of a spiritual genogram with supervisees and clients. The genogram portrays religious and spiritual traditions, conversions or other changes in adherence to a faith, closeness and conflicts between family members based in their beliefs, and significant events in the family and religious community (e.g., first communion, death of a well-loved rabbi). Multigenerational patterns and themes are revealed through examination of the genogram, providing self-awareness for supervisees regarding issues that may affect their work with clients, particularly around "trigger families" (i.e., families with issues similar to those of the counselor's family of origin).

Supervision Settings

Suggestions for site supervisors of school counseling interns were addressed in three articles. Noting the lack of supervisor training for most school counselors, Nelson and Johnson (1999) described an integrated approach based in the discrimination model (Bernard, 1997) and the stage outline of Littrell, Lee-Borden, and Lorenz (1979). Sequential stages (orientation, working, transition, and integration stages) across an internship experience are described. Later, Nelson, Johnson, and Thorngren (2000) applied the same approach to supervision of interns in mental health settings. Roberts, Morotti, Herrick, and Tilbury (2001) addressed more practical issues for school counseling site supervisors, including being clear of expectations and evaluating whether these can be met (e.g., intern taping requirements, adequate space for an intern, potential dual relationships). Roberts et al. also highlighted the critical role modeling that site supervisors provide to interns, ways to enhance communication between site supervisors and university faculty members, and the need for supervisor training for site supervisors. Studer (2005) provided an overview of the supervision process, stages, and strategies for site supervisors. She addressed not only clinical supervision but also administrative supervision that allows interns to gain experience in all aspects of a comprehensive, developmental school counseling program.

Magnuson and her colleagues wrote two post-degree supervision "consumers' guides," one for licensure applicants seeking supervision (Magnuson, Norem, & Wilcoxin, 2002) and one for supervisors considering working with them (Magnuson, Norem, & Wilcoxin, 2000). Licensure applicants were encouraged to view themselves as "consumers of supervision" and gather relevant information and recommendations regarding prospective supervisors. The authors suggested topics licensure applicants can cover in interviews as they seek a good supervisor-supervisee fit. Guidelines for the supervisor included a discussion of the differences between university-based supervision and supervision of licensure applicants, an overview of needed documentation (e.g., professional disclosure statements, supervision contract, assessment protocols), and an emphasis on risk management concerns (e.g., vicarious liability, confidentiality).

Pearson (2001) also addressed supervision of pre-licensed counselors. Using a detailed case example, he illustrated the application of the discrimination model (Bernard, 1997) and a developmental model (Stoltenberg, McNeill, & Delworth, 1998) in assessing the supervisee, choosing supervision topics, and determining supervisor roles. Relatedly, Pearson (2000) outlined potential challenges in the supervisory relationship (e.g., transference, countertranference, resistance), including ways to recognize and address problematic interactions. More recently, Pearson (2004) outlined strategies to help mental health counseling students prepare for supervision and help them be "proactive participants who impact the quality of their supervision experience" (p. 371).

Supervisor Training

The lack of supervisor training for counselors in the field was of concern to other authors, who proposed ways to address the concern. Britton, Goodman, and Rak (2002) described a one-day workshop they presented to counselors in community mental health agencies. Britton et al. covered the supervisory relationship, models of supervision, ethics, resistance, and multicultural issues. They also included experiential activities, such as role plays.

Manzanares, O'Halloran, McCartney, Filer, Varhely, and Calhoun (2004) chose a different approach. They created a CD-ROM for their site supervisors. Contents included materials and forms related to the counseling program and internship expectations, as well as brief video clips of faculty members discussing various supervision topics. Evaluations of both approaches by participants were positive.

Getz (1999) described a more involved training process that she has used in academic and practice settings. In particular, Getz outlined seven core competencies, drawn from the ACES curriculum guide for training supervisors (Borders et al., 1991). She also outlined structured procedures the supervisors-in-training use in sessions with their supervisees as well as in supervised supervision sessions, designed to address each competency area.

Ethical and Legal Issues

Ethical and legal issues continue to be of concern to counseling supervisors, and several authors addressed a variety of topics in this area. Herlihy, Gray, and McCollum (2002) described ethical issues particularly salient for school counselors, both in terms of the need for clinical supervision for these practitioners and issues for the school counselor who provides supervision (e.g., competence, confidentiality, dual relationships). Blackwell, Strohmer, Belcas, and Burton (2002) discussed these and other issues (e.g., due process, informed consent) as applied to rehabilitation counselor supervision. Blackwell et al. emphasized the importance of training for supervisors, as outlined in the rehabilitation counselor-clinical supervisor credential, and the need for a supervisor professional disclosure statement (sample included). Cobia and Boes (2000) discussed professional disclosure statements in some detail, emphasizing that use of a strong statement and a formal plan (or individualized learner contract) can minimize the potential for ethical conflicts. These documents clearly set forth the rights and responsibilities of the supervisor and supervisee, supervision approaches, evaluation methods, desired outcomes, potential risks and benefits, and mutually agreed upon goals for the supervision experience. Such documentation also may help the supervisor avoid liability to the supervision. Guest and Dooley (1999) noted that the trend toward credentialing supervisors meant increased accountability for their actions. They applied the elements of malpractice to the supervisory relationship to examine supervisor vulnerability to a malpractice charge from a supervisee. They concluded that all malpractice components–legal duty of care, standard of care, harm, and proximate cause–existed in the supervisory relationship.

Cobia and Pipes (2002) explored the theoretical and empirical bases supporting mandated supervision for practitioners who are under discipline from a regulatory board (e.g., licensure board). They noted that, although there is a consensus that mandated supervision in such cases can be effective, there is no empirical evidence for its success. They found some theoretical support for the practice in developmental models of supervision, interpersonal influence process theories, and social learning theory. Nevertheless, Cobia and Pipes suggested supervisors take on mandated supervision cases with great caution, given the lack of empirical support and potential legal risks.

Muratori (2001) examined another difficulty situation: supervisees who believe they are working with an impaired supervisor. Muratori discussed the range of impairments (e.g., burnout, substance abuse, sexual exploitation) and emphasized that assessing the nature and severity of the impairment is key to determining an appropriate course of action. Applying a developmental perspective, Muratori noted the vulnerability of neophyte counselors, and urged middle-level counselors, "who may be scrutinizing their supervisors through a resistant and somewhat distorted lens" (p. 48), to carefully assess the accuracy of their perceptions. Muratori also provided an ethical decision-making model to help supervisees determine what course of action, if any, will be pursued regarding the impaired supervision.

Multicultural Supervision

Multicultural issues in supervision have received increased attention over the last five years, including a special issue of the *Journal of Multicultural Counseling and Development* (Constantine, 2001), which included two conceptual articles (empirical articles are discussed in the next section). Hird, Cavalieri, Dulko, Felice, and Ho (2001) summarized ongoing discussions between a supervisor (Hird) and his supervisees (coauthors) regarding how multicultural supervision is conceptualized, how cultural differences affect the supervisory relationship, and how supervisors and supervisees might introduce multicultural issues into the relationship. Drawing from their own experiences, the authors illustrated the deleterious effects of *not* discussing multicultural issues directly in supervision. They also emphasized that such conversations should begin early in supervision and described three possible approaches: (1) the use of semi-structured questions to begin the discussion (e.g., What cultural variables construct your cultural identity? How do you feel about your client's race?); (2) a mutual exchange regarding supervisor-supervisee differences and how these may affect their work together, initiated by the supervisor; and (3) a more personal approach in which the supervisor self-discloses his or her own process of becoming multicultural aware.

Also within the special issue, Garrett et al. (2001) presented a paradigm for increasing supervisors' effectiveness in communicating about cultural differences. Drawing on both counseling and anthropology literature, the authors described a VISION model that includes discussion of *V*alues and belief systems, *I*nterpretation of experiences, *S*tructuring the relationship and process, *I*nteractional style preferences, *O*perational strategies for working toward goals, and *N*eeds, expectations, and desired outcomes. Supervisors are encouraged to use the VISION model to address cultural differences proactively, from the beginning of supervision.

Estrada, Frame, and Williams (2004) echoed these writers' emphasis on early discussions of cultural issues, particularly race and ethnicity. In fact, Estrada et al. argued that supervisors often resist addressing race and ethnicity in their work with supervisees, even when there are racial and ethnic differences among the supervisor, supervisee, and client. The authors described several potential (and observed) errors in cross-cultural supervision, such as failing "to challenge clients' cultural practices, even when these practices limit clients psychologically or result in harm, in a misguided notion that to challenge a client's values is tantamount to imposing one's values on the client" (p. 312). To enhance cross-cultural supervision, Estrada et al. suggested using cultural genograms or racial identity assessments to identify supervisor's and supervisee's culturally-based beliefs and assumptions, and an open discussion of the results in an initial supervision session. They also emphasized the importance of learning about clients' racial and ethnic contexts through conversations with colleagues with a similar background, reading professional literature, and experiencing the music and stories of clients of color.

International journals also included multicultural supervision articles. Robinson, Bradley, and Hendricks (2000) provided an overview of supervisor cultural awareness and dynamics in the supervision relationship. They provided suggestions for integrating cultural concepts into various theory-based approaches (e.g., psychotherapeutic, behavioral) to supervision. Richards (2000) identified cultural and social issues in Zimbabwe (e.g., colonial history, family hierarchy, spirituality and mysticism) that impact the supervision process. She offered specific suggestions for supervisors working in that country (e.g., use of group supervision rather than individual supervision, recognition of the value of traditional network of helpers).

More recently, Hays and Chang (2003) addressed White privilege, oppression, and racial identity development within supervision, acknowledging that although client populations are becoming increasingly diverse, most counselors are White. Thus, the need to address White privilege within supervision is paramount. Following a review of the literature on the identified constructs, Hays and Chang suggested several approaches for introducing a discussion of White privilege in supervision, including questions to facilitate awareness (e.g., What values and traditions do you associate with your White heritage?), supervisors' open discussion of their own heritage and its influences on their counseling and supervision relationships, expanding discussions to other forms of privilege (e.g., men, heterosexuals), and focusing on group dynamics in group supervision (e.g., Who in the supervision group do you feel most similar to?).

Finally, Fuertes (2004) explored issues salient in supervision of bilingual counseling. First, Fuertes offered explanations and suggestions regarding language, including client and supervisee preferences, dynamics related to "language mixing" and "language switching," and language-based conceptions of wellness, illness, and coping. He also discussed acculturation levels and acculturation stress, the need for flexibility in theory and technique in counseling and supervision, and the role of counselors and supervisors in advocating for clients' needs (e.g., housing, health care, immigration issues).

THE EMPIRICAL LITERATURE

The empirical literature on counseling supervision during the five-year span appeared in a number of journals (see Table 1). Not surprisingly, the vast majority of these were published in *Counselor Education and Supervision*, the official journal of the Association for Counselor Education and Supervision (ACES). Both quantitative and, increasingly, qualitative studies were published on an array of topics and issues. In the following section, these research articles have been grouped into categorizes by the main focus of the research questions; some could have been included in more than one section. Table 2 provides a more comprehensive view, as each study was counted in each category (variable) represented in the study.

School Counseling

During the 1990s, researchers documented the lack of clinical supervision for school counseling practitioners–and their growing need and desire for it (Borders & Usher, 1992; Roberts & Borders, 1994; Sutton & Page, 1994). Unfortunately, more recent studies reveal little change. Page, Pietrzak, and Sutton (2001) conducted a follow-up survey of a national random sample of ASCA members who were practicing school counselors ($n = 267$). Few respondents reported they were currently receiving individual (13%) or group (11%) clinical supervision. Of these, their primary purposes for seeking supervision were improving their school counseling skills (46%) and preparing for licensure (35%). Over half (57%) said they wanted to receive clinical supervision in the future, while 33% reported no need for supervision. Participants also rated the importance of a set of supervision goals. The highest rated goals were "taking appropriate action with client problems," "developing skills and techniques," and "improving skills in diagnosis." These skills-oriented statements, however, accounted for small amounts of the variance in an exploratory factor analysis. Three factors were revealed: Developing Self as a Counselor (44% of the variance), Treatment Planning and Assessment (9.9%), and Developing Skills and Taking Action (6.5%). Page et al. noted the similarity of these factors to the three focus areas in the discrimination model (Bernard, 1997).

School counselors in Australia ("guidance officers") also receive little supervision, according to McMahon and Patton (2001). In fact, almost half the participants ($n = 227$) in focus groups and a follow-up survey indicated they received supervision twice a year or less. Similar to the United States participants in Page et al.'s (2001) survey, the Australian school counselors expressed strong desires for clinical supervision, and cited a number of supervision benefits such as support, new ideas and strategies, reducing stress and burnout, and personal growth. Participants described in detail their use of informal support networks to meet their supervision needs. McMahon and Patton (2000) reported similar results from focus groups of senior guidance officers (supervisors) and supervised and unsupervised guidance officers (school counselors). All perceived inadequate time was devoted to supervision, and all viewed supervision as important. Reasons for needing supervision identified by the participants included support, accountability, induction of new professionals, isolation, and professional, personal, and skill development. Participants also reported their observations of lack of development without supervision.

School counselors in Israel *do* receive supervision, although they also have expressed a desire to receive more systematic supervision (Shechtman & Wirzberger, 1999). To determine needs and preferred supervisor style, Shechtman and Wirzberger sent questionnaires to Israeli school counselors. Respondents (n = 202) were divided into four groups: novices (no more than 2 years experience), less experienced counselors (3-7 years experience), more experienced counselors (8 or more years), and counselor supervisors (those who have completed a 2-year training program in counseling supervision). In line with developmental models of supervision, the counselor supervisors and more experienced counselors reported fewer needs for supervision overall, and novice and less experienced counselors wanted a more structured teaching style of supervision. Shechtman and Wirzberger also noted the areas for which most of the school counselors wanted supervision: working with teachers, working with parents, innovations in counseling, learning disabilities, suicide prevention, eating disorders, testing in counseling, and coping with conflict and resistance.

Agnew, Vaught, Getz, and Fortune (2000) reported on one Virginia school system's efforts to address the lack of supervision for elementary school counselors through a peer group clinical supervision program. During the first year of the program, a credentialed supervisor (consultant) met monthly with the school counselors to demonstrate and teach various peer group supervision methods (e.g., Interpersonal Process Recall, Kagan, & Kagan, 1997; structured peer group supervision, Borders, 1991). During the second year, the counselors met periodically in peer groups of four, received feedback from the consultant, and modeled their process for each other. The groups continued to meet on their own in the third and subsequent years. During the sixth year, Agnew et al. conducted a qualitative program evaluation, including structured interviews and ratings of program effects, strengths, and weaknesses, as well as archival data (e.g., ratings of job satisfaction and burnout). The researchers reported peer group participants "had high job satisfaction and significantly low burnout levels" (actual data not reported). In addition, almost all participants (97%) reported gains in skills, professionalism, and personal areas (e.g., confidence), although gains in skills were lower than the other areas. Peer support was the most frequently cited strength of the program; weaknesses included not enough time and the need for more supervision training. There was some indication that participants gave each other less confrontive feedback over time.

Although this evaluation report had many limitations, the results reinforce those found in earlier studies (e.g., Crutchfield & Borders, 1997). Clinical supervision for school counselors is a challenge. In contrast to many community mental health agencies, there is not an expectation of clinical supervision–and no clinical supervisors on staff–in school systems. Peer group supervision is one viable approach, and it meets some needs. Notably, however, peer groups do not seem to enhance counseling skills (Agnew et al., 2000; Crutchfield & Borders, 1997). Given that a substantial percentage of counselor education program graduates are school counselors, with consistent documented needs and wishes for clinical supervision, in conjunction with hurdles presented by the school system structure, this is an area needing innovative programs and research that includes outcome variables of interest to school administrators (e.g., students' academic achievement).

Although school counselors in the United States rarely receive supervision, nevertheless training in supervision, they often serve as on-site supervisors for interns. Kahn (1999) investigated how these school counselors allocated their supervision time. Retrospective data were collected from counselors in Pennsylvania (n = 119) who had supervised an intern within the last five years. Respondents indicated they spent most of their time supervising the interns' individual and group counseling/crisis intervention (34%) and consultation work (22%). Middle school counselors devoted more supervision time to counseling work than did elementary and high school counselors. Kahn also interviewed 12 counselors who had had supervision training. These counselors reported their supervision training enabled them to prioritize supervision time according to the interns' needs and be more effective.

Counselors in Other Settings

A few studies of counselors in other settings also were reported during the last five years. McMahon (2003) conducted focus groups and surveyed members of a professional career counseling organization in Australia. Fewer than half reported they received clinical supervision, although they cited a variety of benefits of supervision (e.g., support, new ideas and strategies). Participants with backgrounds in counseling, psychology, and social work demonstrated a greater understanding of supervision and were more open to it than were those from human resource development backgrounds.

Schultz, Ososkie, Fried, Nelson, and Bardos (2002) sent questionnaires to rehabilitation counselors employed in the public sector in two western states. Of the 111 respondents, 73% reported no regularly scheduled contact with their supervisor. About half (53%) reported 30 minutes or less of supervision each week, and respondents often cited staff meetings as supervision time. Shultz et al. concluded that clinical supervision of rehabilitation counselors was irregular, inconsistent, reactive, and crisis-oriented, and noted an "extensive misunderstanding as to what constitutes supervision" (p. 219). The authors noted the need for continued study of clinical supervision and supervisor training to advance the field of rehabilitation counseling.

Thielsen and Leahy (2001) contributed to this effort through a study designed to identify essential knowledge and skills for clinical supervisors in rehabilitation counseling. Randomly selected rehabilitation counselors (n = 774) rated 95 knowledge and skill items generated via the Delphi method. Principal components analysis with varimax rotation yielded a six-component solution that accounted for 46.3% of the variance. Of the six factors, "rehabilitation counseling knowledge" and "ethical and legal issues" were rated most important. The other four were rated important, but less so: theories and models, intervention techniques and methods, evaluation and assessment, and supervisor relationship. There were some differences by demographic variables. Women rated 5 of the 6 factors as more important than did the men. Respondents with a doctoral degree, training in clinical supervision, and those with counseling specialties other than rehabilitation and social work all rated "theories and models" higher in importance. Thielson and Leahy also reported a majority of the respondents supported establishing specific training (67.5%) and experience (70.5%) requirements for clinical supervisions in rehabilitation counseling.

Culbreth and Borders (1999) investigated substance abuse counselors' perceptions of the supervisory relationship. The counselors (n = 360) were employed in public mental health centers in North Carolina. Of interest was the impact of a match or mismatch of counselor and supervisor recovery status, a unique dynamic in the substance abuse field. No main effects for counselor or supervisor recovery status were found. There was, however, a significant two-way interaction effect for recovery status (match or mismatch) for all satisfaction and relationship measures. Both recovering and non-recovering counselors reported significantly higher ratings when their recovery status matched that of their supervisor. Culbreth (1999) found similar results in a national survey of substance abuse counselors ($n = 134$). Overall, the counselors reported satisfaction with their supervision, including session mechanics (e.g., frequency), supervisor competence, and the supervisory relationship. Those who considered themselves in recovery wanted significantly more supervision than did non-recovery counselors, and were significantly more likely to prefer a supervisor who also was in recovery.

Supervisor Training

The effectiveness of supervisor training programs were investigated in two studies. Baker, Exum, and Tyler (2002) used Watkins' (1994) supervisor complexity model as the framework in a study of a doctoral-level academic course. Twelve students who had completed a supervision theory and research class and who were currently enrolled in a supervision practicum made up the experimental group. Seven doctoral students not yet enrolled in either course made up the control group. All students completed a scale designed to measure Watkins' supervisor development model at the beginning, middle, and end of the semester. In addition, students participated in retrospective interviews at mid-semester and one month after the end of the course. The interviews also involved questions based in Watkins' model. Dependent t tests indicated the experimental groups' developmental scores significantly increased from the beginning to mid-semester and from mid-semester to the end of the course. Independent t tests indicated the experimental and control groups were not significantly different at the beginning of the course, but were different at mid-semester and the end, with the experimental group being higher each time. Ratings of the students' interview responses were less clear, as the judges could not always agree on the developmental stages represented in the comments. There was the most agreement of growth of one stage in the students' cognitive/skills focus over the semester. There seemed to be little observable growth in more affective areas such as dealing with supervisee feelings and confronting supervisees. These results are in line with those reported by Borders and Fong (1994), who found their supervisors-in-training were particularly challenged by situations requiring interventions related to relationship dynamics and were reluctant to address counselor's personal concerns. Also, given the calls for including both didactic and experiential (i.e., supervised supervision) activities in supervisor training programs (e.g., Borders et al., 1991), it is interesting to note that the two groups of students scored similarly on the objective developmental measure at the beginning of the semester, even though the experimental group had completed the didactic portion of their training and the control group had not. It appears that *supervised supervision* experiences have a unique influence on supervisor development and, perhaps, their effectiveness.

McMahon and Simons (2004) provided an intensive four-day supervision training workshop for 15 practicing counselors (experimental group) in a variety of work settings throughout Queensland, Australia. Learning objectives were based on the competency areas identified in the ACES curriculum guide for training counseling supervisors (Borders et al., 1991), and included both didactic and experiential components. There also was a control group, made up of 42 counselors who had indicated an interest in the training but could not attend. The researchers constructed a measure based on the learning objectives and covering theoretical and conceptual knowledge, practical skills and abilities, and confidence and self-awareness. The measure was administered to both groups before the training, to the experimental group at the end of training, and to both groups six months later. There were no differences between the two groups on the pretest, and the control group's scores had not changed six months later. In contrast, there was a significant increase in the experimental group's scores from pretest to posttest, and then a slight (non-significant) decline at the six months follow-up. Nevertheless, the experimental group had significantly higher scores than the control group did at the six month point.

It is challenging to conduct research on supervisor training programs, whether in academic or field settings. It is particularly difficult to obtain a sample size large enough for anything than fairly basic research designs. Clearly, Baker et al. (2002) and McMahon and Simons (2004) faced these and other limitations. In both studies, supervisor gains were assessed with self-report measures with limited psychometric support, rather than actual behaviors. Few measures specific to supervisor performance exist, however, and the use of a control group in each study is notable.

Wheeler and King (2000) surveyed counseling supervisors in Britain about supervision of supervision. They were prompted by an ethical requirement for supervisors to arrange for supervision for their work (British Association for Counselling, 1996). Of the 70 respondents to the survey, 90% reported they had supervision of their supervision;

about half (55.7%) had the same supervisor for supervision as for their counseling. Half (51%) also indicated they currently were providing supervision for other supervisors, and this group rated supervision of supervision significantly higher in importance than did respondents not currently engaged in providing such supervision. Respondents also listed issues they had discussed with their supervisor of supervision during the last year as well as what issues their supervisees (supervisors) had raised. In both instances, ethical issues were the most frequently discussed topic, followed by boundary issues and competence of supervisees.

Supervisor Competence

Only one study related to supervisor competence was located. Magnuson, Wilcoxon, and Norem (2000) set out to characterize ineffective supervision in a qualitative study of 11 counselors and counselor educators. Interview data yielded six nearly unanimous overarching principles of "lousy supervision": unbalanced (e.g., too focused on details rather than the large picture), developmentally inappropriate, intolerant of differences (e.g., not flexible), untrained (e.g., not able to manage boundaries or difficult issues), professionally apathetic, and providing a poor model of professional and personal attributes (e.g., does not mentor, behaves unethically). The researchers also delineated three general spheres of lousy supervision: organizational/administrative (e.g., fails to clarify expectations, not prepared), technical/cognitive (e.g., perceived as unskilled or unreliable, provides vague feedback), and relational/affective (e.g., intrusive, insensitive, avoids relational issues). In short, ineffective supervisors were characterized as unskilled and/or not invested. The need for supervision training seems a clear implication of this study.

Supervisory Relationship

Over the last five years, researchers have investigated various aspects of the supervisory relationship and its impact. Most operationalized the supervisory relationship in terms of the working alliance (Bordin, 1983). Some used an adapted measure of scales designed to measure the counseling working alliance, while others used a measure developed specific to the supervisory relationship (Efstation, Patton, & Kardash, 1990). (One additional study of the working alliance [Gatmon et al., 2001] is reviewed in the multicultural supervision section.)

In one of the few theory-based studies (across all studies reviewed here), White and Queener (2003) investigated the relevance of attachment theory in explaining the working alliance. They included one additional variable, social provisions (i.e., quality of one's support network), in their quest to identify individual well-being characteristics of the supervisee and supervisor relevant to the supervisory relationship. They gathered data from 67 dyads, supervisees in practica or internship (mostly female master's students) and their supervisors (mostly female, onsite supervisors). Preliminary analyses indicated that gender, theoretical orientation, and number of supervision sessions were not related to any of the criterion variables. Supervisees' attachments and social provisions predicted neither their own perceptions of the working alliance nor their supervisors' perceptions. In contrast, supervisors' attachments (but not their social provisions) predicted both the supervisees' and supervisors' perceptions of the working alliance. When either supervisees or supervisors reported a more favorable supervisory working alliance, the supervisors were more comfortable with closeness in relationships and depending on others when in need, two aspects of more secure attachment.

Ladany and his colleagues published a series of studies of the supervisory relationship, beginning with his dissertation (Ladany, Ellis, & Friedlander, 1999). Ladany et al.'s (1999) study was based in Bordin's (1983) theory of the working alliance, specifically testing whether changes in supervisees' perceptions of the working alliance would predict their self-efficacy as counselors. They recruited a national sample of counseling and psychology interns (n = 107, mostly White female doctoral students) who reported perceptions of their work with their supervisors (mostly males) near the beginning and the end of the semester. Preliminary analyses revealed that months of supervised counseling experience did not correlate significantly with any of the predictor or criterion variables. Self-efficacy increased significantly over time. In terms of the theoretical research question, a multivariate multiple regression analysis was significant. Follow-up analyses, however, indicated that changes in the supervisees' perceptions of the working alliance were not related to reported changes in their self-efficacy. In addition, only one working alliance factor, emotional bond, predicted supervisees' satisfaction with supervision. When supervisees perceived the emotional bond became stronger over time, they also reported increases in satisfaction (e.g., more positive perceptions of supervisor's personal qualities and performance, their own supervisory behavior, and their comfort in expressing ideas in supervision). Ladany et al. speculated that their measure of the working alliance may have been inappropriate, since it was an adaptation of a scale designed to measure the therapeutic working alliance and did not include items related to evaluation.

In several follow-up studies, Ladany and colleagues explored the role of self-disclosure in the supervisory relationship. First, Ladany and Lehrman-Waterman (1999) gathered supervisees' reports of supervisor self-disclosures, including frequency and content of these disclosures. Supervisees ($n = 105$, mostly White females in counseling and psychology programs) both described actual supervisor self-disclosures and completed an index of frequency of types of disclosures (e.g., favorable or unfavorable, intimate or non-intimate). Supervisees reported an average of 5.46 supervisor self-disclosures, most often in the categories of personal issues (73%), neutral counseling experiences (55%) (e.g., how supervisor handled a suicidal client), and counseling struggles (51%). Least reported self-disclosures included experiences as a supervisor (8%) (mostly negative), didactic mentoring (12%), supervisory relationship (12%), and dynamics of the training site (13%). Ladany and Lehrman-Waterman expressed some concern over the high frequency of supervisor disclosures regarding their own personal issues and the few didactic or mentoring statements. In further planned analyses, the researchers found some relationships among supervisor styles, working alliance, and content and frequency of self-disclosures. For example, supervisees reported that supervisors with a more attractive (i.e., collegial) style made more disclosures overall, more task-oriented supervisors made fewer disclosures of personal issues, and more interpersonally-sensitive supervisors were less likely to reveal neutral counseling experiences. Supervisees who reported more supervisor disclosures also rated the supervisory working alliance higher, on all three subscales (goals, tasks, emotional bond). More self-disclosures of counseling struggles were related to a stronger emotional bond.

Ladany and Melincoff (1999) provided an interesting contrast in their study of supervisor reports of nondisclosures. Ninety supervisors (mostly White females, doctoral level) in a variety of settings (e.g., mental health agencies, schools, private practice, prisons) described actual nondisclosures ($n = 519$) and explained their reasons ($n = 711$) for not disclosing. Categories of the most frequently listed nondisclosures were negative reactions to a supervisee's counseling and professional performance (74%), supervisor personal issues (67%), and negative reactions to a supervisee's behavior in supervision (56%). The least cited categories included positive reactions of a supervisee's counseling and professional performance (11%), supervisor attraction to a supervisee

(10%), reactions to a supervisee's clients (4%), and supervisor's experiences with other trainees (4%). Thus, based on their self-reports, supervisors were more likely to share positive reactions and not share negative evaluations with their supervisees. The most cited reasons for nondisclosure were not relevant (77%), supervisor's own issue (71%), and anticipated negative reactions from supervisee (64%). There were several significant relationships between type of nondisclosure and reason for not disclosing. When supervisors did not disclose negative reactions to a supervisee, they were more likely to cite reasons that the supervisee "will discover when developmentally ready" and "addressed indirectly." When personal issues were not disclosed, supervisors were more likely to explain with "not relevant." Interestingly, supervisors in this study reported they typically did not disclose personal issues (67%) while supervisees in Ladany and Lehrman-Waterman (1999) cited personal issues as the most frequent self-disclosure of their supervisors (74%).

In a third study, Ladany, Walker, and Melincoff (2001) gathered supervisors' (n = 137) self-reports of self-disclosure frequency, supervisory style, and working alliance with respect to their work with a current supervisee. Supervisor style significantly predicted the working alliance. Follow-up analyses revealed that the attractive style predicted all three components of the working alliance, agreement on goals, agreement on tasks, and emotional bond. Interpersonally-sensitive and task-oriented styles predicted agreement on tasks only. In addition, supervisor style significantly predicted frequency of supervisor self-disclosure; supervisors who reported greater use of attractive and interpersonally sensitive styles also reported more frequent self-disclosures. Ladany et al. (2001) encouraged supervisors to be flexible, since each style seemed to contribute in a unique way to the working alliance.

In two other studies, the role of gender within the supervision relationship was explored. Although these two studies could have been discussed in the multicultural and diversity issues section, the research questions were so specific to the supervisory relationship that I have elected to include them here.

Wester, Vogel, and Archer (2004) focused on male supervisees and the impact of their socialized restricted emotionality (RE) within the supervision relationship. The researchers theorized that supervisor gender and supervisee defensive style were important moderators in supervision. They used a supervisory working alliance scale (Efstation, Patton, & Kardash, 1990) as a measure of the "turning-against-object" defensive style, and a counseling self-efficacy scale (Larson et al., 1992) as a measure of the "turning-against-self" defensive style. Psychology interns (n = 103) reported lower restrictive emotionality scores than published scores for men in the general population but higher than published scores for practicing counselors. A series of ANOVAs indicated that male supervisees with higher RE scores had significantly lower self-efficacy scores, but RE scores had no effect on working alliance scores. Supervisor gender had a main effect on working alliance scores, with male-male dyads reporting poorer perceptions of the supervisory relationship.

Finally, Granello (2003) investigated the impact of gender and age on the interactions of supervisor and supervisee. She analyzed transcripts of supervision sessions for 42 interns and their onsite supervisors, using a revised form of the Blumberg Interaction Analysis System (BIA). For gender, there was a main effect only for supervisee gender (no interaction effect or main effect for supervisor gender) on four BIA categories. Supervisors of both genders were more likely to accept or build on the suggestions and ideas of female supervisees, an unexpected finding. Supervisors of both genders also asked for more opinions, analysis, and evaluations from male supervisees. Male supervisees gave more suggestions and female supervisees gave more praise, support, and agreement comments to their supervisors. In a second MANOVA, gender and age had a significant interaction effect for two BIA categories. Although male supervisees scored higher than female supervisees in both categories, males who were older than their supervisors were asked for their opinions and gave their opinions more often than supervisees (male or female) in other age configurations. These differences were particularly apparent in comparing the scores of older male and older female supervisees. Granello discussed the symbiotic nature of the supervisory relationship as revealed by the different patterns of interactions of supervisors with male versus female supervisees, and the status apparently afforded to older male supervisees.

Supervisor Style

Supervisor style continues to be a popular variable in research, often in terms of the role of style in the supervisory relationship, as previously discussed (e.g., Culbreth & Borders, 1999; Ladany, Walker et al., 2001; Ladany & Lehrman-Waterman, 1999). Four other studies explored other aspects of supervisor style. Most relied on Friedlander and Ward's (1984) conceptualization and measure, which delineates three fairly distinct styles: attractive, interpersonally-sensitive, and task-oriented.

Ladany, Marotta, and Muse-Burke (2001) investigated supervisees' (n = 100, mostly White females) preference for supervisor style based on their counseling experience, familiarity with specific client symptoms and diagnoses, and complexity of their case conceptualizations of these clients. A series of multivariate multiple regression analyses revealed that supervisee general experience (i.e., months of counseling experience, months of supervised counseling experience, and total number of clients seen) vs. specific experience (i.e., number of clients seen with the specified diagnoses) predicted the complexity of the supervisees' case conceptualizations. Those with more experience wrote more integrated and complex case conceptualizations (for both diagnoses). No measures of supervisee experience predicted supervisor style preference for the specified client, and complexity of case conceptualizations also did not predict style preference. Most supervisees preferred a mixture of styles for the specified client, suggesting the need for supervisors to be flexible in their approach. Having used multiple measures relevant to counselor developmental level (i.e., experience and cognitive complexity), Ladany et al. concluded, "It is likely that the relationship between trainee developmental level and supervisor approach is more complex than anticipated" (p. 216).

Fernando and Hulse-Killacky (2005) hypothesized that supervisor story would predict master's-level interns' satisfaction with supervision and their perceived self-efficacy. Interns (n = 82, mostly White females) from six different training programs participated. The two multiple regression analyses were significant. However, the interpersonally sensitive style was the only significant predictor of satisfaction, and the task-oriented style was the only significant predictor of perceived self- efficacy. Satisfaction with supervision and perceived self-efficacy were not significantly correlated. Like Ladany, Marotta et al. (2001), Fernando and Hulse-Killacky concluded that supervisors need to be proficient in all three styles and be flexible in their use.

Steward, Breland, and Neil (2001) explored the influence of novice supervisees' preferences for supervisor style on their self-evaluations. The supervisees (n = 36, mostly White females) completed a non-standardized counselor competence rating scale at the end of the semester. Their supervisors also evaluated them using the same scale. Supervisory styles did not significantly predict supervisees' self-evaluations nor their supervisors' evaluations of them. Supervisor style was a significant predictor of the accuracy of supervisees' self-evaluations (i.e., how close their evaluations were to their supervisors' evaluations). The attractiveness style explained 37% of the variance in the difference between supervisees' and supervisors' evaluations. The more attractive the supervisor, the greater was the difference in the evaluations. The authors provided several, somewhat contradictory, possible explanations for these results, and concluded their results underscore the need for supervisor support and challenge. In addition, supervisees' and supervisor's evaluations were significantly correlated, with supervisees tending to give themselves lower scores than their supervisors gave them.

Hart and Nance (2003) tested a different model, based in Adaptive Counseling and Therapy, which involves four styles: telling, teaching, supporting, and delegating. Supervisees (n = 168) and their supervisors (n = 90) (both groups, mostly White females) rank ordered 150 word descriptions of the styles twice. As a pretest, they rank ordered their preferences. As a post-test, they rank ordered based on the supervisors' actual behaviors across ten weeks of individual supervision sessions. Not surprisingly, more directive styles were negatively correlated with less directive styles. Supervisees' and supervisors' rankings were somewhat consistent at pretest and post-test, with "supportive teacher" ranked high and "consultant/integrative" ranked low each time.

Supervisor Feedback and Evaluation

Despite the critical role of supervisor feedback in counselor development there have been few studies specific to this part of the process. Two were located during the five-year span of this review, both by Larson and her colleagues.

Larson, Day, Springer, Clark, and Vogel (2003) described the development of an observational feedback rating scale. They described optimal supervisory feedback as specific, constructive, and with a balance of positive and negative comments, and devised a 4-point rating scale to measure the presence of each of these four dimensions (1 = absent, 4 = present to a large degree). Transcripts of two supervisor-supervisee dyads in a university counseling center were rated. Of the 31 hours of tape, 199 feedback statements were identified. Interestingly, low numbers of both positive (M = 2.08, SD = .83) and negative (M = 1.32, SD = .54) statements were reported. The supervisor statements more often evidenced constructive (M = 2.91, SD = .96) and specific (M = 3.04, SD = .86) feedback. Larson et al. reported initial estimates of construct validity and concurrent validity, and found that undergraduates could rate the statements reliably. These results suggest that the supervisors used fewer than 7 feedback statements during each supervision hour, a result that echoes earlier findings by Friedlander, Siegel, and Brenock (1989), who also found feedback was given rarely.

Daniels and Larson (2001) conducted an experimental study to test the impact of performance feedback (positive or negative) on counseling students' self-efficacy and anxiety. Participants (n = 45, mostly White females) completed a self-efficacy pretest, conducted a 10-minute mock counseling session, estimated his or her own performance, completed an anxiety pretest, and then received either positive or negative feedback (bogus, somewhat exaggerated, randomly assigned) that rated the counseling students' performance in comparison to others. Repeated measures ANOVAs revealed an interaction effect between feedback and self-efficacy. Positive feedback significantly increased self-efficacy scores and decreased anxiety, while negative feedback had the opposite effects. Given the difficulty of finding measurable effects with only one, brief treatment in research, these results are impressive. Daniels and Larson concluded that the optimal feedback for novice counselors enhances the positives and provides specific suggestions for improvement.

Supervision Interventions

As in previous decades of supervision research, there were few investigations of specific interventions in individual supervision; only two were located in counseling journals over the last five years. Neswald-McCalip, Sather, Strati, and Dineen (2003) reported on their own experiences in a "creative supervision group." An open-ended, evolving qualitative approach is described, with an emphasis on process observations. The group leader and group members reported that the creative approaches used contributed to a more collaborative atmosphere.

Clingerman and Bernard (2004) explored the use of student-initiated e-mail as a supplemental supervisory tool, with a particular focus on whether e-mail enhanced supervisees' growth in personalization (self-awareness). E-mails of 19 master's level practicum students (mostly White females in school counseling) were coded in terms of their reference to interventions, conceptualization, personality, professional behavior/practicum site, and professional behavior/practicum class. E-mails were divided into time periods representing the beginning, middle, and final weeks of the semester. There was a significant decrease in the number of e-mails across the time periods. Personalization messages were significantly greater than other message types during each time period. Clingerman and Bernard concluded that their results supported other claims that e-mail encourages greater intimacy than face-to-face interactions.

Group Supervision

Holloway and Johnston (1985) described group supervision research as "widely practiced but poorly understood" (p. 332). Four studies around group supervision helped address this gap in the literature.

Christensen and Kline (2000) set out to address the lack of research regarding the process of group supervision. They collected various data (e.g., direct observations, researcher's journal, interviews, focus group) for six doctoral students in group supervision of their work with process groups for first-semester master's students. Using grounded theory procedures, four primary constructs were identified: influence of supervisee anxiety (e.g., hesitant to participate, fear of evaluation), the group supervision process (e.g., development of trust, increase in peer feedback), multiphasic learning process (e.g., involvement in group, making sense of learning and applying it), and multiphasic learning outcomes (e.g., personal awareness, group work concepts, group skills).

Later, Christensen and Kline (2001) explored their "process-sensitive peer group supervision" model, in which peers provide feedback based in the three focus areas of Bernard's (1997) discrimination model (i.e., techniques and interventions, conceptualization, personalization). Six master's level interns responded to open-ended questions regarding their experiences in the group at three points across the semester. Data analyses, following grounded theory procedures, yielded two primary themes: peer engagement and supervisor involvement. The most significant aspect of peer engagement was peer feedback, and the supervisees seemed to prefer a more facilitative (vs. directive) role for the supervisor. Three developmental phases also were identified: passive involvement (dependence), learning responsibility (independence), and personal involvement (interdependence and intimacy). Christensen and Kline concluded their results supported previous findings regarding the strengths of peer group supervision (with a supervisor facilitator).

In a third qualitative study, Starling and Baker (2000) explored the efficacy of a structured peer group model, as described by Borders (1991). They conducted intensive interviews of four master's level practicum students at the middle and end of the semester. The interviews included questions about their goals, self-assessed competence, and influence of peers in the group. Four themes emerged from grounded theory-based analyses. Supervisees reported a decrease in confusion and anxiety, greater clarity about their goals, and increased confidence, and emphasized the value of feedback from their peers. Starling and Baker concluded the structured peer group model was an effective approach, and that their results supported previous writings regarding the benefits of group supervision.

Ray and Altekruse (2000) conducted an experimental investigation comparing the effectiveness of large group supervision (8 students), small group supervision (4 students), and combined large group and individual supervision. Of particular interest was whether group supervision alone was as effective as combined group and individual supervision. Master's level practicum students ($n = 64$) were randomly assigned to one of the three treatment groups. They submitted videotaped counseling sessions near the beginning and at the end of the semester. These tapes were rated using a measure of counselor influence by the clients, supervisors, and trained raters. In addition, the students completed pre- and post-test measures of counselor development, and stated their preference for each supervision experience. Across groups, there were significant increases in counselor influence ratings for the supervisors' ratings only. Client ratings had a ceiling effect. An ANCOVA indicated no significant differences in post-test ratings, regardless of source, among the three treatment groups. Across groups, there was a significant increase in supervisees' self-reports of development. An ANCOVA revealed significant differences on one of three development subscales. Students in large group supervision reported greater gains in a sense of autonomy than did students in the other two treatment groups. Finally, students reported a strong preference for individual supervision, regardless of treatment group. Ray and Altekruse acknowledged the limitation of using the counselor influence measure as an indicator of counselor effectiveness, but concluded their results raised some questions regarding the best way to provide supervision (i.e., Is individual supervision necessary?).

Multicultural Supervision

Of the four studies reviewed here, two appeared in a special issue of the *Journal of Multicultural Counseling and Development* (Constantine, 2001). "Multicultural" was defined quite broadly in two of the studies. All involved supervisor-supervisee discussions specific to multicultural variables and the critical influence of these discussions on the supervisory relationship.

Toporek, Ortega-Villalobos, and Pope-Davis (2004) collected critical incidents in multicultural supervision, defined broadly to include race, ethnicity, sex, religion, sexual orientation, socioeconomic status, and physical disabilities. Although most of their supervisees (n = 17 master's students) and supervisors (n = 11 doctoral students) were White females, each dyad differed on at least one of the identified multicultural dimensions. At the end of the semester, participants described one or more critical incidents in which multicultural issues occurred during supervision, including if and how the incident was resolved, and rated the experience as positive, negative, helpful, challenging, supportive, offensive, harmful, or threatening (1-5 Likert scale). Finally, participants described how the critical incident(s) influenced their multicultural competence. Content coding yielded 10 types of critical incident situations, including interpersonal discomfort, contact with cultural differences, supervisor corrected behavior, theoretical discussions, and self-disclosure. In addition, seven influence categories were identified, with awareness (i.e., gain in personal awareness, insight) reflected in 50% of the responses. Toporek et al. also provided a matrix of influences with corresponding critical incident situations and multicultural variables. For example, "recognition of need for more training" arose out of one situation, as did "encouragement from supervisor," regarding only the cultural variable of ethnicity, while "awareness" was generated by a number of situations, regarding a variety of cultural variables. The researchers noted that perceptions and impact of the critical incidents were unique to each dyad, but also concluded that the supervisory relationship "may be a pivotal component of multicultural supervision that moderates how all other experiences are perceived" (p. 80). In response to a request to provide suggestions for improving multicultural supervision, supervisor participants recommended addressing these issues in the initial supervision session, and expressed a need for positive demonstrations of supervisors dealing with multicultural issues.

Gatmon et al. (2001) explored the influence of discussions of cultural variables during supervision on satisfaction and the working alliance. Psychology interns (n = 289, mostly White, heterosexual females) reported whether discussions of ethnicity, gender, and sexual orientation occurred during supervision, who initiated these discussions, and rated (7-point Likert scale) perceived levels of frequency, depth, safety, and satisfaction with the discussions. There were more matches in the three cultural variables than differences among the dyads. Overall, the interns reported low frequencies of discussions of cultural variables, especially for sexual orientation. Discussions of ethnicity, gender, and sexual orientation were significantly more likely (Chi-square analysis) when there were dyad match differences on these variables. A MANOVA was used to assess differences in working alliance between dyads that did discuss similarities and differences and those who did not. Only ethnicity was significant; supervisees who reported discussions of ethnic similarities had higher scores on the bond subscale of the working alliance measure. Tests for group differences in satisfaction (ANOVAs) were significant for gender and sexual orientation, but not ethnicity. Supervisees who reported discussions of similarities and differences in gender and sexual orientation reported higher levels of satisfaction. Supervisors initiated about half of the discussions regarding ethnicity and gender, but only one-third for sexual orientation, a finding that contrasts with suggestions of the supervisors in Toporek et al. (2004) and others (e.g., Hird et al., 2001) that these issues be put on the table in the first session. Gatmon et al. concluded, "it is not the cultural match between supervisor and supervisee itself that is important but the presence and quality of the discussion of difference and similarity" (p. 110).

Duan and Roehlke (2001) focused on cross-racial supervision dyads in university counseling centers. Psychology interns ($n = 60$, 40 men) and their supervisors ($n = 58$, 30 men) were recruited; one person in each dyad was Caucasian. Duan and Roehlke developed a survey of scaled items and open-ended questions regarding perceptions of supervisor-supervisee conflicts, supervisor's behaviors, attitudes, and characteristics. Although both groups reported high satisfaction, there were a number of significant differences in the groups' perceptions. For example, compared to the supervisees, supervisors reported more incidences of addressing multicultural issues, asking supervisees for help in understanding their culture, and acknowledging the power differential, and significantly higher levels of like and respect for their supervisees. Supervisees reported more comfort with self-disclosure than their supervisors perceived. Stepwise multiple regression revealed supervisees' comfort level with self-disclosure and their perceptions of supervisors' positive attitudes toward them significantly predicted supervisees' satisfaction (72% of the variance). For supervisors' satisfaction, three predictors were significant (61% of the variance): their positive attitudes toward supervisees, perceptions of supervisees' comfort with self-disclosure, and the degree to which they believed their supervisees viewed them as expert, trustworthy, and helpful. Much in line with previously discussed studies, Duan and Roehlke encouraged early attention to multicultural issues, with supervisors taking responsibility for initiating these discussions, and urged supervisors to check their self-perceptions of how frequently they address these issues during supervision. Notably, this is the only study reviewed here in which the participants were primarily male, although it is not clear to what extent this influenced the results.

Gainor and Constantine (2002) compared the effects of Web-based peer group and an in-person peer group on supervisees' multicultural competence. School counseling interns ($n = 45$, mostly White females) were randomly assigned to the two groups, both of which followed Constantine's (1997) multicultural supervision framework in weekly group meetings. They completed a multicultural case conceptualization ability exercise before and after the group experience, and a satisfaction questionnaire at post-test. A MANCOVA revealed significant differences on the multicultural case conceptualization measures between the two groups; the in-person peer group had higher etiology and treatment scores. In addition, the in-person group reported significantly greater satisfaction with their group experience than the Web-based group. In contrast to Clingerman and Bernard (2004; reported earlier), Gainor and Constantine concluded that their Web-based format may provide limited perceptual relationship cues and intimacy, particularly around multicultural topics, and suggested Web-based groups be used ideally in conjunction with face-to-face supervision.

Ethical Behavior

Erwin (2000) explored counseling supervisors' levels of moral sensitivity, one's realization that behaviors may affect others negatively or violate a moral principle. He randomly selected from members of ACA who self-identified as counseling supervisors. Participants ($n = 147$, mostly White, with master's degrees) were asked to identify key supervision and counseling issues in two case vignettes, one in which the counselor broke confidentiality and one in which the counselor had a dual role with a client. Their responses were rated for degree of moral sensitivity on a 1 to 5 scale, with scores of 1, 2, and 3 indicating low sensitivity. The supervisors scored significantly higher in moral sensitivity (t test) on the breach of confidentiality case than on the dual relationship case. Nevertheless, 35% scored low on the confidentiality case and 67% scored low on the dual relationship case.

DISCUSSION AND IMPLICATIONS

This review of five years of counseling supervision journal publications provides a snapshot of the models, issues, and dynamics of particular relevance to the field of counseling and counselor education. The number of articles published during this time period, many more than I expected, denotes the continued emphasis on this topic in the counseling field. Most articles, conceptual and empirical, had an applied focus, such as descriptions of supervision strategies, issues specific to various counseling specialties, challenges of conducting on-site supervision, and dialogues concerning multicultural issues. In empirical studies, supervisors were studied more often than supervisees. Familiar variables (e.g., supervisory style) and new ones (e.g., supervisor self-disclosure, technology) were investigated. A number of these studies provided critical directions for supervisor training. Themes, conclusions, and implications are discussed in this section.

1. There is continued evidence of and concern for lack of clinical supervision for counseling practitioners, particularly those in the schools. In addition, there continues to be "extensive misunderstanding" (Schultz et al., 2002, p. 219) of what clinical supervision is, often being confused with staff meetings and administrative oversight. These misunderstandings may be rooted in the lack of supervisor training for master's-level counselors, who typically are the primary supervisors for counseling interns, pre-licensed counselors, and counseling staff members. In several studies reviewed here, those with supervision training better understood their role and function and valued supervision more highly, including supervision of their own work. The need for increased supervisor training, then, is abundantly clear. Innovative approaches are needed to reach practitioners in a variety of field settings, as supervision training students during their master's program can have limited impact. Master's students do not yet have the experience and professional maturity needed to understand the complex levels and nuances of counseling supervision. In fact, at graduation they may be at a developmental level where they question the value of supervision for themselves (Borders & Brown, 2005).

2. The absolute critical role of the supervisory relationship resonates throughout the literature reviewed here, as does the responsibility of the *supervisor* for creating a safe, trusting, challenging, and open environment. This is stated in particularly strong terms by multicultural supervision writers and researchers, who emphasized repeatedly the supervisor's responsibility for introducing cultural variables into the supervisory dialogue, in initial sessions and beyond. Clearly, supervisors need to check out their own self-perceptions of their behavior, as these may be inaccurate, particularly in terms of how often they initiate multicultural discussions (Duan & Roehlke, 2001) as well as what topics they disclose

during supervision (Ladany & Lehrman-Waterman, 1999; Ladany & Melincoff, 1999). In addition, there is some indication that supervisor's characteristics, such as attachment style, have more bearing on relationship dynamics than do supervisees' characteristics (White & Queener, 2003). Again, the responsibility of the supervisor for self-scrutiny regarding supervisory attitudes and behaviors is clear. The relationship can be enhanced by supervisor self-disclosures, particularly disclosures of their own counseling struggles (Ladany & Lehrman-Waterman, 1999).

3. Despite the critical role of the supervisory relationship, there is some evidence that supervisors avoid difficult relationship issues, or at least find them challenging. Both supervisees (Ladany & Lehrman-Waterman, 1999) and supervisors (Ladany & Melincoff, 1999) reported that supervisors infrequently disclosed about the supervisory relationship. Lack of attention to relation issues also was a defining characteristic of "lousy supervision" (Magnuson et al., 2000). It may be that supervisors want to avoid negative reactions from their supervisees, or are unsure of how to handle these reactions. In addition, some supervisors seem to struggle with boundary issues with their supervisees (Wheeler & King, 2000). It appears that greater attention to relationship dynamics in supervisor training is warranted.

4. Multicultural supervision received increased attention, was defined broadly by several authors, and moved to a focus on the supervisor-supervisee dialogue about cultural issues. These issues seem to be discussed more frequently when there are supervisor-supervisee mismatches on cultural variables (Gatmon et al., 2001). Cultural issues are just as prevalent and relevant in matched dyads, however, including White-White dyads, where White privilege may be a powerful if invisible influence (Hays & Chang, 2003). In fact, Gatmon et al. (2001) concluded that the cultural match is much less important than "the presence and quality of the discussion of difference and similarity" (p. 110). Indeed, when cultural issues are discussed supervisees report greater gains in personal awareness and insight (Toporek et al., 2004), stronger emotional bonds with their supervisors, and higher levels of satisfaction (Gatmon et al., 2001). Yet, supervisors may discuss these issues less frequently than they believe they do (Duan & Roehlke, 2001). Sexual orientation may be overlooked more often than other cultural issues (Gatmon et al., 2001). Supervisees want to discuss multicultural issues related to their counseling and supervision interactions, apparently more frequently and with greater comfort than their supervisors realize (Duan & Roehlke, 2001). Although several authors provided strategies

for addressing multicultural issues, particularly in initial sessions (Estrada et al., 2004; Garret et al., 2001; Hays & Chang, 2003; Hird et al., 2001), supervisors may need specific training–and modeling–of effective approaches and productive interactions around this topic (Toporek et al., 2004).

5. Almost all the empirical results covered in this review were based on White female participants. Often, the percentages of Whites and females were as high as 70% and 80%. Unfortunately, these figures reflect the reality of the counseling student population, and present quite a challenge to multicultural supervision researchers. Nevertheless, these researchers designed studies that provided insightful and instructive results, as previously discussed.

6. What is the role of feedback in supervision? What *is* feedback in supervision? The few analyses of session dialogues to date (Friedlander et al., 1989; Larson et al., 2003) have yielded relatively few statements that can be categorized specifically as feedback, yet supervisees require feedback to be able to make changes, add new skills, expand their client conceptualizations, and develop greater self-awareness. Supervisors seem reluctant to give negative feedback and prefer indirect over direct methods of providing this feedback (Ladany & Melincoff, 1999). Indeed, blunt negative statements decreased supervisees' self-efficacy and increased their anxiety in one study (Daniels & Larson, 2001), and ineffective feedback (vague, too focused on details) was a component of lousy supervision (Magnuson et al., 2000). Nevertheless, Larson et al. (2003) also reported low frequencies of positive feedback. Additional studies of effective feedback–direct and indirect–are needed to enhance our knowledge–and supervisor training–in this area.

7. Other supervisor training needs beyond relationship dynamics, discussions of cultural issues, and effective feedback also were indicated. In particular, supervisors reported that ethical issues were particularly challenging (Thielson & Leahy, 2001; Wheeler & King, 2000). In addition, beginning supervisors (at least those who are doctoral students) struggle with the appropriate way to deal with supervisee affect (Baker et al., 2002), perhaps because of their heightened awareness regarding ethical issues in taking on a counselor role with their supervisees (Borders & Fong, 1994). Importantly, this review provided additional empirical evidence that *supervised supervision* experiences are requisite to supervisor development (Baker et al., 2002). As previously outlined (e.g., Borders et al., 1991), supervisor training programs should include experiential components–ongoing practice with feedback–as well as didactic instruction.

8. In terms of counseling specialties, school counseling supervision received the most attention. This seems appropriate given that school counseling is one of the foundations of the counseling field and represents a significant proportion of counseling graduates. In addition, the school setting presents unique challenges, even hurdles, to efforts to provide clinical supervision, which several authors tried to address. Nevertheless, there are many counselors in a number of other settings, and the limited literature indicates these have their own challenges and dynamics. Hopefully, researchers will continue to explore these.

9. The viability of group supervision was supported consistently in the four studies published during the last five years, although perhaps it is best used in combination with individual supervision (Ray & Altekruse, 2000). In three qualitative studies, the key role of peer feedback was highlighted. Interestingly, although all three used the term "peer group supervision," all employed group supervisors. Results seem to support the presence of a facilitative (vs. directive) role for a group supervisor who sets appropriate structure, helps create a safe and trusting environment, encourages peer involvement, and helps generalize learnings and the application of them (cf. Starling & Baker, 2000; Christensen & Kline, 2001). Although peer feedback is valuable in unique and important ways, skills outcomes are enhanced when a supervisor is present (Agnew et al., 2000; Crutchfield & Borders, 1997).

10. Developmental models were a major focus of supervision research in the 1980s and 1990s. Here, these models were mentioned often as a guiding framework for a supervision approach and in interpreting research results. Within this five year span, however, only two empirical investigations of developmental models were located. Measuring "developmental level," a term with a more conceptual than experience basis (e.g., Blocher, 1983), continued to be a challenge. Shechtman and Wirzberger (1999) categorized their counselors by years of experience alone, while Ladany, Marotta et al. (2001) used various measures of counseling experience and a measure of cognitive complexity. Both studies added support to the general tenets of developmental models, although both also indicated matching developmental level with supervisor approach was more complex than perhaps originally described. Researchers in both studies concluded the need for supervisor flexibility, since various styles and approaches are needed, even with the same supervisee.

11. Similarly, Bernard's (1997) discrimination model was frequently used as a framework for describing supervisory approaches to issues as varied as goal-setting (Curtis, 2000) and addressing spirituality (Polanski,

2003). The model was the basis for two studies, one of Israeli school counselors (Shechtman & Wirzberger, 1999) and one of e-mail communications from supervisees (Clingerman & Bernard, 2004). Clearly, the discrimination model continues to be a viable and instructive framework across the spectrum of counseling supervision.

12. Use of technology in supervision was investigated in two studies, with somewhat contradictory results regarding attention to relationship and self-awareness components via technology. Clingerman and Bernard (2004) concluded that e-mail communications encourage greater intimacy than face-to-face supervision, while Gainor and Constantine (2002) reported their Web-based group format limited intimacy, likely due to the lack of perceptual relationship cues. Differences in the supervision formats may have contributed to the different conclusions. Clingerman and Bernard's supervisees were e-mailing their small-group practicum supervisors, who responded to their messages, so they had both e-mail and face-to-face interactions with their supervisors. Gainor and Constantine compared in-person only and Web-based only group supervision formats. As technology evolves and becomes more accessible to supervisors in a variety of settings, studies of more interactive formats will be of interest, particularly since these formats may expand the availability of supervision in some geographical areas (e.g., rural) and other isolated settings.

13. The empirical research on clinical supervision during this time period included both quantitative and, increasingly, qualitative studies. Often, the samples were small and were based in one program, which limits generalizability (cf. Borders & Fong, 1994). Of the quantitative, only five employed an experimental design. The rest were primarily descriptive, *ex post facto* studies, often described as "exploratory," or surveys. The qualitative studies, again often exploratory in nature, varied greatly in their rigor. Lack of attention to potential (or obvious) researcher bias and adherence to a systematic qualitative approach characterized a few of the studies. Nevertheless, a qualitative approach seemed quite appropriate for identified research questions in several studies, particularly those of group supervision, "lousy supervision," and multicultural supervision. Given the lack of standardized measures specific to the supervision enterprise, qualitative approaches may be preferred to, or be seen as a valuable adjunct to, use of researcher-developed scales and surveys that have little to no psychometric support. Indeed, several researchers used a mixed methods approach quite effectively (e.g., Gatmon et al., 2001; Ladany & Lehrman-Waterman, 1999).

14. How should the supervisory relationship be conceptualized and operationalized? In this review, the working alliance was the most frequently chosen theoretical framework. However, both adaptations of therapeutic working alliance scales and the supervision-based scale by Efstation et al. (1990) have been criticized by researchers (although they often continue to use the same measures in subsequent studies). White and Queener (2003) noted that the Efstation et al. scale does not correspond exactly with Bordin's (1983) theory, so that it may not be accurate to operationalize working alliance by using this scale. Ladany et al. (1999) noted that therapeutic working alliance scales do not include items related to evaluation, a key component of the supervisor's responsibility and the power dynamics in supervision.

Perhaps a larger question, implied by these researchers, is whether working alliance is an appropriate conceptualization of the supervisory relationship. Reliance on the working alliance theory may be another example of adopting counseling-based theories as the basis for studying supervision, a practice that is problematic since the two enterprises differ in key ways (Bernard & Goodyear, 2004; Borders & Brown, 2005; Dye & Borders, 1990). To date, the supervisory relationship has not received the same scrutiny as the counseling relationship has enjoyed for some decades, so that the components specific to supervision interactions are still largely unknown. That said, the working alliance has been useful in highlighting the importance of the emotional bond factor in the supervisor-supervisee relationship.

CONCLUSION

Clinical supervision literature in counseling and counselor education continues to cover a broad range of issues, settings, and dynamics. Literature published during the last five years has been instructive, particularly regarding supervisor-supervisee dialogues regarding multicultural issues and the critical role of the supervisory relationship. In addition, the need for supervisor training, including supervised practice, has been further supported. A number of avenues for continued development and research regarding supervision practice have been identified, although several will be challenging to address. Hopefully, over the next five years, counseling researchers will find creative approaches to further enhance supervision practice and refine supervisor training.

REFERENCES

Agnew, T., Vaught, C. C., Getz, H. G., & Fortune, J. (2000). Peer group clinical supervision program fosters confidence and professionalism. *Professional School Counseling*, *4*, 6-12.

Arthur, G. L., & Gfroerer, K. P. (2002). Training and supervision through the written word: A description and intern feedback. *The Family Journal*, *10*, 213-219.

Baker, S. B., Exum, H. A., & Tyler, R. E. (2002). The developmental process of clinical supervisors in training: An investigation of the supervisor complexity model. *Counselor Education and Supervision*, *42*, 15-30.

Baltimore, M. L., & Crutchfield, L. B. (2003). *Clinical supervisor training: An interactive CD-ROM training program for the helping professions.* Boston, MA: Allyn & Bacon.

Barnes, K. L. (2004). Applying self-efficacy theory to counselor training and supervision: A comparison of two approaches. *Counselor Education and Supervision*, *44*, 56-69.

Bernard, J. M. (1997). The discrimination model. In C. E. Watkins, Jr. (Ed.), *Handbook of psychotherapy supervision* (pp. 310-327). New York: Wiley.

Bernard, J. M., & Goodyear, R. K. (2004). *Fundamentals of clinical supervision* (3rd ed.). Needham Heights, MA: Allyn & Bacon.

Bishop, R. D., Avila-Juarbe, E., & Thumme, B. (2003). Recognizing spirituality as an important factor in counselor supervision. *Counseling and Values*, *48*, 34-46.

Blackwell, T. L., Strohmer, D. C., Belcas, E. M., & Burton, K. A. (2002). Ethics in rehabilitation counselor supervision. *Rehabilitation Counseling Bulletin*, *45*, 240-247.

Blocher, D. H. (1983). Toward a cognitive developmental approach to counseling supervision. *The Counseling Psychologist*, *11*(1), 27-34.

Borders, L. D. (1991). A systematic approach to peer group supervision. *Journal of Counseling and Development*, *69*, 248-252.

Borders, L. D. (2001). Counseling supervision: A deliberate educational process. In D. C. Locke, J. E. Myers, & E. L. Herr (Eds.), *The handbook of counseling* (pp. 417-432). Thousand Oaks, CA: Sage.

Borders, L. D., & Benshoff, J. M. (1999). *Learning to think like a supervisor* [instructional videotape]. Alexandria, VA: American Counseling Association.

Borders, L. D., Bernard, J. M., Dye, H. A., Fong, M. L., Henderson, P., & Nance, D. W. (1991). Curriculum guide for training counseling supervisors: Rationale, development and implementation. *Counselor Education and Supervision*, *31*, 58-82.

Borders, L. D., & Brown, L. L. (2005). *The new handbook of counseling supervision.* Mahwah, NJ: Lahaska/Lawrence Erlbaum.

Borders, L. D., & Cashwell, C. S. (1992). Supervision regulations in counselor licensure legislation. *Counselor Education and Supervision*, *31*, 208-218.

Borders, L. D., & Fong, M. L. (1994). Cognitions of supervisors-in-training: An exploratory study. *Counselor Education and Supervision*, *33*, 280-293.

Borders, L. D., & Usher, C. H. (1992). Post-degree supervision: Existing and preferred practices. *Journal of Counseling and Development*, *70*, 594-599.

Bordin, E. S. (1983). A working alliance based model of supervision. *The Counseling Psychologist*, *11*(1), 35-42.

British Association for Counselling. (1996). *Code of ethics and practice for supervisors of counsellors.* Rugby: Author.

Britton, P. J., Goodman, J. M., & Rak, C. F. (2002). Presenting workshops on supervision: A didactic-experiential format. *Counselor Education and Supervision, 42,* 31-39.

Champe, J., & Kleist, D. M. (2003). Live supervision: A review of the research. *The Family Journal, 11,* 268-275.

Christensen, T. M., & Kline, W. B. (2000). A qualitative investigation of the process of group supervision with group counselors. *Journal for Specialists in Group Work, 25,* 376-393.

Christensen, T. M., & Kline, W. B. (2001). The qualitative exploration of process-sensitive peergroup supervision. *Journal for Specialists in Group Work, 26,* 81-99.

Clingerman, T. L., & Bernard, J. M. (2004). An investigation of the use of e-mail as a supplemental modality for clinical supervision. *Counselor Education and Supervision, 44,* 82-95.

Cobia, D. C., & Boes, S. R. (2000). Professional disclosure statements and formal plans for supervision: Two strategies for minimizing the risk of ethical conflicts in post-master's supervision. *Journal of Counseling and Development, 78,* 293-296.

Cobia, D. C., & Pipes, R. B. (2002). Mandated supervision: An intervention for disciplined professionals. *Journal of Counseling and Development, 80,* 140-144.

Constantine, M. G. (2001). Introduction to the special issue: Perspectives on multicultural supervision. *Journal of Multicultural Counseling and Development, 29,* 98-101.

Crutchfield, L. B., & Borders, L. D. (1997). Impact of two clinical peer supervision models on practicing school counselors. *Journal of Counseling and Development, 75,* 219-230.

Culbreth, J. R. (1999). Clinical supervision of substance abuse counselors: Current and preferred practices. *Journal of Addictions and Offender Counseling, 20,* 15-25.

Culbreth, J. R., & Borders, L. D. (1999). Perceptions of the supervisory relationship: Recovering and nonrecovering substance abuse counselors. *Journal of Counseling and Development, 77,* 330-338.

Curtis, R. C. (2000). Using goal-setting strategies to enrich the practicum and internship experiences of beginning counselors. *Journal of Humanistic Counseling, Education and Development, 38,* 194-205.

Daniels, J. A., & Larson, L. M. (2001). The impact of performance feedback on counseling self-efficacy and counselor anxiety. *Counselor Education and Supervision, 41,* 120-130.

DeLucia-Waack, J. L. (1999). Supervision for counselors working with eating disorders groups: Countertransference issues related to body image, food, and weight. *Journal of Counseling and Development, 77,* 379-388.

Duan, C., & Roehlke, H. (2001). A descriptive "snapshot" of cross-racial supervision in university counseling center internships. *Journal of Multicultural Counseling and Development, 29,* 131-146.

Dye, H. A., & Borders, L. D. (1990). Counseling supervisors: Standards for preparation and practice. *Journal of Counseling and Development, 69,* 27-32.

Edwards, J. K., & Chen, M-W. (1999). Strength-based supervision: Frameworks, current practice, and future directions. *The Family Journal, 1,* 349-357.

Efstation, J. F., Patton, M. J., & Kardash, C. M. (1990). Measuring the working alliance in supervision. *Journal of Counseling Psychology, 37*, 322-329.

Erwin, W. J. (2000). Supervisor moral sensitivity. *Counselor Education and Supervision, 40*, 115-127.

Estrada, D., Frame, M. W., & Williams, C. B. (2004). Cross-cultural supervision: Guiding the conversation toward race and ethnicity. *Journal of Multicultural Counseling and Development, 32*, 307-319.

Fernando, D. M., & Hulse-Killacky, D. (2005). The relationship of supervisory styles to satisfaction with supervision and the perceived self-efficacy of master's-level counseling students. *Counselor Education and Supervision, 44*, 293-304.

Fitch, T. J., & Marshall, J. L. (2002). Using cognitive interventions with counseling practicum students during group supervision. *Counselor Education and Supervision, 41*, 335-342.

Foster, V. A., & McAdams, C. R., III. (1999). The impact of client suicide in counselor training: Implications for counselor education and supervision. *Counselor Education and Supervision, 39*, 22-33.

Frame, M. W. (2001). The spiritual genogram in training and supervision. *The Family Journal, 9*, 109-115.

Friedlander, M. L., Siegel, S. M., & Brenock, K. (1989). Parallel process in counseling and supervision. *Journal of Counseling Psychology, 36*, 149-157.

Friedlander, M. L., & Ward, L. G. (1984). Development and validation of the Supervisory Styles Inventory. *Journal of Counseling Psychology, 31*, 541-557.

Fuertes, J. N. (2004). Supervision in bilingual counseling: Service delivery, training, and research considerations. *Journal of Multicultural Counseling and Development, 32*, 84-94.

Gainor, K. A., & Constantine, M. G. (2002). Multicultural group supervision: A comparison of in-person versus web-based formats. *Professional School Counseling, 6*, 104-112.

Garrett, M. T., Borders, L. D., Crutchfield, L. B., Torres-Rivera, E., Brotherton, D., & Curtis, R. (2001). Multicultural supervision: A paradigm of cultural responsiveness for supervisors. *Journal of Multicultural Counseling and Development, 29*, 147-158.

Gatmon, D., Jackson, D., Koshkarian, L., Martos-Perry, N., Molina, A., Patel, N., & Rodolfa, E. (2001). Exploring ethnic, gender, and sexual orientation variables in supervision: Do they really matter? *Journal of Multicultural Counseling and Development, 29*, 102-111.

Getz, H. G. (1999). Assessment of clinical supervisor competencies. *Journal of Counseling and Development, 77*, 491-497.

Granello, D. H. (2000). Encouraging the cognitive development of supervisees: Using Bloom's taxonomy in supervision. *Counselor Education and Supervision, 40*, 31-46.

Granello, D. H. (2003). Influence strategies in the supervisory dyad: An investigation into the effects of gender and age. *Counselor Education and Supervision, 42*, 189-202.

Guest, C. L., Jr., & Dooley, K. (1999). Supervisor malpractice: Liability to the supervisee in clinical supervision. *Counselor Education and Supervision, 38*, 269-279.

Hart, G., Borders, L. D., Nance, D., & Paradise, L. (1995). Ethical guidelines for counseling supervisors. *Counselor Education and Supervision, 34*, 270-276.

Hart, G. M., & Nance, D. (2003). Styles of counselor supervision as perceived by supervisors and supervisees. *Counselor Education and Supervision, 43*, 146-158.

Hays, D. G., & Chang, C. Y. (2003). White privilege, oppression, and racial identity development: Implications for supervision. *Counselor Education and Supervision, 43*, 134-144.

Herlihy, B., Gray, N., & McCollum, V. (2002). Legal and ethical issues in school counselor supervision. *Professional School Counseling, 6*, 55-60.

Hird, J. S., Cavalieri, C. E., Dulko, J. P., Felice, A. A. D., & Ho, T. A. (2001). Visions and realities: Supervisee perspectives of multicultural supervision. *Journal of Multicultural Counseling and Development, 29*, 114-130.

Holloway, E. L., & Johnston, R. (1985). Group supervision: Widely practiced but poorly understood. *Counselor Education and Supervision, 24*, 332-340.

Kagan (Klein), H., & Kagan, N. I. (1997). Interpersonal process recall: Influencing human interaction. In C. E. Watkins Jr. (Ed.), *Handbook of psychotherapy supervision* (pp. 296-309). New York: Wiley.

Kahn, B. B. (1999). Priorities and practices in field supervision of school counseling students. *Professional School Counseling, 3*, 128-136.

Ladany, N., Ellis, M. V., & Friedlander, M. L. (1999). The supervisory working alliance, trainee self-efficacy, and satisfaction. *Journal of Counseling and Development, 77*, 447-455.

Ladany, N., & Lehrman-Waterman, D. E. (1999). The content and frequency of supervisor self-disclosures and their relationship to supervisor style and the supervisory working alliance. *Counselor Education and Supervision, 38*, 143-160.

Ladany, N., Marotta, S., & Muse-Burke, J. L. (2001). Counselor experience related to complexity of case conceptualization and supervision preference. *Counselor Education and Supervision, 40*, 203-219.

Ladany, N., & Melincoff, D. S. (1999). The nature of counselor supervisor nondisclosure. *Counselor Education and Supervision, 38*, 161-176.

Ladany, N., Walker, J. A., Melincoff, D. S. (2001). Supervisory style: Its relation to thesupervisory working alliance and supervisor self-disclosure. *Counselor Education and Supervision, 40*, 263-275.

Larson, L. M., Day, S. X., Springer, S. H., Clark, M. P., & Vogel, D. L. (2003). Developing a supervisor feedback rating scale: A brief report. *Measurement and Evaluation in Counseling and Development, 35*, 230-238.

Larson, L. M., Suzuki, L. A., Gillespie, K. N., Potenza, M. T., Bechtel, M. A., & Toulouse, A. L. (1992). Development and validation of the Counseling Self-Estimate Inventory. *Journal of Counseling Psychology, 39*, 105-120.

Littrell, J. M., Lee-Borden, N., & Lorenz, J. A. (1979). A developmental framework for counseling supervision. *Counselor Education and Supervision, 19*, 119-136.

Magnuson, S., Norem, K., & Wilcoxon, A. (2000). Clinical supervision of prelicensed counselors: Recommendations for consideration and practice. *Journal of Mental Health Counseling, 22*, 176-188.

Magnuson, S., Norem, K., & Wilcoxon, S. A. (2002). Clinical supervision for licensure: A consumer's guide. *Journal of Humanistic Counseling, Education and Development, 41*, 52-60.

Magnuson, S., Wilcoxon, S. A., & Norem, K. (2000). A profile of lousy supervision: Experienced counselors' perspectives. *Counselor Education and Supervision, 39*, 189-202.

Manzanares, M. G., O'Halloran, T. M., McCartney, T. J., Filer, R. D., Varhely, S. C., & Calhoun, K. (2004). CD-ROM technology for education and support of site supervisors. *Counselor Education and Supervision, 43*, 220-231.

McMahon, M. (2003). Supervision and career counsellors: A little-explored practice with an uncertain future. *British Journal of Guidance and Counselling, 31*, 177-187.

McMahon, M., & Patton, W. (2000). Career counsellors, support and lifelong learning: A case for clinical supervision. *International Journal for the Advancement of Counselling, 22*, 157-169.

McMahon, M., & Patton, W. (2000). Conversations on clinical supervision: Benefits perceived by school counsellors. *British Journal of Guidance and Counselling, 28*, 339-351.

McMahon, M., & Patton, W. (2001). Clinical supervision: The perception and experiences ofschool counselors in Australia. *International Journal for the Advancement of Counselling, 23*, 201-214.

McMahon, M., & Simons, R. (2004). Supervision training for professional counselors: An exploratory study. *Counselor Education and Supervision, 43*, 301-309.

Miller, K. L., Miller, S. M., & Evans, W. J. (2002). Computer-assisted live supervision in college counseling centers. *Journal of College Counseling, 5*, 187-192.

Montgomery, M. J., Hendricks, C. B., & Bradley, L. J. (2001). Using system perspectives in supervision. *The Family Journal, 9*, 305-313.

Muratori, M. C. (2001). Examining supervisory impairment from the counselor trainee's perspective. *Counselor Education and Supervision, 41*, 41-56.

Nelson, M. D., & Johnson, P. (1999). School counselors as supervisors: An integrated approach for supervising school counseling interns. *Counselor Education and Supervision, 39*, 89-100.

Nelson, M. D., Johnson, P., & Thorngren, J. M. (2000). An integrated approach for supervising mental health counseling interns. *Journal of Mental Health Counseling, 22*, 45-58.

Neswald-McCalip, R. (2001). Development of the secure counselor: Case examples supporting Pistole & Watkins's (1995) discussion of attachment theory in counseling supervision. *Counselor Education and Supervision, 41*, 18-27.

Neswald-McCalip, R., Sather, J., Strati, J. V., & Dineen, J. (2003). Exploring the process of creative supervision: Initial findings regarding the regenerative model. *Journal of Humanistic Counseling, Education and Development, 42*, 223-237.

Page, B. J., Pietrzak, D. R., & Sutton, J. M., Jr. (2001). National survey of school counselor supervision. *Counselor Education and Supervision, 41*, 142-150.

Pearson, Q. M. (2001). A case in clinical supervision: A framework for putting theory into practice. *Journal of Mental Health Counseling, 23*, 174-183.

Pearson, Q. M. (2004). Getting the most out of clinical supervision: Strategies for mental health counseling students. *Journal of Mental Health Counseling, 26*, 361-373.

Polanski, P. J. (2003). Spirituality in supervision. *Counseling and Values, 47*, 131-141.

Presbury, J., Echterling, L. G., & McKee, J. E. (1999). Supervision for inner vision: Solution-focused strategies. *Counselor Education and Supervision, 39*, 146-155.

Ray, D., & Altekruse, M. (2000). Effectiveness of group supervision versus combined group and individual supervision. *Counselor Education and Supervision, 40*, 19-30.

Richards, K. (2000). Counsellor supervision in Zimbabwe: A new direction. *International Journal for the Advancement of Counselling, 22*, 143-155.

Roberts, E. B., & Borders, L. D. (1994). Supervision of school counselors: Administrative, program, and counseling. *The School Counselor, 41*, 149-157.

Roberts, W. B., Morotti, A. A., Herrick, C., & Tilbury, R. (2001). Site supervisors of professional school counseling interns: Suggested guidelines. *Professional School Counseling, 4*, 208-215.

Robinson, B., Bradley, L. J., & Hendricks, C. B. (2000). Multicultural counselling supervision: A four-step model toward competency. *International Journal for the Advancement of Counselling, 22*, 131-141.

Schultz, J. C., Ososkie, J. N., Fried, J. H., Nelson, R. E., & Bardos, A. N. (2002). Clinical supervision in public rehabilitation counseling settings. *Rehabilitation Counseling Bulletin, 45*, 213-222.

Shechtman, Z., & Wirzberger, A. (1999). Needs and preferred style of supervision among Israeli school counselors at different stages of professional development. *Journal of Counseling and Development, 77*, 456-464.

Sommer, C. A., & Cox, J. A. (2003). Using Greek mythology as a metaphor to enhance supervision. *Counselor Education and Supervision, 42*, 326-335.

Starling, P. V., & Baker, S. B. (2000). Structured peer group practicum supervision: Supervisees' perceptions of supervision theory. *Counselor Education and Supervision, 39*, 162-176.

Steward, R. J., Breland, A., & Neil, D. M. (2001). Novice supervisees' self-evaluations and their perceptions of supervisory style. *Counselor Education and Supervision, 41*, 131-141.

Stoltenberg, C. D., McNeill, B. W., & Delworth, U. (1998). *IDM supervision: An integrated developmental model for supervising counselors and therapists*. San Francisco, CA: Jossey-Bass.

Studer, J. R. (2005). Supervising school counselors-in-training: A guide for field supervisors. *Professional School Counseling, 8*, 353-359.

Sutton, J. M. (1997, January). *A descriptive study of the supervision of counselors as mandated by state statute and rule*. Paper presented at the annual meeting of the American Association of State Counseling Boards, Hot Springs, AZ.

Sutton, J. M., & Page, B. J. (1994). Post-degree clinical supervision of school counselors. *School Counselor, 42*, 32-39.

Thielsen, V. A., & Leahy, M. J. (2001). Essential knowledge and skills for effective clinical supervision in rehabilitation counseling. *Rehabilitation Counseling Bulletin, 44*, 196-208.

Toporek, R. L., Ortega-Villalobos, L., & Pope-Davis, D. B. (2004). Critical incidents in multicultural supervision: Exploring supervisees' and supervisors' experiences. *Journal of Multicultural Counseling and Development, 32*, 67-83.

Watkins, C. E., Jr. (1994). The supervision of psychotherapy supervisor trainees. *American Journal of Psychotherapy, 48*, 417-431.

Wester, S. R., Vogel, D. L., & Archer, J., Jr. (2004). Male restricted emotionality and counseling supervision. *Journal of Counseling and Development, 82*, 91-98.

Wheeler, S., & King, D. (2000). Do counselling supervisors want or need to have their supervision supervised? An exploratory study. *British Journal of Guidance and Counselling*, *28*, 279-290.

White, V. E., & Queener, J. (2003). Supervisor and supervisee attachments and social provisions related to the supervisory working alliance. *Counselor Education and Supervision*, *42*, 203-218.

Žorga, S., Dekleva, B., & Kobolt, A. (2001). The process of internal evaluation as a tool for improving peer supervision. *International Journal for the Advancement of Counselling*, *23*, 151-162.

doi:10.1300/J001v24n01_05

Clinical Supervision in School Psychology: Challenges, Considerations, and Ethical and Legal Issues for Clinical Supervisors

Tony D. Crespi
Jennifer M. B. Dube

SUMMARY. Clinical supervisors face unique challenges in school psychology. It is estimated that approximately one-third of school psychologists will testify in court on issues challenging school psychological assessments. With courts finding against schools and practitioners omitting such aspects as DSM diagnoses, the complexity of practice grows. Still, the issues are not confined solely to assessment and diagnosis. From assessment to counseling and from consultation to interrogations involving school shootings, school psychologists are facing issues of growing complexity. Still, despite acknowledgement that clinical supervision is a highly valued tool for remaining up-to-date, few school psychologists actually receive clinical supervision. This article provides a fundamental look at the literature, to challenge and examine definitions of clinical supervision, and provides a contemporary foundation, through an ex-

---

Tony D. Crespi and Jennifer M. B. Dube are affiliated with the University of Hartford.

[Haworth co-indexing entry note]: "Clinical Supervision in School Psychology: Challenges, Considerations, and Ethical and Legal Issues for Clinical Supervisors." Crespi, Tony D., and Jennifer M. B. Dube. Co-published simultaneously in *The Clinical Supervisor* (The Haworth Press, Inc.) Vol. 24, No. 1/2, 2005, pp. 115-135; and: *Supervision in Counseling: Interdisciplinary Issues and Research* (ed: Lawrence Shulman, and Andrew Safyer) The Haworth Press, Inc., 2005, pp. 115-135. Single or multiple copies of this article are available for a fee from The Haworth Document Delivery Service [1-800-HAWORTH, 9:00 a.m. - 5:00 p.m. (EST). E-mail address: docdelivery@haworthpress.com].

Available online at http://cs.haworthpress.com

doi:10.1300/J001v24n01_06

amination of selected ethical and legal issues, of clinical supervision issues facing school psychologists. doi:10.1300/J001v24n01_06 *[Article copies available for a fee from The Haworth Document Delivery Service: 1-800-HAWORTH. E-mail address: <docdelivery@haworthpress.com> Website: <http://www.HaworthPress.com>*

KEYWORDS. Supervision in school psychology, psychological assessments, clinical supervision

On March 21st, 2005, in Red Lake, Minnesota, public school student Jeff Weise opened fire in his school, resulting in multiple, tragic, school-related deaths. Notably, this shooting is but one in a series of school-related shooting sprees. From Columbine, Colorado, to Red Lake, Minnesota, schools are struggling with dangerous behavior. In fact, school shootings are only one challenge. Crockett (2004) observed that children are facing a vast scope of critical problems, both new as well as existing issues. Childhood maltreatment (Locke & Newcomb, 2003), illegal drugs, threats, and weapons (Kann et al., 1998), violence (Green & Kowalik, 1997), as well as family problems (Crespi & Howe, 2001) are all increasing pressures to more effectively integrate mental health services into the schools. Truly, the issues facing schools are profound and growing. How can school psychologists develop new competencies to meet these challenges, and generally facilitate effective delivery of school psychological services?

Within school psychology, clinical supervision has often been cited as an important but frequently missing ingredient in the effort to develop maximally effective school psychological services (McIntosh & Phelps, 2000; Crespi & Fischetti, 1997; Ross & Goh, 1993). Yet, while clinical supervision is well acknowledged as a key to developing competence (Borders & Cashwell, 1992), and while 95% of school-based mental health professionals have supported the importance of clinical supervision (Zins, Murphy, & Wess, 1989), the most recent national studies on clinical supervision in school psychology have reported low participation. Chafouleas, Clonan, and Vanauken (2002), for instance, noted severe lapses in clinical supervision, documenting a desire for more supervision.

Welsh, Stanley, and Wilmoth (2003) indicated that far too little attention has been paid to supervision issues in school psychology. Indeed, Harvey and Struzziero (2000) indicated that a broad research base on clinical supervision in school psychology is simply missing.

Are school supervisors up-to-date on the issues? Looking at school shootings, for instance, are supervisors knowledgeable about threat assessments? What additional concerns can be cited? At present, in school psychology a maximum of 10% of practicing school psychologists actually participate in clinical supervision (Fischetti & Crespi, 1999). Thus, it appears an overlooked area. Of course, looking at a sister profession, school counseling, it has been noted that clinical supervision in school counseling has also been largely overlooked (Page, Pietrzak, & Sutton, 2001; Crespi, 1998; Barett & Schmidt, 1986), with a majority of school counselors indicating that while a desire exists for clinical supervision, the majority do not receive clinical supervision.

In point of fact, then, while clinical supervision is valuable, it has been largely overlooked both in the practice arena as well as in the supervision literature in school psychology. This article highlights the need for clinical supervision, reviews definitions, examines critical ethical and legal challenges impacting contemporary practice, and underscores the necessity of school psychologists becoming active participants in clinical supervision as a component to continuing education and professional development.

THEORY AND PRACTICE

With a rising population of children in need of school-based services (Crespi, Nissen, & Lopez, 2000), and with a growing acknowledgement that parents and communities are turning to school mental health professionals, such as school psychologists, for psychological services (Reeder et al., 1997), school-based mental health professionals face an array of challenges. In fact, it has been observed that as many as one quarter of all adolescents are at risk for behaviors that can seriously impact their health (Carnegie Council on Adolescent Development, 1996).

Clinical supervision represents one important component in meeting the changing needs of children (Crespi & Fischetti, 1997), as clinical supervision is a useful tool to teach new skills and refine practice. Still, within school psychology, how is clinical supervision defined?

Knoff (1986) defined clinical supervision as follows:

> An intensive, hierarchical, interpersonally focused relationship involving a supervisor who oversees the development of a supervisees professional knowledge, skill, confidence, objectivity, and

> interpersonal interactions on behalf of or with a specified client for the purpose of facilitating and/or improving competence and effective service delivery and promoting accountability in the field. (p. 529)

McIntosh and Phelps (2000) defined clinical supervision similarly:

> Supervision is an interpersonal interaction between two or more individuals for the purpose of sharing knowledge, assessing professional competencies, and providing objective feedback with the terminal goals of developing new competencies, facilitating effective delivery of psychological services, and maintaining professional competencies. (pp. 33-34)

More generally, Strein (1996) defined supervision as key to facilitating effective delivery of school psychological services and promoting professional development in practitioners. Fischetti and Crespi (1999) defined administrative supervision as involving record keeping, policy, and attendance issues. Of course, more globally, from counseling psychology, Ladany, Walker, and Melincoff (2001) noted that supervisors can have different roles, styles, and approaches. Stoltenberg and McNeill (1997) suggested a teaching role with early career practitioners, while Muse-Burke, Ladany, and Deck (2001) spoke to a broad range of complexity in developing the supervisory relationship.

Functionally, then, areas of clinical responsibility for school practitioners may be important to understand as a starting framework. Three major areas of practice in school psychology include the following:

1. Assessment

   Assessment remains an important area of practice for school psychologists. Dumont and Willis (2003) noted that assessment is fundamental to school psychological practice and requires direct and frequent assessment to avoid legal and ethical pitfalls. In fact, not only are cognitive, personality, and psychoeducational assessments vital in identification and classification for special education and related services, but new instrumentation, skills, and standards must be continually integrated into practice.

   With refinements in cognitive, personality, and neuropsychological assessment, supervision affords a viable vehicle for up-dating skills. Moreover, increasingly, assessment requires a growing knowledge of psychopathology, and special education law in order to precisely address the classification and diagnostic outcomes of testing.

2. Counseling

   Counseling remains a cornerstone of practice for school psychologists. Unfortunately, the supervision literature on this area is virtually entirely related to counseling and clinical psychology with limited attention to school psychology (Welsh et al., 2003). With advances in our understanding of empirically supported interventions, growth in integrating multicultural perspectives, and advances in ethical and legal issues related to counseling, a strong need exists to update practitioner knowledge of counseling theory and practice issues.

   Unfortunately, from a supervision framework, no research has been conducted specific to school psychology. On the other hand, from neighboring specialties, Worthen and McNeill (1996) noted too little time is spent examining counseling supervision in mental health as a broad practice area. For schools, this means an important challenge.

3. Consultation

   Cramer and Rosenfield (2003) indicated that after a period of neglect interest in consultation has risen, although the process of supervision on consultation remains a area of little attention. Still, it is noted that supervision can enhance competence and develop greater expertise when applied to consultation.

   Teacher, parent, and administrator consultation are three areas in which schools are intimately involved. New consultation models, new research on classroom consultation, advances in mental health consultation, and behavioral and organizational consultation theory and intervention models are continually evolving. Both supervisors and supervisees can benefit from increased focus and on basic research examining this component.

Chafouleas et al. (2002) noted great lapses in clinical supervision in school psychology. In fact, practitioners report that clinical supervision is unsatisfactory (Fischetti & Crespi, 1999; Coll, 1995). More specifically, Fischetti and Crespi (1999) indicated that while 70% of a national sample of school psychologists reported a desire for clinical supervision, only 10% of their sample indicated participation.

Taken together, results of multiple studies indicate that clinical supervision is generally not in place in school psychology. Results indicate practitioners are interested in supervision, and it is acknowledged that while clinical supervision is a valuable continuing education tool, it is lacking an agenda on both a local and national level. In addition, while supervisors and supervisees are aware of the benefits of supervision, they have not been successful in raising it to a priority level, nor are they aware of potential problems and pitfalls.

CLINICAL SUPERVISION

Despite more than 30 years of recognition of its viability as a tool for professional development (Pierce & Schauble, 1970) clinical supervision remains poorly placed in public education and in school psychology in particular. For supervisors content itself, as noted, represents one challenge. In addition, though, unethical supervisory practices (Cobia & Boes, 2000), sexualized supervision (Barnett-Queen & Larrabee, 2000), wrong supervision (Kadushin, 1999), bad practices (Allen, Szollos, & Williams, 1986), and lack of training in supervision (Crespi & Lopez, 1998) represent a sampling of difficulties that can confound the issues. Sadly, a dearth exists in research on multiple areas of practice in school psychology.

Looking at counseling, Nelson and Friedlander (2001) noted that supervisors can display as many problems as clinicians in psychotherapy. In fact, Bernard and Goodyear (1998), drawing from counselor education and supervision, indicated that negative factors within both supervisor and supervisee can create negative consequences. Given the importance of supervision, it is vital to foster a successful match with a suitable supervisor (Ramos-Sanchez et al., 2002). Otherwise, negative experiences can result.

Functionally, clinical supervisors must possess knowledge of both clinical practice as well as the clinical supervision process. Highlighting the former, the depth and breadth of knowledge in school psychology is expanding exponentially. With more than 450 identifiable forms of psychotherapy noted in clinical and counseling psychology (Karasu, 1986), supervisors addressing counseling and psychotherapy must, themselves, be thoroughly up-to-date, understand contemporary changes in practice, and supervisors must also possess a solid understanding of both their supervisory style, and the concomitant impediments to developing a solid supervisory process.

Supervision provides feedback about performance, offers guidance, provides alternate views about client dynamic and interventions, refines supervisee identity, and serves as a base for learning (Hoffman, 1994;

Greben, 1991). Unfortunately, not all supervisors have the same skills, nor even similar levels of interest in supervision. Knowledge can vary. Skills can vary. Interest and motivation can vary. In addition, style can vary. Drawing from counseling psychology, Friedlander and Ward (1984) indicated that the distinctive approach (i.e., style) that supervisors use can impact supervisees. Three styles they note include (A) Attractive, (B) Sensitive, and (C) Task-oriented. Somewhat similarly (but more recently), Bernard (1997) identified three styles: (A) Consultant, (B) Counselor, and (C) Teacher. A summary follows:

A. Attractive/Consultant (warm, friendly, supportive),
B. Sensitive/Counselor (invested, perceptive), and
C. Task-Oriented/Teacher (goal-directed, focused, structured).

To comprehensively develop supervision models in school psychology, then, supervisors must possess considerable knowledge and skills. Further, potential problems should be considered. Adapting eight potential problems identified in psychotherapy supervision (i.e., Rodenhauser, 1997), the following points should be thoughtfully considered if supervision is to be comprehensively instituted:

1. Uniform standards for training in assessment, counseling, and consultation have not been established;
2. Social, political, and economic pressures are rapidly changing the configuration and accessibility of school psychological services;
3. While standards for administrative supervision are in place in schools, they are lacking in providing supervision in assessment, counseling, and consultation;
4. Supervisors may lack skill diversity and flexibility with a variety of theories and practices in assessment, counseling, and consultation; and
5. Legal and ethical issues are continually changing school practice.

In essence, supervisors can begin by recognizing the challenging complexity of supervision. Because clinical supervisors provide feedback, offer guidance, provide alternative views, and provide insights into ethical and legal issues, supervisors themselves must be actively engaged in a comprehensive program of professional development. Bernard and Goodyear (1998) suggested that clinical supervisors be senior members of the profession. Ideally, senior members will themselves have participated in supervision, have actively pursued professional development activities, and possess considerable depth and breadth of knowledge.

Indeed, then, how can sufficient depth and breadth be maximally developed? There are supervisors who pursue supervision of their supervision in order to refine supervision skills. More generally, professional development activities represent another tool to maintain and extend skills. At a basic level, it is helpful for supervisors to possess at least a minimal understanding of the professional development literature, be up-to-date clinically, and be able to actively understand how to integrate clinical supervision into a professional development program for supervisees.

ETHICAL AND LEGAL ISSUES SHAPING SUPERVISION IN SCHOOL PSYCHOLOGY

McIntosh and Phelps (2000) noted that overall association professional standards are often not adequately linked to clinical supervision. More recently, in a major work prepared for the National Association of School Psychologists Crespi and Politikos (2005) analyzed contemporary ethical and legal challenges facing clinical supervisors overseeing school psychologists. Key data, presented in a question and answer format, follow.

Case Illustrations

Legal Dilemmas In School Psychology Practice

Legal Case: Question Area: Diagnosis In Psychological Evaluations

Example: A school psychologist, after consultation with a supervisor, determines not to include diagnoses in evaluations. It is felt this must be done by doctoral, licensed, practitioners.

Legal Case: Answer: Diagnosis In Psychological Evaluations

Case: Montgomery County Public Schools, 40 IDELR 60 (SEA MD 2003).

A Maryland administrative judge concluded that district school psychologist's evaluation that an 8-year-old student had Asperger's syndrome was improper for several reasons and ordered the district reimburse the parent for an independent evaluation. The judge determined the school psychologist did not consider the DSM in the evaluation, provide a differential diagnosis of Asperger's with ADHD and focus on the child's current diagnosis.

Of note, this means parents may be reimbursed for independent evaluations if they can demonstrate the district evaluation contained improper methods. An appropriate diagnosis comparing and contrasting issues and adequate discussion may be required.

The judge concluded that the school psychologist's evaluation failed to properly evaluate the child, and ordered reimbursement on the independent evaluation diagnosing ADHD. He was troubled by the fact that the school psychologist refused to consider the DSM IV "a standard diagnostic classification system for evaluating or diagnosing a child with a learning disability in a school setting under the IDEA." The judge noted the psychologist had failed to engage in a differential diagnosis, and did not address the ADHD issue. The psychologist had also failed to focus the report on the child's current diagnosis and educational needs.

Ethical Case: Question Area: Standardizing Assessment Batteries (IV, C, 1a)

Example: The district uses a standard battery when assessing students referred for L.D. What ethical problems, if any, may this cause?

Ethical Case: Answer: Standardizing Assessment Batteries (IV, C, 1a)

IV C 1. School psychologists maintain the highest standard for educational and psychological assessment and direct and indirect interventions.

In conducting psychological, educational, or behavioral evaluations or in providing therapy, counseling, or consultation services, due consideration is given to individual integrity and individual differences.

Legal Case: Question Area: Mother Requests Father Not Receive Information

Example: A mother of an elementary student tells the school that if the father requests information, they must not provide any information as the mother has legal custody. The practitioner explains that unless father has had rights terminated, the school has a policy to provide the same information both the custodial and non-custodial parent. When the mother offers a copy of the custody order as verification, the practitioner suggests seeing the principal.

Legal Case: Answer: Mother Requests Father Not Receive Information

All parents, both custodial and non-custodial, have rights and responsibilities for the welfare of their children and have legal rights.

Connecticut CGS Section 46B-56 states:

> "Parent not granted custody of a minor child shall not be denied rights of access to the academic, medical, hospital, or health records unless otherwise ordered by the court." In addition, CGS 20-7C provides a caveat. The provider does not have to turn over records if the provider "reasonably determines that the information is detrimental to the physical or mental health of the patient, or is likely to cause the patient to harm himself or another." This provides a basis for refusing to turn over sensitive records of treatment to a potentially abusing parent.

Legal Case: Question Area: Written Permission for Counseling

Example: A high school counseling department, in which a school psychologist operates, is notified by the principal that from this day forward a student's parent or guardian must sign a written permission before counseling. Because counseling services are routinely offered, the Department feels this is not necessary.

Legal Case: Answer: Written Permission for Counseling

Individual state laws can vary widely on this issue. Certainly it should be noted that written consent is the most advantageous way to proceed. Of note, though, in Connecticut, General Statute Sec 19a-14c notes that a psychologist may provide treatment without consent or notification of a parent if

1. Requiring consent or notification would cause the minor to reject treatment,
2. The provision of treatment is clinically indicated,
3. Failure to provide treatment would be seriously detrimental,
4. The minor has knowingly and willingly sought the treatment, and
5. The minor is mature enough to participate in treatment.

Records must be documented to show the above and the minor needs to sign a statement that he or she is voluntarily seeking the treatment and discussed issue of parental notification, has determined it is not in his or her best interests to involve parents and has been given ample opportunity to ask questions about treatment. After 6 sessions, parents must be notified unless notification would be seriously detrimental to the child's well-being. This determination must be made every 6 sessions and noted in the record.

Question Area: Computer-Generated Reports (NASP IV, E, 3)

Example: One or more tests you use require you to derive scores through a computer-generated data analysis. You are unable to determine scores through hand calculations. What ethical (and legal) issues does that raise?

Answer: Computer-Generated Reports (NASP IV, E, 3)

IV E 3. School psychologists do not promote or encourage inappropriate use of computer generated test analyses or reports. In accordance with this principle, a school psychologist would not even offer an unedited computer report as his or her own writing or use a computer-scoring system for tests in which he or she has no training. The psychologists should select scoring and interpretation services on the basis of accuracy and professional alignment with the underlying decision rules.

Question Area: Confidentiality (NASP III, A, 9, 11, III, B, 2)

Example: A child you are testing displays bruises on his arms. When asked, he indicates his mother's boyfriend hits him when they play rough. What do you do?

Answer: Confidentiality (NASP III, AS, 9, 11)

III A 9. School psychologists respect the confidentiality of information obtained during their professional work. Information is revealed only with the informed consent of the child, or the child's legal guardian, except in those situations in which failure to release information would result in clear danger to the child or others.

III A 11. School psychologists inform children and other clients of the limits of confidentiality at the outset of establishing a professional relationship.

Question Area: Conflicts Between Ethics and Law (NASP III, D, 5)

Example: You receive a summons to produce all records on a child you tested and counseled. You object, knowing your ethical beliefs do not allow the dissemination of these records. What do you do?

Answer: Conflicts Between Ethics and Law

III D 5. School psychologists adhere to federal, state, and local laws and ordinances governing their practice and advocacy efforts. If regulations conflict with ethical guidelines, school psychologists seek to resolve such conflict through positive, respected, and legal channels, including advocacy efforts involving public policy.

Question Area: Unethical Practice (NASP III, A, 8)

Example: You have observed one of your colleagues responding positively to solicitous behaviors displayed by a high school student. What do you do?

Answer: Unethical Practice (NASP III, A, 8)

III A 8. School psychologists attempt to resolve suspected detrimental or unethical practices on an informal level. If informed efforts are not productive, the appropriate professional organization is contacted for assistance, and procedures established for questioning ethical practice are followed.

Question Area: Service, Parents Do Not Provide Consent (NASP III, C, 4)

Example: A depressed and withdrawn student asks you to talk with her, saying she has thought about taking her life. You contact her parents who inform you that no crazy psychologist is going to see their daughter. What do you do?

Answer: Service, Parents Do Not Provide Consent (NASP III, C, 4)

III C 4. School psychologists respect the wishes of parents who object to school psychological services and attempt to guide parents to alternative community resources.

Question Area: Exceeding Boundaries of Competence (NASP III, E, 5)

Example: Your supervisor asks you to do an evaluation of a child referred for autism. You have no training or experience in conducting such an evaluation. What do you do?

Answer: Exceeding Boundaries of Competence (NASP III, E, 5)

III E 5. The child or other client is referred to another professional for services when a condition or need is identified that is outside the professional competencies or scope of the school psychologist.

Question Area: Record Restrictions/Confidentiality (NASP IV, D, 1, 2, 3)

Example: You present your report to the IEP committee, including the parents, during the meeting. What ethical problems, if any, may this cause?

Answer: Record Restrictions/Confidentiality (NASP IV, D, 1, 2, 3)

IV D 1. School psychologists ascertain that information about children and other clients reaches only authorized persons.

School psychologists adequately interpret information so that the recipient can better help the child or other clients. School psychologists assist agency recipients to establish procedures to properly safeguard confidential material.

IV D 2. School psychologists communicate findings and recommendations in language readily understood by the intended recipient. These communications describe potential consequences associated with proposals.

IV D 3. School psychologists prepare written reports such form and style that the recipient of the report will be able to assist the child or other clients. Reports should emphasize recommendations and interpretations: unedited computer-generated reports, pre-printed "check-off" or "fill in the blank" reports, and reports that present only test scores or global statements regarding eligibility for special education without specific recommendations for intervention are seldom useful. Reports should include an appraisal of the degree of confidence that could be assigned to the information. Alterations of previously released reports should be done only by the original author.

Question Area: Record Storage and Disposal (NASP IV, D, 5)

Example: The district is running out of storage room and thus will need to shred all but the first page of all protocols. What ethical problems may this cause?

Answer: Record Storage and Disposal (NASP IV, D, 5)

IV D 5. School psychologists comply with all laws, regulations, and policies pertaining to the adequate storage and disposal of records to maintain appropriate confidentiality of information.

Question Area: Maintaining Test Security (NASP IV, E, 1)

Example: An attorney for parents requests copies of all tests used in your assessment. What ethical (and legal) issues does this raise?

Answer: Maintaining Test Security (NASP IV, E, 1)

IV E 1. School psychologists maintain test security, preventing the release of underlying principle and specific content that would undermine the use of the device. School psychologists are responsible for the security requirements specific to each instrument used.

Question Area: Electronic Transmission of Reports (NASP IV, E, 6)

Example: You and the parents agree to exchange information weekly via the internet as to their son's behavior at school and home. What ethical issues does this raise?

Answer: Electronic Transmission of Reports (NASP IV, E, 6)

IV E 6. To ensure confidentiality, student/client records are not transmitted electronically without a guarantee of privacy. In line with this principle, a receiving fax machine must be in a secure location and operated by employees cleared to work with confidential files, and e-mail messages must be encrypted or else stripped of all information that identifies the student/client.

SUPERVISION AS PROFESSIONAL DEVELOPMENT

Continuing education has long been acknowledged as a hallmark of professionalism (Livneh & Livneh, 1999; Mullen, Holcomb, & Fasser, 1988). In fact, it has been well over two decades that leaders of professional organizations have supported continuing education (Houle, 1980).

Within the schools, more than decade has passed since continuing education was highlighted as specifically important for school psychologists (Crespi & Rigazio-DiGilio, 1992). Of course, placed in a larger context, most licensed psychologists have been described as actively participating in continuing education (Vandecreek, Knapp, & Brace, 1990).

Broadly, continuing education has been deemed critical for teachers and educators (Livneh & Livneh, 1999). In fact, it is noted that school personnel need continuing education in order to keep up-to-date with knowledge and skills, to be able to analyze job functions and prepare and for new roles, and to consider environmental, professional, and contexts of practice. Further, continuing education is required in many states for recertification and continuing practice. Given that school-based mental health professionals are working at the praxis of education and psychology, the support of both constituents on the importance of continuing education is noteworthy.

As the knowledge base in school psychology continues to evolve, clinical supervision increasingly can be conceptualized as a key component to continuing education. Crespi and Rigazio-DiGilio (1992) indicated that the acceptance of the National School Psychology Certification System, with a mandate for professional development, extended the agenda of continuing education to all nationally certified school psychologists in the US and employed in US Department of Defense Schools throughout the world.

Paisley and McMahon (2001) indicated that school mental health professionals must participate in clinical supervision to develop professionally. Topics addressed in supervision of importance to school-based practitioners can be wide ranging, including such issues as depression, violence, ADHD, counseling and psychotherapeutic interventions, ethics and laws, assessment, and consultation.

In a broader framework, post-degree supervision is a vital ingredient to quality practice, and outside schools, is actually required for independent practice in both psychology and counseling (Crespi, 1994; Borders & Cashwell, 1992).

Watkins (1995) noted the following:

> Supervisors are ultimately responsible for their supervisees' therapy conduct and performance, can contribute substantially to the growth and development of their supervisees' therapy knowledge and skill, and serve as a vital quality-assurance control function vis-à-vis their supervisees and the public, it seems only right that more theoretical and research emphasis would be given to the subject. (p. 573)

School psychologists encounter challenging cases. One child may be violent, and potentially very dangerous. A second child may be suicidal. Yet a third may pose a difficult assessment dilemma. For too long, and too often, cases fall beyond the scope of graduate training (Gysbers & Henderson, 1988). Supervision, on the other hand, is one important vehicle for professional development (Crespi & Fischetti, 1997), and can enhance services for children, families, and the schools.

Synthesizing these points, since continuing education is actively suggested for educators and mental health professionals, and given that school psychologists largely do, indeed, participate in continuing education in order to main State Department of Education credentialing, and given the substantial value of clinical supervision, practitioners need to build systems whereby this can occur. Actually, just as supervisors have a responsibility to increase the awareness of supervisees of the importance of supervision, so practitioners need to educate administrators and supervisors about the overall responsibility of building in supervision systems. This can enhance services to children. And increase skills.

CONCLUSIONS

School psychologists have an obligation to meet the highest standards of mental health practice. That is, they have an obligation to provide effective services consistent with the most contemporary standards of practice. Unfortunately, practice issues are too often not linked with supervision (McIntosh & Phelps, 2000). With schools facing a growing array of challenges, the need to refine and update skills is increasing. Crockett (2004) observed a vast scope of critical problems. Childhood maltreatment (Locke & Newcomb, 2003), drugs and weapons (Kann et al., 1998), extreme violence (Green & Kowalik, 1997), family problems (Crespi & Howe, 2001), as well more generalized counseling needs (Borders & Drury, 1992) are illustrative of the rising challenges facing schools and school psychologists.

School psychologists can maximize professional skills to meet these demands through clinical supervision. Clinical supervision is an acknowledged vehicle to developing contemporary skills, and is presently recognized as an important ingredient for the effective delivery and enhancement of school mental health services (Crespi, 2003; Welsh et al., 2003).

Unfortunately, while clinical supervision is a documented tool to develop and refine clinical competence and while 95% of school-based mental health professionals have supported the importance of clinical supervision (Zins et al., 1989), recent national studies on clinical supervision in school psychology have noted a paucity of participation and research on clinical supervision. Welsh et al. (2003) as well as Harvey and Struzziero (2000) indicated that a broad lack of research exists relative to clinical supervision in school psychology. In fact, McIntosh and Phelps (2000) note that supervision, when it occurs, is more typically on an "as-needed basis as opposed to being provided during regularly scheduled, structured, times" (p. 35).

Despite the acknowledgement that clinical supervision is valuable, it has remained overlooked in schools. Specifically, Chafouleas et al. (2002) noted great lapses in clinical supervision in school psychology. More specifically, Fischetti and Crespi (1999) indicated that while 70% of a national sample of school psychologists reported a desire for clinical supervision, only 10% of their sample indicated participation. Moreover, it has been generally overlooked both in the practice arena as well as in the area of the supervision literature in school psychology. This article reviewed critical definitions of clinical supervision, delineated the distinction between clinical and administrative supervision, examined relevant issues, and suggested that rising ethical and legal issues can serve as a foundation for both research and practice on supervision in school psychology.

Fundamentally, clinical supervision represents a critical ingredient in the education, training, and professional development of mental health professionals (Crespi & Fischetti, 1997). Dumont and Willis (2003) indicated that with increasing complexity in assessment, for instance, and with a need for new competencies and skills, "Supervision should . . . be provided conscientiously for all aspects of the evaluation process" (p. 175). The points raised in this article, and complemented by the points of the authors in this volume, suggest a strong need for a national agenda emphasizing clinical supervision practices in the schools. As noted in numerous works, both popular and professional, schools throughout the United States are coping with dramatic challenges. At the same time, school-mental health practice is growing. What is on the horizon for new innovations? As child clinicians, we must continually remain current. We must be ready for new challenges. We must meet the needs of children, families, and the schools. Clinical supervision is one way to help meet these challenges in school psychology.

REFERENCES

Allen, G.J., Szollos, S.J., & Williams, B.E. (1986). Doctoral students' comparative evaluations of best and worst psychotherapy supervision. *Professional Psychology: Research and Practice*, *17*, 91-99.

Barett, R.L., & Schmidt, J.J. (1986). School counselor certification and supervision: Overlooked professional issues. *Counselor Education and Supervision*, *26*, 50-56.

Barnett-Queen, T., & Larrabee, M.J. (2000). Sexually oriented relationships between educators and students in mental-health education programs. *Journal of Mental Health Counseling*, *22*, 68-84.

Bernard, J.M., & Goodyear, R.K. (1998). *Fundamentals of clinical supervision* (2nd ed). Boston: Allyn & Bacon.

Borders, L.D., & Cashwell, C.S. (1992). Supervision regulations in counselor licensure legislation. *Counselor Education and Supervision*, *31*, 208-218.

Carey, J.C., Reinat, M., & Fontes, L. (1990). School counselors' perceptions of training needs in multicultural counseling. *Counselor Education and Supervision*, *29*, 155-169.

Carnegie Council on Adolescent Development (1996). *Great transitions: Preparing adolescents for a new century*. New York: Author.

Chafouleas, S.M., Clonan, S.M., & Vanauken, T.L. (2002). A national survey of current supervision and evaluation practices of school psychologists. *Psychology in the Schools*, *39*, 317-325.

Cobia, D.C., & Boes, S.R. (2000). Professional disclosure statements and formal plans for supervision: Two strategies for minimizing the risk of ethical conflicts in post-master's supervision. *Journal of Counseling and Development*, *78*, 293-296.

Coll, K.M. (1995). Clinical supervision of community college counselors: Current and preferred practices. *Counselor Education and Supervision*, *35*, 111-117.

Cramer, K., & Rosenfield, S. (2003). Clinical supervision of consultation. *The Clinical Supervisor*, *22*, 111-124.

Crespi, T.D. (1998). School counselors and clinical supervision: perspectives to facilitate counseling services in the schools. *Special Services in the Schools*, *13*, 107-114.

Crespi, T.D. (1994). *Licensure in professional psychology: Preparatory techniques.* Washington, DC: Taylor & Francis.

Crespi, T.D., & Fischetti, B.A. (1997). Clinical supervision for school psychologists: Bridging theory and practice. *School Psychology International, 18*, 41-48.

Crespi, T.D., & Howe, E.A. (2001). Facing the family treatment crisis: Changing parameters in marriage and family therapy education. *Family Therapy, 28*, 32-38.

Crespi, T.D., & Lopez, P.G. (1998). Practicum and internship supervision in the schools: Standards and considerations for school psychology supervisors. *The Clinical Supervisor, 17*, 113-126.

Crespi, T.D., Nissen, K.S., & Lopez, P.G. (2000). Managed health care and school-based services: Present status and contemporary case deliberations–Applications for school practice. *Special Services in the Schools, 16*, 95-109.

Crespi, T.D., & Politikos, N.N. (2005). *Ethical and legal challenges for supervisors: Clinical and administrative considerations* (Cassette Recording No. 350AB WS18). Bethesda, MD: National Association of School Psychologists.

Crespi, T.D., & Rigazio-DiGilio, S.A. (1992). Professional development and continuing education: Implications for the school psychologist. *School Psychology International, 13*, 347-355.

Crockett, D. (2004). Critical issues facing children in the 2000s. *School Psychology Review, 33*, 78-82.

Dumont, R., & Willis, J.O. (2003). Issues regarding the supervision of assessment. *The Clinical Supervisor, 22*, 159-176.

Ellis, M.V. (2001). Harmful supervision, a cause for alarm: Comment on Gray et al. (2001) and Nelson and Friedlander (2001). *Journal of Counseling Psychology, 48*, 401-406.

Fischetti, B.A., & Crespi, T.D. (1999). Clinical supervision for school psychologists: National practices, trends, and future implications. *School Psychology International, 20*, 278-288.

Friedlander, M.L., & Ward, L.G. (1984). Development and validation of the Supervisory Styles Inventory. *Journal of Counseling Psychology, 4*, 541-557.

Granet, R.B., Kalman, T.P., & Sacks, M.H. (1980). From supervisee to supervisor: An unexplored aspect of the psychiatrist's education. *American Journal of Psychiatry, 137*, 1443-1446.

Greben, S.E. (1991). Interpersonal aspects of the supervision of individual psychotherapy. *American Journal of Psychotherapy, 45*, 306-316.

Green, W.H., & Kowalik, S.C. (1997). Violence in child and adolescent psychiatry. *Psychiatric Annals, 27*, 745-750.

Gysbers, N.C., & Henderson, P. (1988). *Developing and managing your school guidance program.* Alexandria, VA: American Counseling Association.

Harvey, V.S., & Struzziero, J.A. (2000). *Effective supervision in school psychology.* Bethesda, MD: National Association of School Psychologists.

Hoffman, L.W. (1994). The training of psychotherapy supervisors: A barren scape. *Psychotherapy in Private Practice, 13*, 23-42.

Houle, C.O. (1980). *Continuing learning in the professions.* San Francisco, CA: Jossey-Bass.

Kadushin, A. (1999). What's wrong, what's right with social work supervision. *The Clinical Supervisor, 18*, 3-19.

Kann, L., Kinchen, S.A., Williams, B.I., Ross, J.G., Lowery, R., Hill, C.V., Grunbaum, J.A., Blumson, P.S., Collins, J.L., Kolbe, L.J., & State and Local Coordinators. (1998). *Youth risk behavior surveillance–United States, 1997* [CDC MMWR Surveillance Summaries No. SS-3]. Atlanta, GA: Centers for Disease Control and Prevention.

Karasu, T.B. (1986). Psychotherapies: Benefits and limitations. *American Journal of Psychotherapy, 40*, 324-342.

Ladany, N., Hill, C.E., Corbett, M.M., & Nutt, E.A. (1996). Nature, extent, and importance of what psychotherapy trainees do not disclose to their supervisors. *Journal of Counseling Psychology, 43*, 10-24.

Ladany, N., Walker, J.A., & Melincoff, D.S. (2001). Supervisory style: Its relation to the supervisory working alliance and supervisor self-disclosure. *Counselor Education and Supervision, 40*, 263-275.

Livneh, C., & Livneh, H. (1999). Continuing professional education among educators: Predictors of participation in learning activities. *Adult Education Quarterly, 49*, 91-109.

Locke, T.F., & Newcomb, M.D. (2003). Childhood maltreatment, parental alcohol/drug related problems, and global parental dysfunction. *Professional Psychology: Research and Practice, 34*, 73-79.

McIntosh, D.E., & Phelps, L. (2000). Supervision in school psychology: Where will the future take us? *Psychology in the Schools, 37*, 33-38.

Montgomery County Public Schools. (2003). 40 IDELR 60. (SEA MD 2003).

Mullen, P.D., Holcomb, J.D., & Fasser, C.E. (1988). Selected allied health professionals' self-confidence in health promotion counseling skills and interest in continuing education programs. *Journal of Allied Health, 17*, 123-133.

Muse-Burke, J.L., Ladany, N., & Deck, M. (2001). The supervisory relationship. In J.L. Bradley & N. Ladany (Eds.), *Counselor supervision: Principles, process, & practice* (3rd ed., pp. 28-62). Philadelphia: Brunner-Routledge.

National Association of School Psychologists. (2000). *Professional Conduct Manual: Principles for professional ethics and guidelines for the provision of school psychological services.* Bethesda, MD: Author.

Nelson, M.L., & Friedlander, M.L. (2001). A close look at conflictual supervisory relationships: The trainee's perspective. *Journal of Counseling Psychology, 48*, 384-395.

Page, B.J., Pietrzak, D.R., & Sutton, J.M. (2001). National survey of school counselor supervision. *Counselor Education and Supervision, 41*, 142-150.

Paisley, P.O., & McMahon, H.G. (2001). School counseling for the twenty-first century: Challenges and opportunities. *Professional School Counseling, 5*, 106-115.

Pierce, R.M., & Schauble, P.G. (1970). Graduate training of facilitative counselors: The effects of individual supervision. *Journal of Counseling Psychology, 17*, 210-215.

Ramos-Sanchez, L., Esnil, E., Goodwin, A., Riggs, S., Touster, L.O., Wright, L.K. et al. (2002). Negative supervisory events: Effects on supervision satisfaction and supervisory alliance. *Professional Psychology: Research and Practice, 33*, 197-202.

Reeder, G.D., Maccow, G.C., Shaw, S.R., Swerdlik, M.E., Horton, C.B., & Foster, P. (1997). School psychologists and full service schools: Partnerships with medical mental health, and social services. *School Psychology Review, 26*, 603-621.

Rodenhauser, P. (1994). Toward a multidimensional model for psychotherapy supervision based on developmental stages. *Journal of Psychotherapy Practice And Research, 3*, 1-15.

Rodenhauser, P. (1997). Psychotherapy supervision: Prerequisites and problems in the process. In C.E. Watkins (Ed.), *Handbook of psychotherapy supervision* (pp. 527-548). New York: John Wiley.

Ross, R., & Goh, D. (1993). Participating in supervision in school psychology: A national survey of practices and training. *School Psychology Review, 22*, 63-80.

Shanfield, S.B., & Gil, D. (1985). Styles of psychotherapy supervision. *Journal of Psychiatric Education, 9*, 225-232.

Stoltenberg, C.D., & McNeill, B.W. (1997). Clinical supervision from a developmental perspective: Research and practice. In C.E. Watkins (Ed.), *Handbook of psychotherapy supervision* (pp. 184-202). New York: John Wiley.

Strein, W. (1996). Professional supervision. T.K. Fagan & P.G. Worden (Eds.), *Historical encyclopedia of school psychology* (pp. 297-298). Westport, CT: Greenwood.

Sutton, J.M., & Page, B.J. (1994). Post-degree clinical supervision of school counselors. *The School Counselor, 42*, 32-39.

Vandecreek, L., Knapp, S., & Brace, K. (1990). Mandatory continuing education for licensed psychologists: Its rationale and current implementation. *Professional Psychology: Research and Practice, 21*, 135-140.

Watkins, C.W. (1995). Psychotherapy supervision in the 90's: Some observations and reflections. *American Journal of Psychotherapy, 49*, 568-582.

Welsh, J.S., Stanley, J.D., & Wilmoth, C. (2003). Competency-based pre-internship supervision of school psychologists: A collaborative training model. *The Clinical Supervisor, 22*, 189.

Worthen, V., & McNeill, B.W. (1996). A phenomenological investigation of "good" supervision events. *Journal of Counseling Psychology, 43*, 25-34.

Zins, J.E., Murphy, J.J., & Wess, B.P. (1989). Supervision in school psychology: Current practices and congruence with professional standards. *School Psychology Review, 18*, 56-63.

doi:10.1300/J001v24n01_06

Current Supervision Scholarship in Psychology: A Five Year Review

Rodney K. Goodyear
Keyondria Bunch
Charles D. Claiborn

SUMMARY. This paper reviewed five years of supervision-related articles that had been published in psychology journals. Almost one-fourth of the articles were published in *Professional Psychology: Research & Practice.* The other journals most frequently represented in this review were the *Journal of Counseling Psychology*, *Journal of Clinical Psychology*, and *Psychotherapy: Theory, Research, Practice, Training.* The largest single category of articles during this five-year period concerned supervision that in some way was harmful. Surprisingly few articles,

Rodney K. Goodyear and Keyondria Bunch are affiliated with the University of Southern California. Charles D. Claiborn is affiliated with the Arizona State University.

Address correspondence to: Rodney K. Goodyear, 1100A WPH, University of Southern California, Los Angeles, CA 90089-0031 (E-mail: goodyea@usc.edu).

Earlier versions of this article were presented both at the Clinical Supervision Planning Committee meeting in October 2004 and at the First International Interdisciplinary Clinical Supervision Conference in Amherst, NY, June 2005. The authors thank Catharina Chang and Jack Culbreth for their helpful feedback.

[Haworth co-indexing entry note]: "Current Supervision Scholarship in Psychology: A Five Year Review." Goodyear, Rodney, Keyondria Bunch, and Charles D. Claiborn. Co-published simultaneously in *The Clinical Supervisor* (The Haworth Press, Inc.) Vol. 24, No. 1/2, 2005, pp. 137-147; and: *Supervision in Counseling: Interdisciplinary Issues and Research* (ed: Lawrence Shulman, and Andrew Safyer) The Haworth Press, Inc., 2005, pp. 137-147. Single or multiple copies of this article are available for a fee from The Haworth Document Delivery Service [1-800-HAWORTH, 9:00 a.m. - 5:00 p.m. (EST). E-mail address: docdelivery@haworthpress.com].

Available online at http://cs.haworthpress.com

doi:10.1300/J001v24n01_07

though, concerned issues of race or culture. The most frequent type of article was theoretical or conceptual in nature. However, when the various categories of article that were in one way or another research-based were combined, this comprised the largest overall category. doi:10.1300/J001v24n01_07

KEYWORDS. Research and practice, counseling psychology, clinical psychology, clinical supervision, supervision training

In their now-classic work, Henry, Sims, and Spray (1971) suggested that the practice of psychotherapy comprised a supraordinate "fifth profession" that bound together the four professions of social work, clinical psychology, psychiatry, and psychoanalysis. Other mental health professions have since joined these four at center stage of the mental health arena. But all continue to share in common this one activity of psychotherapy.

It is possible to think of the relationships among these professions in terms of a Venn diagram in which the point of common overlap is psychotherapy. If psychotherapy is common across the mental health professions, and if clinical supervision is the primary means by which to prepare trainees for its practice, it is reasonable then to argue that clinical supervision *also* will be common across those professions.

Shulman (2005) has introduced the term "signature pedagogies" to describe distinctive, profession-specific ways of instructing. In the education of physicians, the signature pedagogy is that of clinical rounds, in which a "multigenerational" team of residents and medical school students visit a prescribed set of patients (who each comprise the "curriculum"). For each patient they visit, someone is to report to the team what has happened since the group last had their rounds at that bed, and then to field questions from the team. In law school, on the other hand, the signature pedagogy involves an instructor singling out students to call upon without warning to ask that they tell the class about a particular case or that they offer to state the ways in which they agree or disagree with a legal argument another student has just presented.

To the extent that there is a signature pedagogy for the mental health professions, it must be clinical supervision. However, although it is a shared signature, each of those professions puts its own flourish on it.

Supervision can differ with respect to style, format, focus, and so on (Bernard & Goodyear, 2004); the differences are profession-linked. Moreover, the type of supervisory phenomena likely to be of interest to scholars will differ by profession, as will the tools of inquiry.

The grounding assumption of this paper was that whereas the mental health professions have clinical supervision in common, each approaches it differently in practice and in research. The purpose was to focus on the supervision-related scholarship of a single mental health profession–psychology–during one five-year period. Of primary interest was the kind of research being conducted, with respect to topics and methods. Also of interest was the particular journals and authors most frequently contributing to this literature.

METHOD

To be included in this review, an article had to have been published in 1999 or later and to focus in some way on clinical supervision. Our strategy to locate these articles was to employ two primary search engines: *PsychInfo* and *Google* (including *Google Scholar*). The reference lists of articles identified in this way also were consulted in order to locate additional articles that would meet our inclusion criteria.

We employed three *exclusion* rules as well:

1. Foremost, we focused only on those journals that explicitly identified with the profession of psychology. (Because it might not be clear from its title that *Psychotherapy: Theory, Research, and Practice* is a psychology journal, we would note here that it is a publication of the American Psychological Association's Division of Psychotherapy.)
2. We eliminated from consideration any article that addressed a training issue (e.g., an examination of the extent to which psychology programs provided training with respect to domestic violence) and not supervision per se.
3. We restricted the search to English language journals. Therefore, even though Norwegian psychologists Reichelt and Skjerve seem to be engaged in an active supervision research program, we did not include in this review their Norwegian publications (Reichelt & Skjerve, 2004; Skjerve, Flåm, Haugstvedt, Stalsberg, & Ogaard, 2003; Skjerve & Reichelt, 2003)–though did include one they had published in an English language journal (Reichelt & Skjerve, 2002).

RESULTS

We identified 49 supervision articles published during the past five years, in 11 psychology journals. These are indicated in the reference list with an asterisk (*).

Table 1 summarizes the number of articles published in each of the 11 journals in which they occurred. Nearly a fourth of the articles were published in *Professional Psychology: Research & Practice* (11; 22.4%). The other journals publishing the most supervision-related articles were *Journal of Counseling Psychology* (9; 18.4%), *Journal of Clinical Psychology* (7; 14.3%), and *Psychotherapy: Theory, Research, Practice, and Training* (7; 14.3%).

Table 2 summarizes both the type of article and the content. For each, we have offered a very brief indication of the focus of the article. As well, we coded each according to the extent that it fit one (or, in some cases, two) of the following nine broader categories: countertransference; self-disclosure; relationship/alliance; harmful processes; ethics; cultural issues; competency/evaluation; supervision types/modalities; and supervision in general (or "other").

The largest category concerned supervision that in some way was harmful (10 of the articles). The next most frequently-occurring category was that of "Competency/Evaluation" (8 articles), and then "Ethical/Legal" issues (6). Only two of these articles addressed any aspect of race, ethnicity, or culture.

Nineteen of the articles were what we categorized as "Conceptual/Theoretical." That is, they were advancing an argument of some type.

TABLE 1. Psychology Journal Sources of Articles on Supervision.

Journal	*Number of Articles*
Australian Psychologist	*2*
British Journal of Clinical Psychology	*2*
Canadian Psychology	*1*
Journal of Clinical Psychology	*7*
Journal of Counseling Psychology	*9*
Professional Psychology: Research & Practice	*11*
Psychoanalytic Psychology	*5*
Psychotherapy Research	*1*
Psychotherapy: Theory, Research, Practice, Training	*7*
The Counseling Psychologist	*3*
New Zealand Psychologist	*1*
Total	*49*

TABLE 2. Types and Content of Supervision Articles in Psychology Journals: 1999-2005.

Article	Content	Type of Article	Counter-transference	Self-Disclosure	Relationship/Alliance	Harmful Processes	Ethics	Cultural Issues	Competency/Evaluation	Supervision Types or Modalities	Other
Aten & Hernandez (2004)	Religion in supervision	Conceptual/Theoretical									X
Azar (2000)	CBT sup & burnout	Conceptual/Theoretical								X	
Bob (1999)	Narrative approaches	Conceptual/Theoretical								X	
Borg (2005)	Blind supervisees	Case Study									X
Burrian & Slimp (2000)	Dual relationships	Conceptual/Theoretical					X				
Chen & Bernstein (2000)	Working alliances	Quantitative			X						
Davis (2002)	Countertrans/self-discl	Conceptual/Theoretical	X	X							
DeMayo (2000)	Sexual harassment	Survey					X				
Ellis (2001)		Comment				X					
Ellis et al. (2002)	Supervisee anxiety	Quantitative									X
Elman & Forrest (2004)	Supervisee remediation	Qualitative				X					
Enyedy et al. (2003)	Group supervision	Quantitative				X					
Falender et al. (2004)	Competencies	Conceptual/Theoretical							X		
Farber (2003)	Self-disclosure	Conceptual/Theoretical		X							
Forrest et al. (1999)	Trainee impairment	Review							X		
Freitas (2004)	Supervision outcomes	Review							X		
Gizara & Forrest (2004)	Supervisee impairment	Qualitative							X		
Gonsalvez et al. (2002)	A supervision model	Conceptual/Theoretical									
Gray et al. (2001)	Counterproductive supervision	Qualitative				X					
Hahn (2001)	Supervisee shame	Conceptual/Theoretical				X					
Hamilton & Spruill (1999)	Reducing sexual misconduct	Conceptual/Theoretical				X	X				
Johnson & Stewart (2000)	Supervisor preparation	Survey									X
Kanz (2001)	On-line supervision	Conceptual/Theoretical								X	
Ladany et al. (1999)	Ethical issues	Mixed Quant & Qual			X		X				
Ladany et al. (2000)	Supervisor countertransference	Qualitative	X								

TABLE 2 (continued)

Article	Content	Type of Article	Counter-transference	Self-Disclosure	Relationship/Alliance	Harmful Processes	Ethics	Cultural Issues	Competency/Evaluation	Supervision Types or Modalities	Other
Ladany et al. (2003)	Self-disclosure	Conceptual/Theoretical		X							
Ladany (2004)	Issues in sup research	Conceptual/Theoretical									X
Lamb et al. (2003)	Sexual relationships	Survey				X	X				
Lambert & Hawkins (2001)	Using client test data	Conceptual/Theoretical									X
Lehrman-Waterman & Ladany (2001)	Evaluation Instrument	Instrument Development							X		
McKinney (2000)	Supervisory relationships	Conceptual/Theoretical			X						
Milne & James (2000)	CBT supervision	Review								X	
Milne & James (2002)	Training outcomes	Quantitative							X		
Nelson & Friedlander (2001)	Conflictual supervision	Qualitative			X						
Nelson et al. (2001)		Comment			X						
Nilsson & Anderson (2004)	International sup-ees	Survey						X			
Norrie et al. (2003)	Sup effectiveness	Quantitative									X
Ögren et al. (2005)	Group sup processes	Quantitative								X	
Peake et al. (2002)	List of sup references	Bibliography									X
Ramos-Sanchez et al. (2002)	Neg supervision events	Quantitative				X					
Reichelt & Skjerve (2002)	Correspondence of Sup-or/sup-ee perceptions	Quantitative			X						
Scott et al. (2000)	Supervisor training	Survey							X		
Sutter et al. (2002)	Contracting	Conceptual/Theoretical					X				X
Tummala-Narra (2004)	Race/culture dynamics	Conceptual/Theoretical						X			
Tyler et al. (2002)	Faculty sup. practices	Survey									X
Veach (2001)		Comment			X	X					
Vespia et al. (2002)	Sup utilization rating	Instrument Development							X		
Yerushalmi (1999)	Group supervision	Conceptual/Theoretical								X	
Yourman (2003)	Shame & self-disclosure	Conceptual/Theoretical		X		X					

Of the remaining, we coded them as Quantitative (8), Survey Reports (6), Qualitative (5), Literature Review (3), Comment (including rejoinders) (3), Instrument Development (2), Mixed-Method, quantitative/qualitative (1), Case Study (1), and Bibliography (1).

DISCUSSION

Of the psychology specialties, counseling psychology has been most identified with supervision research and training. It is not a surprise, then, that the *Journal of Counseling Psychology* has published a relatively large proportion of the supervision-related articles. Interestingly, though, *Professional Psychology: Research & Practice* was the larger source. In fact, articles in it accounted for nearly one-fourth of those we identified. This does make sense in that this journal provides an outlet for work that targets all of professional psychology rather than a single specialty (although counseling psychologists provided most of these articles). In fact, an associated, APA journal devoted exclusively to supervision and training is about to be spun-off of *Professional Psychology: Research & Practice.*

The largest category of article topics concerned supervision that in some way was harmful to the supervisee. We suspect that this must reflect the (important) growing realization that if supervision is an intervention that is potent enough to have positive effects, it also is potent enough to cause harm. Because the person of the supervisee is so closely related to the work he or she does, that harm actually can extend beyond the supervisee's competencies. So the topic is important, as the volume of these articles suggests.

What was surprising, given the current emphasis on multicultural competencies, was how little research focused on any aspect of race, ethnicity, or culture. Supervision is central in the development of these competencies. It is possible, of course, that this actually is a ubiquitous focus of supervision practice, but simply is not showing up in the literature. The more likely explanation, though, is that more attention needs to be given this area of supervision.

With respect to type of scholarship, it should be unsurprising that the most frequent type of article was "Conceptual/Theoretical." It is gratifying, though, to see that a substantial subset actually were research-based in some way. These included quantitative, qualitative, mixed methods, instrument development, and survey-based studies and when these were grouped into a supraordinate category, it actually was largest of all. Although supervision is maturing as an area of focus, it still lags substantially behind psychotherapy as an area of inquiry and so such research is to be encouraged.

We almost certainly will have failed to include some articles that would have met inclusion criteria. Nevertheless, we are confident that the review is sufficiently thorough, and that we have provided here an accurate snapshot of the supervision scholarship that has appeared in psychology journals during the past five years.

By themselves, these data are interesting. But their value will increase to the extent that similar data are obtained for the other mental health professions. It would be of interest to compare the between-profession methodologies and topics of supervision research.

REFERENCES

*Aten, J. D., & Hernandez, B. C. (2004). Addressing religion in clinical supervision: A model. *Psychotherapy: Theory, Research, Practice, Training, 41*(2), 152-160.

*Azar, S.T. (2000). Preventing burnout in professionals and paraprofessionals who work with child abuse and neglect cases: A cognitive behavioral approach to supervision. *Journal of Clinical Psychology, 56*(5), 643-663.

*Bob, S.R. (1999). Narrative approaches to supervision and case formulation. *Psychotherapy: Theory, Research, Practice, Training, 36*(2), 146-153.

*Borg, M. B. J. (2005). "Superblind": Supervising a blind therapist with a blind analysand in a community mental health setting. *Psychoanalytic Psychology, 22*(1), 32-48.

*Burian, B.K., & Slimp, A. O. (2000). Social dual-role relationships during internship: A decision-making model. *Professional Psychology: Research & Practice. Special Issue: Training and employment of professional psychologists, 31*(3), 332-338.

*Chen, E.C., & Bernstein, B.L. (2000). Relations of complementarity and supervisory issues to supervisory working alliance: A comparative analysis of two cases. *Journal of Counseling Psychology, 47*(4), 485-497.

*Davis, J.T. (2002). Countertransference temptation and the use of self of self-disclosure by psychotherapists in training: A discussion for beginning psychotherapists and their supervisors. *Psychoanalytic Psychology, 19*(3), 435-454.

*DeMayo, R.A. (2000). Patients' sexual behavior and sexual harassment: A survey of clinical supervisors. *Professional Psychology: Research & Practice, 31*(6), 706-709.

*Ellis, M.V. (2001). Harmful supervision, a cause for alarm: Comment on Gray et al. (2001) and Nelson and Friedlander. *Journal of Counseling Psychology, 48*(4), 401-406.

*Ellis, M.V., Krengel, M., & Beck, M. (2002). Testing self-focused attention theory in clinical supervision: Effects of supervisee anxiety and performance. *Journal of Counseling Psychology, 49*(1), 101-116.

*Elman, N.S., & Forrest, L. (2004). Psychotherapy in the remediation of psychology trainees: Exploratory interviews with training directors. *Professional Psychology: Research & Practice, 35*(2), 123-130.

*Enyedy, K.C., Arcinue, F., Puri, N.N., Carter, J.W, Goodyear, R.K., & Getzelman, M.A. (2003). Hindering phenomena in group supervision: Implications for practice. *Professional Psychology: Research & Practice, 34*(3), 312-317.

*Falender, C.A., Cornish, J.A., Goodyear, R. et al. (2004). Defining competencies in psychology supervision: A consensus statement. *Journal of Clinical Psychology. Special Competencies Conference: Future Directions in Education and Credentialing in Professional Psychology, 60*(7), 771-785.

*Farber, B.A. (2003). Self-disclosure in psychotherapy practice and supervision: An introduction. *Journal of Clinical Psychology. Special Issue: In session: Self disclosure, 59*(5), 525-528.

*Forrest, L., Elman, N., Gizara, S., & Vacha-Haase, T. (1999). Trainee impairment: A review of identification, remediation, dismissal, and legal issues. *Counseling Psychologist, 27*(5), 627-686.

*Freitas, G.J. (2002). The impact of psychotherapy supervision on client outcome: A critical examination of 2 decades of research. *Psychotherapy: Theory, Research, Practice, Training, 39*(4), 354-367.

*Gizara, S.S., & Forrest, L. (2004). Supervisors' experiences of trainee impairment and incompetence at APA-accredited internship sites. *Professional Psychology: Research & Practice, 35*(2), 131-140.

*Gonsalvez, C. J., Oades, L. G., & Freestone, J. (2002). The objectives approach to clinical supervision: Towards integration and empirical evaluation. *Australian Psychologist, 37*, 68-77.

*Gray, LA., Ladany, N., Walker, J.A., & Ancis, J.R. (2001). Psychotherapy trainees' experience of counterproductive events in supervision. *Journal of Counseling Psychology, 48*(4), 371-383.

*Hahn, W.K. (2001). The experience of shame in psychotherapy supervision. *Psychotherapy: Theory, Research, Practice, Training, 38*(3), 272-282.

*Hamilton, J.C., & Spruill, J. (1999). Identifying and reducing risk factors related to trainee-client sexual misconduct. *Professional Psychology: Research & Practice, 30*(3), 318-327.

Henry, W., Sims, J. H., & Spray, L. S. (1971). *The fifth profession.* San Francisco: Jossey-Bass.

*Johnson, E.A., & Stewart, D.W. (2000). Clinical supervision in Canadian academic and service settings: The importance of education, training, and workplace support for supervisor development. *Canadian Psychology, 41*(2), 124-130.

*Kanz, J.E. (2001). Clinical-supervision.com: Issues in the provision of online supervision. *Professional Psychology: Research & Practice, 32*(4), 415-420.

*Ladany, N. (2004). Psychotherapy supervision: What lies beneath. *Psychotherapy Research, 14*(1), 1-19.

*Ladany, N., Constantine, M.G., Miller, K., Erickson, C.D., & Muse-Burke, J.L. (2000). Supervisor countertransference: A qualitative investigation into its identification and description. *Journal of Counseling Psychology, 47*(1), 102-115.

*Ladany, N., Lehrman-Waterman, D., Molinaro, M., & Wolgast, B. (1999). Psychotherapy supervisor ethical practices: Adherence to guidelines, the supervisory working alliance, and supervisee satisfaction. *Counseling Psychologist, 27*(3), 443-475.

*Ladany, N., & Walker, J.A. (2003). Supervision self-disclosure: Balancing the uncontrollable narcissist with the indomitable altruist. *Journal of Clinical Psychology. Special Issue: In session: Self disclosure, 59*(5), 611-621.

*Lamb, D.H., Catanzaro, S.J., & Moorman, A.S. (2003). Psychologists reflect on their sexual relationships with clients, supervisees, and students: Occurrence, impact, rationales and collegial intervention. *Professional Psychology: Research & Practice, 34*(1), 102-107.

*Lambert, M. J., & Hawkins, E. J. (2001). Using information about patient progress in supervision: Are outcomes enhanced? *Australian Psychologist, 36*, 131-138.

*Lehrman-Waterman, D., & Ladany, N. (2001). Development and validation of the evaluation process within supervision inventory. *Journal of Counseling Psychology, 48*(2), 168-177.

*McKinney, M. (2000). Relational perspectives and the supervisory triad. *Psychoanalytic Psychology, 17*(3), 565-584.

*Milne, D., & James, I. (2000). A systematic review of effective cognitive-behavioral supervision. *British Journal of Clinical Psychology, 39*(2), 111-127.

*Milne, D.L., & James, I.A. (2002). The observed impact of training on competence in clinical supervision. *British Journal of Clinical Psychology, 41*(1), 55-72.

*Nelson, M.L., & Friedlander, M.L. (2001). A close look at conflictual supervisory relationships: The trainee's perspective. *Journal of Counseling Psychology, 48*(4), 384-395.

*Nelson, M.L., Gray, L.A., Friedlander, M.L., Ladany, N., & Walker, J.A. (2001). Toward relationship-centered supervision: Reply to Veach (2001) and Ellis (2001). *Journal of Counseling Psychology, 48*(4), 407-409.

*Nilsson, J.E., & Anderson, M.Z. (2004). Supervising international students: The role of acculturation, role ambiguity, and multicultural discussions. *Professional Psychology: Research Practice, 35*(3), 306-312.

*Norrie, J., Eggleston, E., & Ringer, M. (2003). Quality parameters of supervision in a correctional context. *New Zealand Journal of Psychology, 32*, 76-83.

*Ögren, M., Jonsson, C., & Sundin, E. C. (2005). Group supervision in psychotherapy: The relationship between focus, group climate, and perceived attained skill. *Journal of Clinical Psychology, 61*, 373-388.

*Peake, T.H., Nussbaum, B.D., Tindell, S.D. (2002). Clinical and counseling supervision references: Trends and needs. *Psychotherapy: Theory, Research, Practice, Training, 39*(1), 114-125.

*Ramos-Sanchez, L., Esnil, E., Goodwin, A., Riggs, S., Touster, L., Wright, L.K., Ratanasiripong, P., & Rodolfa, E. (2002). Negative supervisory events: Effects on supervision and supervisory alliance. *Professional Psychology: Research & Practice, 33*(2), *197-202.*

*Reichelt, S., & Skjerve, J. (2002). Correspondence between supervisors and trainees in their perception of supervision events. *Journal of Clinical Psychology, 58*(7), 759-772.

Reichelt, S., & Skjerve, J. (2004). Supervision of supervision: What is important in supervisor training?/Veiledning av veiledning: Hva er viktig i veilederutdanning? *Nordisk Psykologi, 56*, 107-127.

*Scott, K.J., Ingram, K.M., Vitanza, S.A., & Smith, N.G. (2000). Training in supervision: A survey of current practices. *Counseling Psychologist, 28*(3), 403-422.

Shulman, L. (February 6-8, 2005). The signature pedagogies of the professions of law, medicine, engineering, and the clergy: Potential lessons for the education of Teachers. Paper presented at the Math Science Partnerships (MSP) Workshop: "Teacher Education for Effective Teaching and Learning," Hosted by the National Research Council's Center for Education. Irvine, CA (Available on-line at http://hub.mspnet.org/media/data/Shulman_Signature_Pedagogies.pdf?media_000000001297.pdf).

Skjerve, J., Flåm, A. M., Haugstvedt, E., Stalsberg, V., & Ogaard, C. (2003). Clinical supervision of psychology students: Group-supervision using two supervisors/Tromso-modellen for klinisk veiledning av studenter: Bruk av to veiledere. *Tidsskrift for Norsk Psykologforening, 40*, 1039-1045.

Skjerve, J., & Reichelt, S. (2003). Supervision in training of specialists in clinical psychology: Results from a questionnaire inquiry/Veiledning til den kliniske specialiteten: Resultater fra en sporreskjemaundersokelse. *Tidsskrift for Norsk Psykologforening, 40*, 2-11.

*Sutter, E., McPherson, R.H., & Geeseman, R. (2002). Contracting for supervision. *Professional Psychology: Research & Practice, 33*(5), 495-498.

*Tummala-Narra, P. (2004). Dynamics of race and culture in the supervisory encounter. *Psychoanalytic Psychology, 21*(2), 300-311.

*Tyler, J.D., Sloan, L.L., & King, A.R. (2000). Psychotherapy supervision practices of academic faculty: A national survey. *Psychotherapy: Theory, Research, Practice, Training, 37*(1), 98-101.

*Veach, P.M. (2001). Conflict and counterproductivity in supervision–when relationships are less than ideal: Comment on Nelson and Friedlander (2001) and Gray et al. (2001). *Journal of Counseling Psychology, 48*(4), 396-400.

*Vespia, K.M., Heckman-Stone, C., & Delworth, U. (2002). Describing and facilitating effective supervision behavior in counseling trainees. *Psychotherapy: Theory, Research, Practice, Training, 39*(1), 56-65.

*Yerushalmi, H. (1999). The roles of group supervision of supervision. *Psychoanalytic Psychology, 16*(3), 426-447.

*Yourman, D.B. (2003). Trainee disclosure in psychotherapy supervision: The impact of shame. *Journal of Clinical Psychology. Special Issue: In session: Self disclosure, 59*(5), 601-609.

doi:10.1300/J001v24n01_07

Clinical Supervision in Nursing: What's It All About?

Janice M. Jones

SUMMARY. Clinical supervision in nursing has been largely defined by practicing nurses in the U.K., Australia, and New Zealand. In this context, it generally refers to a reflective practice on the part of a novice or new nurse (the supervisee) and the expert nurse or supervisor. It is considered a mandatory and obligatory process both in the execution and development of the clinical supervisory relationship. Clinical supervision in the U.S., however, has been defined as the relationship between faculty or preceptor and student in a clinical nursing practice setting. Reflective practice through the use of inquiry is only one tool used in the evaluation process of the student. Clinical supervision also is known in the clinical setting as the relationship between the nursing staff and an administrative clinical staff member. This relationship is primarily supportive and evaluative in function and does not meet the criteria for clinical supervision as defined in the U.K. This manuscript describes the definition and use of clinical supervision outside of the U.S. and its utility within the academic and clinical nursing community within the U.S., especially its use in the magnet hospital accreditation process. A

Janice M. Jones, PhD, RN, CNS, is Clinical Associate Professor of Nursing, University at Buffalo, The State University of New York, 910 Kimball Tower, Buffalo, NY 14214 (E-mail: jsylakow@buffalo.edu).

[Haworth co-indexing entry note]: "Clinical Supervision in Nursing: What's It All About?" Jones, Janice M. Co-published simultaneously in *The Clinical Supervisor* (The Haworth Press, Inc.) Vol. 24, No. 1/2, 2005, pp. 149-162; and: *Supervision in Counseling: Interdisciplinary Issues and Research* (ed: Lawrence Shulman, and Andrew Safyer) The Haworth Press, Inc., 2005, pp. 149-162. Single or multiple copies of this article are available for a fee from The Haworth Document Delivery Service [1-800-HAWORTH, 9:00 a.m. - 5:00 p.m. (EST). E-mail address: docdelivery@haworthpress.com].

Available online at http://cs.haworthpress.com

doi:10.1300/J001v24n01_08

comprehensive bibliography is provided that may be useful to other disciplines utilizing and conducting research in the area of clinical supervision. doi:10.1300/J001v24n01_08 *[Article copies available for a fee from The Haworth Document Delivery Service: 1-800-HAWORTH. E-mail address: <docdelivery@haworthpress.com> Website: <http://www.HaworthPress.com>*

KEYWORDS. Clinical supervision, nursing

The construct of clinical supervision has been widely studied and described in the nursing literature during the past 10 years. Prior to 1996, few substantial studies had been published on the topic in nursing publications (Faugier, 1996). The preponderance of research and clinical articles related to clinical supervision in regards to the nursing profession has come from the United Kingdom, Australia and New Zealand, and the Scandinavian countries.

Clinical supervision research in non-U.S. countries has dealt primarily with supervisors who are expert nurses in their particular field and supervisees who are novice or new nurses to the field or subspecialty. Various subpopulations of nurses have been studied but the majority of the research has been with psychiatric nurses (see Figure 1).

Fowler (1996b) identified five areas of literature review related to the construct of clinical supervision: the need for clinical supervision for nurses, uses of the concept in practice, perception of good supervision, models of supervision, and preparation for supervisors.

DEFINITIONS OF CLINICAL SUPERVISION

The term "clinical supervision" has taken on numerous definitions. The most comprehensive definition is that by Winstanley and White (2003) who defined clinical supervision as "focusing upon the provision of empathetic support to improve therapeutic skills, the transmission of knowledge and the facilitation of reflective practice. The participants have an opportunity to evaluate, reflect and develop their own clinical practice and provide a support system to one another" (p. 8). Although there is disagreement as to the defining characteristics of clinical supervision, various aspects have been agreed upon by nurse researchers:

- It is a formal growth focused relationship or arrangement
- Provides an opportunity for the nurse to review the professional development of a new practitioner
- Provides a forum for the practice of care and the discussion of problems
- Allows colleagues to learn from each and encourage each other thereby reducing professional isolation, emotional strain and stress
- May lead to the development of practice theory

(Rafferty & Coleman, 2001, p. 85; Porter, 1997)

THE PURPOSE OF CLINICAL SUPERVISION: NECESSITY OR EXTRANEOUS?

The necessity for clinical supervision for nurses was first identified by Butterworth in the early 1990s in the United Kingdom (Butterworth & Faugier, 1992). Early models of supervision were taken from psychotherapy and adapted to nursing practice. Government mandates from

FIGURE 1. A U.K./U.S. model of clinical supervision in nursing

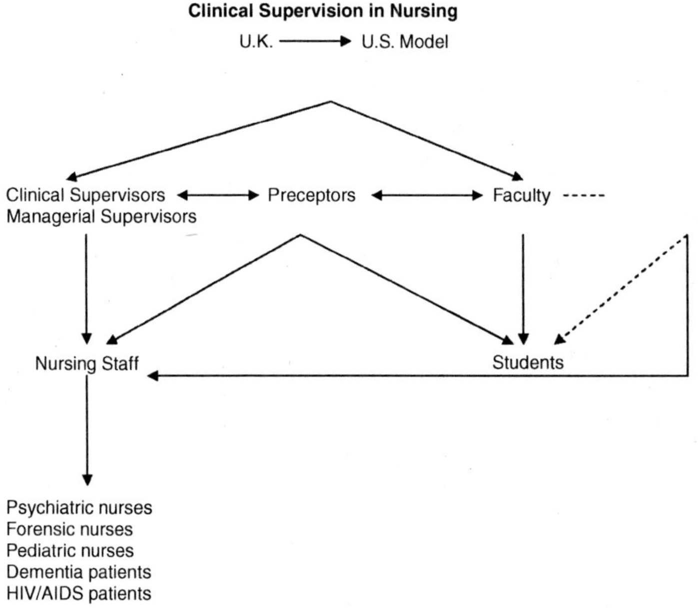

the U.K. Department of Health and U.K. Code of Professional Conduct made the implementation of clinical supervision necessary. The biggest undertaking was the Clinical Supervision Evaluation Project (CSEP) in 1996. The project was conducted over 23 sites in National Health Services Trusts from England and Wales. The purpose of the project was to look at the effects of the implementation and evaluation of clinical supervision on the nursing workforce in these countries. This study has generated the largest database from nurses involved in clinical supervision activities thus far (Winstanley, 2001).

Porter (1997) has identified various purposes of clinical supervision. He described the process as one of the supervisee telling their story to the supervisor. During this process, client problems are identified and clarification of the nurse's actions are evaluated in terms of client outcomes. This process can reduce the risk to the client and enhance nursing care. It also provides collegial support to the novice nurse and positive reinforcement for a job well done. Education and quality practice get reinforced through the discussions that follow. For example, Mr. Jones may be developing a pressure ulcer on his sacral area. In discussions with the supervisor, the novice nurse must report his or her assessment findings that may be validated by the supervisor. The pair may then consult as to the proper care for this client incorporating institutional policies and procedures and clinical practice guidelines that the novice nurse may be unaware of. The client thus receives a higher quality of care and a better outcome through this collaborative process than if the novice nurse were to care for this client alone.

Other alleged benefits of clinical supervision for clinicians have been described by various researchers (Lyth, 2000; Sloan, 1999; Winstanley & White, 2003). These include:

- Increased feelings of support and person well being
- Improved client care through gaining knowledge and awareness of possible solutions to clinical problems
- Increased confidence in practice
- Stress reduction, lessened emotional strain and decreased incidence of burnout
- Higher staff morale and satisfaction leading to a decrease in staff sickness/absence and increased staff satisfaction
- Increased participation in reflective practice
- Increased self-awareness
- A resultant effect of increased job satisfaction

All of the above contribute to diminishing the theory-practice gap inherent to those new in clinical practice. Contrary to the benefits of this collaborative process, Winstanley and White (2003) reported that there is little empirical evidence to show that the process of clinical supervision improves the delivery of care or affects client outcomes in a positive manner. The evidence stems from qualitative data and anecdotal evidence, which surmises that client care is improved but other factors may also be at play. The implication is that nurses who are satisfied with their jobs tend to provide better client care. To date, it has been difficult to link job satisfaction with improved client outcomes as variables such as nurse:client ratio, client acuity levels, education, and tenure have also been identified as contributing factors to improved client outcomes in U.S. hospital settings.

MODELS OF CLINICAL SUPERVISION

Various models have been developed in the nursing literature describing the process of clinical supervision as a mentorship process. These include the growth and support model, the integrative approach model, and the more encompassing, three-function interactive model of supervision.

Model 1. Growth and Support Model

In 1992, Faugier put forth a growth and support model of clinical supervision. In this model, the supervisor facilitates growth both educationally and personally and assists in developing clinical autonomy in the supervisee. Key features of this model include an openness and willingness to learn in a trust relationship that is both practical and personal. The art of supervision should be both thoughtful and thought-provoking, thus providing a win-win relationship for both the supervisor and the supervisee. The focus of this model is primarily on the relationship aspect of clinical supervision and includes the concept of mentorship in nursing practice. Benefits to the supervisee and also to the client appear tangential to the mentorship relationship. A dichotomous approach to the relationship forms with the supervisor assuming an autocratic, almost parental role.

Model 2. Integrative Approach

Hawkins and Shohet (1989) proposed a more integrative-interactive model that included the client and the work environment. The model divides supervision into four components: Supervisor, Supervisee, Client, and Work Context. In the supervisory relationship, there is a contract involving the supervisor and supervisee with negotiated shared tasks and goals. This model provides more of a true mentorship relationship than the previous model. Outcomes beneficial to the client or impacting his or her care form as a direct result of the relationship. The environment in which this relationship takes place or the work environs has important ramifications for the nature of the relationship and to what degree it progresses.

Model 3. Proctor's Three-Function Interactive Model of Supervision

Procotor's (1986) three-function interactive model of clinical supervision is the one most widely adopted by clinical supervisors. Her model for clinical supervision in nursing is based on three key elements or functions of supervision. The normative or managerial function deals with promoting and complying with organizational policies and procedures. Standards are developed that contribute to a clinical audit and quality control. The formative or educative function of the supervision relationship is composed of skills development on the part of the supervisee including the development of evidence-based nursing practice. The two roles of the supervisor are therefore education and development of new skills and new knowledge in the supervisee. The third function, the restorative or pastoral support function, helps nursing practitioners to understand and manage the emotional stress of nursing practice and provide emotional and psychological support for nursing staff.

In 1998, Bond and Holland contributed to and enhanced Proctor's model through which the normative function is also incorporated into the restorative and formative functions. Thus, organizational guidelines form the basis for the educative function and serve as a guide to the pastoral function in diverse settings to better benefit the supervisee and, ultimately, his or her clients.

MEASURING CLINICAL SUPERVISION

Methods for evaluating clinical supervision have ranged from the quasi-experimental approach to a qualitative approach. Although notable progress has been made in the development of validated and sophisticated instruments, few empirical studies have been published. A preponderance of the studies has been via a qualitative approach using focus group interviews, semi-structured interviews, and Delphi survey research.

Using a quantitative approach, self-completion questionnaires have developed such as the Experience of Supervision Questionnaire (ESQ) and the Nursing in Context Questionnaire, which contains 18 attitude statements divided into three factors that are designed to be sensitive to the effects of supervision. These instruments have been used in conjunction with the Minnesota Job Satisfaction Scale and the Maslach Burnout Inventory. Only these two instruments have been validated to be sensitive to the components of clinical supervision. Both of these tools have been used widely in nursing research studies in the U.S.

Winstanley (2000) developed the Manchester Clinical Supervision Scale from the CSEP data collected on clinical supervision in nursing in the U.K. and Wales. The Manchester Clinical Supervision Scale is the only internationally validated research instrument to measure the effectiveness of clinical supervision on supervisors, supervisees, and the quality of care provided (Winstanley & White, 2003). Seven factors were identified, which included all three components of Proctor's model. The factors include trust/rapport, supervisor advice/support, improved care/skills, importance value of clinical supervision, finding time, personal issues, and reflection. This 36-item questionnaire has been shown to have a Cronbach above 0.8 with the intraclass correlation coefficients for test-retest reliability above 0.9. The scale can be viewed and/or purchased at *<http://www.clinicalsupervisionscale.com>*.

The quantitative scale can allow researchers to link the process of clinical supervision directly to patient outcomes (Winstanley, 2001). Other scales that measure nurse job satisfaction, patient satisfaction, and quality indicators can now be correlated with the process of clinical supervision to evaluate the effects of clinical supervision on the nursing workforce and client care outcomes.

BARRIERS TO THE IMPLEMENTATION OF CLINICAL SUPERVISION

Johns (2003) described an organizational culture non-supportive to the practice of clinical supervision to be a primary barrier in its development and implementation within an organization. Organizational culture is the shared beliefs, values, and norms an organization espouses both covertly and overtly (Schein, 1992). A culture change may take as long as 10 years to occur. A paradigm shift towards clinical supervision would require the commitment from top administrators as well as empowering the clinical supervisors and supervisees in the process. Ownership of the process is paramount to its success and belongs to the dual practitioner partnership and their commitment for its success. Due to the lack of data regarding outcomes as related to clinical supervision, a cost-benefit analysis would need to be conducted to support the clinical supervision program. Supervision training is required and may be both cost and labor intensive, thus creating a further shortage of nurses on the clinical unit. Workload schedules must be adjusted to provide time for clinical supervision training and, thereafter, provide time for clinical supervision itself.

Time is also perceived to be a major barrier to the development and implementation of a clinical supervision program. Everyday nursing practice with a nursing shortage at hand and large nurse:client ratios make clinical supervision a "nice idea" but low priority on the nurses' lists of things to do. The clinical supervisor must also be careful that in implementing such program, the work sessions do not turn out to be "complaint sessions," which negates the premise and positive effects of instituting a clinical supervision program. Nursing practitioners must learn to value the process of clinical supervision, establish it as a priority in their practice, and make accommodations to incorporate it into their everyday work life. Johns (2001) raised the question of the "real agenda" of clinical supervision: "Will it enable and empower nurses to develop and realize their vision of nursing practice, or will it become a surveillance system to ensure an efficient and docile workforce?" (p. 32). Other problems identified with initiating or maintaining a clinical supervision program include a scarcity of supervisors and lack of educational preparation by supervisors.

BENEFITS TO THE IMPLEMENTATION OF CLINICAL SUPERVISION

Given the barriers to clinical supervision, the benefits far outweigh what might be conceived as a cumbersome process. Clinical supervision can be viewed as a supportive, educational, and quality assurance process. In 1992, Butterworth and Faugier described clinical supervision as the major force in improving clinical standards and enhancing the quality of care (Butterworth & Faugier, 1992, p. 232). Promoting standards of care has been a the hallmark of the nursing profession and has been identified as a major aspect of the magnet credentialing program sponsored by the American Nurses Credentialing Center, the credentialing arm of the American Nurses Association. For further information on the magnet program in the U.S., go to *<http://www.nursingworld.org/ancc/magnet/index.html>*.

Other benefits have been identified by various researchers:

1. Increased feelings of support and personal well-being (Butterworth et al., 1996; Cutcliffe & McFeely, 2001),
2. Increased knowledge and awareness of possible solutions to clinical problems (Dudley & Butterworth, 1994; Cutcliffe & McFeely, 2001),
3. Increased confidence, decreased incidence of emotional strain and burnout (Halberg & Norberg, 1993),
4. Higher staff morale leading to a decrease in staff sickness/absence, increased staff satisfaction (Butterworth et al., 1996),
5. Increased participation in reflective practice (Hawkins & Shohet, 1989), and
6. Increased self-awareness (Cutliffe & Epling, 1997).

These benefits serve to promote life-long learning in addition to promoting standards and quality of care. Thus, the recipients of such benefits are the clients themselves along with their care givers.

U.S. MODEL: CONFUSING TERMS AND TITLES

Clinical supervision in the United States is perhaps most synonymous with the terms mentorship or preceptorship. Both terms imply a relationship between the expert nurse and the novice nurse as defined by Benner (1984) in her landmark work, *From novice to expert*. The underpinnings of clinical supervision can be most readily seen in the teacher-student, preceptor-student, or new nurse-preceptor relationships. Although the U.S. literature embodies a body of publications relating to both topics, neither has been formally based on the construct of clinical supervision as described and implemented in the European countries and Australia. The term "supervisor" in the U.S. is equated with supervision as a function of nursing management. This formal role carries with it the functions of personnel management. Managerial supervision thus focuses on the direct supervision of nursing care in practice and differs from clinical supervision.

CLINICAL SUPERVISION AND NURSING: FUTURE RESEARCH, A PLACE IN THE U.S.?

Several questions come to mind in reviewing the literature and examining its application to nursing practice in the U.S. The first question is, "Is the U.K. model one that should be adopted for U.S. nurses? For all nurses or selected settings such as psychiatric services?" Given the benefits to clinical supervision it would seem that the resounding answer should be "Yes." However, the nursing shortage today is so widespread that its practical application would probably fall on deaf ears. Yet this model may find a place in psychiatric nursing where reflective practice with another nurse will truly benefit all concerned. Fowler (1996) reiterated the usefulness of clinical supervision for all nurses but stated that the process or model must be tailored to meet the specific needs of staff.

The above prompts question number 2: "Can clinical supervision of nurses be linked to improved client outcomes such as length of stay, reduced incidence of infections and complications, etc.?" If advanced practice nurses such as clinical nurse specialists and nurse practitioners can be utilized as the expert nurse, they can serve as a valuable reference source for even the senior staff nurses.

Is the model appropriate for preceptors who supervise undergraduate nursing students and/or nurse practitioner students who already are RNs and are seeking a Master's degree? This is the area perhaps where clinical supervision would have the greatest impact. Training for preceptors would be needed to enhance their skills for reflective practice and the inquiry process. Generally, time is allotted for preceptors to meet with their students to problem-solve and discuss select nursing practice issues.

Many U.S. hospitals are currently seeking magnet status. Could the implementation of a clinical supervision program be an additional variable to accreditation, e.g., part of clinical self-governance? The magnet hospital program recognizes those hospitals known for excellence in nursing care and autonomy in nursing practice. The use of reflective inquiry in a clinical supervisory relationship could augment the standards of care and quality that would enhance nursing care.

In reviewing the quantitative aspect of the construct of clinical supervision, in what settings is the Manchester Clinical Supervision Scale appropriate? Could it be adapted for nurse preceptors in the U.S.? This would require psychometric evaluation of the scale and its use in relation to preceptors. The scale measures many elements of a supervisory relationship for preceptor-student conferences and could be used by nursing faculty to judge the effectiveness of the preceptor as well as the preceptor-student relationship.

CONCLUSION

Perhaps the best source of information related to clinical supervision comes from those in the forefront of supervision research: *Fundamental themes in clinical supervision* by Cutcliffe, Butterworth, and Proctor (2001). Although clinical supervision has been a hallmark for nursing practice in the U.K., it has many applications to nursing practice in the U.S. Articles related to reflective practice are just beginning to make their way into the U.S. nursing literature, taking on many aspects of the European clinical supervisory model.

At this time, a meta-analysis of the qualitative studies should be undertaken to determine best practice for nurses currently using clinical supervision to enhance practice. A psychometric evaluation of the Manchester Clinical Supervision Scale and its applicability to preceptors should also be done by U.S. nursing researchers to test its applicability with undergraduate and advanced practice nursing students. Clinical supervision should also be examined as a useful tool for those hospitals seeking magnet accreditation. Guidelines for clinical supervision would need to be established within the framework of professional nursing practice in the U.S. For those further interested in the topic, a bibliography is provided rather than simply a reference list of readings.

Clinical supervision can be a win-win strategy for the client or student, for the novice nurse, and for the supervisor, preceptor, or expert nurse. Incorporating the process into a busy work environment remains a challenge as the nursing shortage propagates work-heavy schedules and a hectic work environment.

REFERENCES

Arvidson, B., & Fridlund, B. (2005). Factors influencing nurse supervisor competence: A critical incident analysis study. *Journal of Nursing Management, 13*, 231-237.

Arvidson, B., Lofgren, H., & Fridlund, B. (2000). Psychiatric nurses' conceptions of how group supervision in nursing care influences their professional competence. *Journal of Nursing Management, 8*, 175-185.

Begat, I., Berggren, I., Ellefsen, B., & Severinsson, E. (2003). Australian nurse supervisors' styles and their perceptions of ethical dilemmas within health care. *Journal of Nursing Management, 11*, 6-14.

Begat, I., Ellefsen, B., & Severinsson, E. (2005). Nurses' satisfaction with their work environment and the outcomes of clinical nursing supervision on nurses' experiences of well-being–A Norwegian study. *Journal of Nursing Management, 13*, 221-230.

Benner, P. (1984). *From novice to expert: Excellence and power in clinical nursing practice*. Menlo Park, CA: Addison-Wesley Publishing Co.

Berggren, I., Barbosa da Silva, A., & Severinsson, E. (2005). Core ethical issues of clinical nursing supervision. *Nursing and Health Sciences, 7*, 21-28.

Bond, M., & Holland, S. (1998). *Skills of clinical supervision for nurses: A practical guide for supervisees, clinical supervisors and managers*. Buckingham: Open University Press.

Butterworth, T., Carson, J., Jeacock, J., & White, E. (1999). Stress, coping, burnout and job satisfaction in British nurses: Findings from the clinical supervision evaluation project. *Stress Medicine, 15*, 27-33.

Butterworth, T., & Faugier, J. (1992). *Clinical supervision and mentorship in nursing*. London: Chapman & Hall.

Clouder, L., & Sellars, J. (2004). Reflective practice and clinical supervision: An interprofessional perspective. *Journal of Advanced Nursing, 46*(3), 262-269.

Cutcliffe, J. R., Butterworth, T., & Proctor, B. (2001). *Fundamental themes in clinical supervision*. London: Routledge.

Cutcliffe, J., & McFeely, S. (2001). Practice nurses and their 'lived experience' of clinical supervision. *British Journal of Nursing, 10*(5), 312-323.

Devine, A., & Baxter, T. (1995). Introducing clinical supervision: A guide. *Nursing Standard, 9*(40), 32-34.

Dimond, B. (1998a). Legal aspects of clinical supervision 1: Employer vs. employee. *British Journal of Nursing, 7*(7), 393-395.

Dimond, B. (1998b). Legal aspects of clinical supervision 2: Professional accountability. *British Journal of Nursing, 7*(8), 487-489.

Faugier, J. (1992). The supervisory relationship. In T. Butterworth & J. Faugier (Eds.) *Clinical supervision and mentorship in Nursing*. London: Chapman and Hall.

Faugier, J. (1996). Clinical supervision and mental health nursing. In T. Sandford & K. Gourney (Eds.) *Perspectives in mental health nursing*. London: Bailliere Tindall.

Fowler, J. (1996a). How to use models of clinical supervision in practice. *Nursing Standard, 10*(29), 42-47.

Fowler, J. (1996b). The organization of clinical supervision within the nursing profession: A review of the literature. *Journal of Advanced Nursing, 23*(3), 471-478.

Gray, J. (1995). Opening the debate on clinical supervision. *Nursing Standard, 9*(18), 15.

Hawkins, P., & Shohet, R. (1989). *Supervision in the helping professions*. Milton Keynes: University Press.

Hyrkas, K., Appelqvist-Schmidlechner, K., & Kivimaki, K. (2005). First-line managers' views of the long-term effects of clinical supervision: How does clinical supervision support and develop leadership in health care? *Journal of Nursing Management, 13*, 209-220.

Hyrkas, K., Koivula, M., & Paunonen, M. (1999). Clinical supervision in nursing in the 1990s–Current state of concepts, theory and research. *Journal of Nursing Management, 7*(3), 177-187.

Johns, C. (2001). Depending on the intent and emphasis of the supervisor, clinical supervision can be a different experience. *Journal of Nursing Management, 9*(3), 139-145.

Johns, C. (2003). Clinical supervision as a model for clinical leadership. *Journal of Nursing Management, 11*(1), 25-34.

Landmark, B., Hansen, G. H., Bjones, I., & Bohler, A. (2003). Clinical supervision–Factors defined by nurses as influential upon the development of competence and skills in supervision. *Journal of Clinical Nursing, 12*(6), 834-841.

Lyth, G. M. (2000). Clinical supervision: A concept analysis. *Journal of Advanced Nursing, 31*(3), 722-729.

Porter, N. (1997). Clinical supervision: The art of being supervised. *Nursing Standard, 11*(45), 44-45.

Proctor, B. (1986). Supervision: A co-operative exercise in accountability. In M. Marken & Payne (Eds.) *Enabling and ensuring*. Leicester: National Youth Bureau and Council for Education and Training n Youth and Community Work.

Rafferty, M., & Coleman, M. (2001). Educating nurses to undertake clinical supervision in practice. *Nursing Standard, 10*(45), 38-41.

Schein, E. H. (1992). *Organizational culture and leadership*. San Francisco: Jossey-Bass.

Severinsson, E. I. (1994). The concept of supervision in psychiatric care–compared with mentorship and leadership. A review of the literature. *Journal of Nursing Management, 2*(6), 271-278.

Sloan, G. (1999). Good characteristics of a clinical supervisor: A community mental health nurse perspective. *Journal of Advanced Nursing, 30*(3), 713-722.

Spouse, J. (2001). Bridging theory and practice in the supervisory relationship: A sociocultural perspective. *Journal of Advanced Nursing, 33*(4), 512-522.

Tveiten, S. (2005). Evaluation of the concept of supervision related to public health nurses in Norway. *Journal of Nursing Management, 13*, 13-21.

Winstanley, J. (2000). Manchester Clinical Supervision Scale. *Nursing Standard, 14*(19), 31-32.

Winstanley, J. (2001). *Developing methods for evaluating clinical supervision*. In J. R. Cutcliffe, T. Butterworth, & B. Proctor (Eds.) *Fundamental themes in clinical supervision*. London: Rutledge.

Winstanley J., & White, E. (2003). Clinical supervision: Models, measures and best practice. *Nurse Researcher, 10*(4), 7-38.

Wood, J. A.V., Miller, T. W., & Hargrove, D. S. (2005). Clinical supervision in rural settings: A telehealth model. *Professional Psychology: Research and Practice, 36*(2), 173-179.

Yegdich, T. (1999). Clinical supervision and managerial supervision: Some historical and conceptual considerations. *Journal of Advanced Nursing, 30*(5), 1195-1204.

Yegdich, T. (1998). How not to do clinical supervision in nursing. *Journal of Advanced Nursing*, *28*(1), 193-202.

Yegdich, T., & Cushing, A. (1998). An historical perspective on clinical supervision in nursing. *Australian and New Zealand Journal of Mental Health Nursing*, *7*, 3-24.

doi:10.1300/J001v24n01_08

Field Instruction in Social Work: A Review of the Research Literature

Marion Bogo

SUMMARY. A review of recent literature on field education revealed an extensive body of knowledge consisting of theoretical, educational, and empirical work. This paper reviews 40 studies on field education undertaken in the past five years. A number of relevant themes emerged from this review related to the context of field education, processes of field instruction, assessment of student learning and competence, training field instructors, and international practicum. Despite methodological limitations, these studies are building towards evidence-based field education practices. doi:10.1300/J001v24n01_09 *[Article copies available for a fee from The Haworth Document Delivery Service: 1-800-HAWORTH. E-mail address: <docdelivery@haworthpress.com> Website: <http://www.HaworthPress.com> © 2005 by The Haworth Press, Inc. All rights reserved.]*

KEYWORDS. Field instruction, field education, practicum, student supervision

DEFINITION

Field education, also referred to as field practicum or field work, is the component of social work education where students learn to practice

Marion Bogo is Professor, Faculty of Social Work, University of Toronto.

[Haworth co-indexing entry note]: "Field Instruction in Social Work: A Review of the Research Literature." Bogo, Marion. Co-published simultaneously in *The Clinical Supervisor* (The Haworth Press, Inc.) Vol. 24, No. 1/2, 2005, pp. 163-193; and: *Supervision in Counseling: Interdisciplinary Issues and Research* (ed: Lawrence Shulman, and Andrew Safyer) The Haworth Press, Inc., 2005, pp. 163-193. Single or multiple copies of this article are available for a fee from The Haworth Document Delivery Service [1-800-HAWORTH, 9:00 a.m. - 5:00 p.m. (EST). E-mail address: docdelivery@haworthpress.com].

Available online at http://cs.haworthpress.com

doi:10.1300/J001v24n01_09

social work through delivering social work services in agency and community settings. Field education is a required and integral component of the curriculum in all undergraduate and graduate programs in accredited schools of social work in the United States (EPAS, 2002). It is organized in a systematic manner, directed by the university in partnership with a range of community organizations and settings, and evaluated in relation to the mission and goals of the academic program. The Council on Social Work Education Accreditation standards requires a minimum of 400 hours of field education for baccalaureate programs and 900 hours for master's programs.

Through field education students learn to integrate and apply theory to practice, and to examine, critique, and test out in action the knowledge, values, and principles studied in academic courses. Students are exposed to a wide range of intervention approaches and learn to use practice techniques, skillfully adapted to the unique dynamics of particular situations. They develop competence in performing social work functions through educationally-focused feedback about their actual practice with a range of clients, groups, communities, and in administration, planning, or policy development activities.

Educationally-focused field instruction is provided by agency-based social workers. These experienced professionals are appointed by the university as field instructors to assist students in achieving the educational objectives of the field program. Many social work students and alumni consider the practicum as the core of their educational preparation for professional practice and personal development as a social worker, and the field instructor is central to their learning (Kadushin, 1991; Tolson & Kopp, 1988). Schools develop policies, criteria, and procedures for selecting agencies and field instructors. For baccalaureate students, field instructors must hold a baccalaureate degree from an accredited program, and for masters students they must hold a masters degree. Exceptions are made to these requirements when schools use settings that are relevant to social work but do not employ social workers. Examples of such settings are innovative community programs, agencies in under-serviced fields, or agencies in a locale where there are no social workers. The school provides liaison to the staff appointed as the onsite field instructor to ensure the incorporation of a social work focus.

Field instructors guide students through the practicum. They have primary responsibility for linking the student to the setting; teaching, coordinating, and evaluating the student's learning; ensuring that the agency's service standards are met; and liaising with the university.

They have current practice experience and a commitment to social work education. Training is provided to new and continuing field instructors. Schools also appoint a faculty member as field liaison to link the agency and the school's program, to assist in student learning through monitoring and evaluating student progress, and to consult on educational issues (Faria, Brownstein, & Smith, 1988; Rosenblum & Raphael, 1983). As schools have experienced both diminishing resources and rising expectations for scholarly productivity of faculty members, the commitment and interest in liaison work has diminished and faculty have become less engaged with field teaching and liaison roles (Kilpatrick, Turner, & Holland, 1994). Schools have adopted a trouble-shooting model for problem solving purposes (Fortune et al., 1995) or hired adjunct part-time faculty to provide liaison (Wayne, Bogo, & Raskin, 2006).

Efforts to professionalize the work force in public social services and child welfare have resulted in increased numbers of students entering social work educational programs who are currently employed in social service positions. Since 1992, to accommodate the needs of these students they have been able to complete their field education requirements in their agency of employment, as long as their field education experiences are different from their typical activities in their jobs (Wayne et al., 2006).

In earlier eras field education was referred to as field work and reflected an apprenticeship model rather than the current educationally focused approach (George, 1982). In the apprenticeship model, the terminology of agency practice was used and social work field instructors or field educators were referred to as student supervisors. While remnants of this approach may still exist, these terms are misleading and do not accurately represent the essence of the educationally oriented field learning experience. Since in some studies reviewed for this article the researchers still refer to "student supervision," this term is only used to reflect the work of these authors.

MODALITIES

The primary method of providing field education is through the one-to-one field instructor and student dyad. Students are matched or assigned to one field instructor who coordinates all of their learning in the field setting and is the primary teacher. Indeed, many students and alumnae report that this relationship is key to their learning and researchers have found it predicts satisfaction with all aspects of the field experience such as learning, the agency, and the overall field experience (Alperin, 1998; Raskin, 1989). Frequently the primary field instructor will also involve other social workers or staff in related disciplines in the student's education. This can occur through assigning the student to colleagues to learn specific activities, for example to conduct a group or provide play therapy. The relationship between the primary field instructor and these task instructors is defined in advance, especially their contribution to the final evaluation of student learning.

Group supervision is frequently proposed as an economical adjunct or alternative to the resource intensive individual tutorial method (Globerman & Bogo, 2002; Jarman-Rohde, McFall, Kolar, & Strom, 1997; Tebb, Manning, & Klaumann, 1996) and there are anecdotal descriptions of this approach (Geller, 1994; Tebb et al., 1996) and a growing empirical literature that will be reviewed later in this paper. More recently social work educators have introduced rotation models in field education where students in hospitals rotate between various services and field instructors through the course of the academic term (Cuzzi, Holden, Rutter, Rosenberg, & Chernack, 1996, 1997).

REVIEW OF RESEARCH ON FIELD EDUCATION IN SOCIAL WORK

Following the request of the editors of *The Clinical Supervisor* journal, peer-reviewed journal articles on research on field education published in the past five years were sought, from 1999-2004. A search was conducted using the Social Work Abstracts database for the keywords of "social work" and "field instruction" and "field education." Over the five-year period, a total of eighty-three peer-reviewed journal articles on field instruction in social work were located. The author and a research assistant reviewed all identified articles independently to locate empirical studies. Forty articles were identified for inclusion in the review. Articles were excluded for the following reasons: not specific to social work, editorials, and papers that were theoretical or clinical with selected case examples to illustrate the author's point (see Note).

A number of studies were found on field education on a wide range of themes from context, to techniques, to assessment of learning. The majority of these studies were single stand alone projects on specific topics. Therefore, appropriate caution must be exercised in generalizing conclusions and recommendations. There were, however, a few studies that are part of ongoing programs of research that aim to illuminate crucial aspects of field education and contribute to theory building and evidence-based field teaching and learning. The following review of the research literature includes both single studies and reports from continuing projects and is organized according to salient themes that emerged: the context of field education, contributions towards evidence-based field education, assessment of student learning and competence, training field instructors, and international comparisons.

The Context of Field Education

Characteristics of Organizations

Field education occurs through the voluntary participation of community agencies with schools of social work. Four studies examine the types of organizations used and their relationships with universities. In Fortune, McCarthy, and Abramson's (2001) study of student learning processes, they reported that in one school of social work the majority of first year placements (59%) were in host organizations such as hospitals and residential settings, most were in public organizations (52%) and 34% of the agencies were described as small. Students in the first year perceived that they received a better quality of field instruction when in social work settings as compared to those in host settings. Students in smaller agencies reported more satisfaction with the field experience. In the second year, the type of agency did not affect students' perception of quality or satisfaction.

Field education settings for social work students who were also enrolled in a gerontology certificate program were reported by Euster (1999) who found micro level practicum in a wide range of community and institutional settings and macro level practicum in community-based organizations and government commissions. International placements were offered, in Rai's (2004) survey of twenty-five responding US schools, through international organizations and in human service agencies in other countries. A similar survey about international field placements obtained a response from 446 accredited schools of social work (Panos, Pettys, Cox, & Jones-Hart, 2004). The researchers found that approximately one in five programs place students in international field settings. Schools committed to international practicum are developing sites which they repeatedly use over time.

As noted, field education depends on the collaboration of service organizations and universities. While analysis and strategies to strengthen these partnerships received attention in an earlier era (Cohen, 1977; Frumkin, 1980; Tropman, 1980), only one recent study was found that investigated these inter-organizational relationships. From a review of the anecdotal and descriptive literature, Bogo and Globerman (1999) developed and tested a framework consisting of four components: (1) commitment to education, (2) provision of organizational resources and supports, (3) effective interpersonal relationships, and (4) reciprocal activities. They examined the presence of each component in three categories of agencies: (1) organizations with a formal and continuous link to the university, (2) organizations with one or more field instructors who have a semi-formal relationship with the university, and (3) organizations where one social worker independently volunteers to offer field instruction. They found that organizations with formal agreements had more complex student programs and more reciprocal activities than the other two types of organizations. However, field instructors in all agencies offered a range of learning activities for students and reported positive relationships with university counterparts.

Changes to organizations offering field education has been of concern in the social work literature in the past decade and three studies investigate the impact of managed care on field instruction. Field instruction was found to be less well supported by agencies since managed care resulted in an emphasis on maximizing revenues. Staff in the greater Boston area could not bill for the time they spent in student supervision (Donner, 1996) and had larger caseloads and less time to supervise (Bocage, Homonoff, & Riley, 1995). In a national survey of 70 responding field directors, similar reasons were found for a loss of placements: reduced resources, increased caseloads, and lack of billable hours for field instruction, especially on the East Coast and in urban centers (Raskin & Blome, 1998).

Learning opportunities have also been significantly affected in health and mental health. For example, in settings funded by managed care plans there were fewer inpatient opportunities, more crisis intervention, and more contract workers with no time allotted for field instruction (Raskin & Blome, 1998). While students wanted to learn long-term practice, more placements offered short-term, crisis- and task-oriented practice, and employers expected a high level of skill from graduating students. Respondents perceived that most students were not prepared for the reality of practice in a managed care environment. Similarly, when hospitals reorganize and adopt a program management model and eliminate central social work departments, field education may lose priority. In a sample of nine such hospitals in one Canadian center, it was found that the decision to offer field education had become an individual matter and required individual social workers to negotiate with their multi-professional teams for agreement to take a social work student (Globerman & Bogo, 2002). In the absence of a director of social work, there were no longer senior level advocates to ensure that education for students in the health professions included education for social work students. In response to such changes in the health care system, Long and Heydt (2000) argued for developing new types of placements and present a qualitative case study of one BSW field placement in a hospital-owned physician practice at a skilled nursing facility. The innovation was evaluated as successful by a variety of respondents including a client, the student, the physician, the instructor, and the facility administrator.

In summary, the agency context affects student learning in a number of ways including the availability of practicum, the types of opportunities available, and student perception of the quality of their experience. Managed care funding and program management in hospitals influenced field offerings and field instructors' potential to provide instruction. Hence, relationships between schools of social work and field agencies are crucial and vary based on a range of dimensions that could be strengthened to produce more continuous and complex field programs. Studies are needed to design and evaluate different models for offering field education, including university-agency collaborations that result in institutionalized partnerships. The impact of agency context on student learning has yet to be investigated.

Field Instructors

Since social workers' ability to provide field instruction depends on their agencies' support, these changing contextual issues have led researchers to study field instructors' experiences, motivations, and the factors that influence their participation and satisfaction. Three studies were found on this topic. In a study of field instructors in 11 schools in Illinois and Wisconsin, field instructor satisfaction was significantly related to satisfaction with the liaison, operationally defined as access to the liaisons' evaluations, the liaisons' readiness to provide consultation, and the frequency of the liaison contact (Bennett & Coe, 1998). Agency support such as release time, support for the field instructor, and valuing field instruction was also significant. Three supports at the agency-person level found to be significant were lack of burnout, job certainty, and regular meetings with other field instructors. Finally, personal rewards such as a belief that field instruction enhanced professional skills and development were important.

In a qualitative study Globerman and Bogo (2003) interviewed 20 experienced field instructors and found, similar to Bennett and Coe (1998), that professional and personal issues were motivators. Professional factors included the responsibility to contribute and give back as well as the professional growth that resulted from students who were challenging and energizing. Personal factors included enjoyment derived from teaching and mentoring. They also found a third factor related to the organization: its commitment to education and professional development in general, a belief that the agency had something special to teach, and recognizing the agency benefits from students' work and their new ideas.

Using concepts from object relations and self psychology to examine the development of the professional self in social work, Urdang (1999) conducted a qualitative study and interviewed 19 field instructors after their first year of supervising students. These respondents discussed how the experience of offering clinical supervision contributed to their professional development. It stimulated them to further analysis and reflection about their own practice, to developing deeper self-awareness, and to new insights and perceptions about their student experiences. Providing supervision helped many respondents appreciate their own professional competence and value.

Changes in the University

A recent theme in the literature on social work education has noted that changing academic expectations of faculty members have led to less engagement in field liaison and that schools are hiring part-time personnel for this role. Researchers are concerned that this arrangement will undermine the integration of theory and practice, lessen the importance given to field education and the practice of social work, and create a two-tiered full-time faculty and field faculty system (Bennett & Coe, 1998; Kilpatrick et al., 1994). In an analysis of survey data from 69 schools of social work, it was found that 62% of the schools did not assign full-time faculty members to the faculty field liaison role (Burke, Condon, & Wickell, 1999). Larger programs were more likely to have a separate field department and less likely to use faculty in the field liaison role. Similar to others' findings, field instructor satisfaction was significantly related to satisfaction with the liaison. Similarly, in a survey of fifty-three field instructors in one rural BSW program, respondents rated agency visits by the faculty liaison the second highest as a perceived support, with orientation to field expectations as the first source of support (Unger, 2003). Other valued support activities were orientation to the social work department and curriculum, and resource materials on supervision.

This group of studies on field instructors and schools of social work reveal similar findings: that field instructors' motivation to voluntarily offer field education is related to personal/professional factors, agency support factors, and connection to the university program and its faculty members. Since a consistent theme in the literature highlights the importance of field instructors to providing a quality educational experience to students, it is timely to design and evaluate various models or strategies used to respond to the factors that have been identified as influencing field instructors' motivation. Maintaining a committed core of experienced field instructors is a universal concern; for example, the difficulty in obtaining field instructors was reported as the most critical issue in an international comparative survey of 163 schools of social work (Skolnik, Wayne, & Raskin, 1999).

Finally with respect to changes in the university, despite the recent growth in distance education in social work programs, only one study compared the experiences and perceptions of students on campus with those in distance locations in one school. Using a multi-method approach, more positive student assessments about adequacy of local resources, agency structure and culture, and field office resources were found in students in the two distance sites (McFall & Freddolino, 2000). The authors speculated that the innovative nature of the new distance programs might have provided a level of energy not present in the traditional on-campus program.

Towards Evidence-Based Field Education

Characteristics of Students

A few studies have examined various aspects of student characteristics that might affect field learning. These characteristics include demographic factors, degree of anxiety about the field practicum, learning style, and psychiatric disability. An exploratory study by Zosky and colleagues (Zosky, Unger, White, & Mills, 2003) found that field instructors rated the field performance of non-traditional undergraduate students more highly than the performance of traditional students. Field instructors assessed non-traditional students as more competent on all skill-based activities, value-based variables including boundaries and self-determination, and viewed them as more prepared for the field. Non-traditional students were defined as over the age of 21, out of school for three years or more, or occupying multiple roles (parent, employee, student) with prior life experience.

Gelman (2004) conducted an exploratory study to assess MSW students' level of anxiety and found self-ratings of 46% of students as moderately anxious or higher although the students did not think their anxiety would interfere with learning. Students reported anxiety about their lack of skills, experience, and preparedness. They were concerned that clients would be mandated, resistant, lack motivation, have complex and multiple problems, and be different in a variety of ways. They were concerned about the quality of supervision in terms of content and time. Students under 25 years had higher levels of anxiety than older students. The authors suggested that students receive training about expectations of the supervisory relationship and how it can be maximized.

Learning styles are considered a useful concept for understanding field learning and, using Kolb's learning styles inventory, researchers found that among both students and field supervisors accommodators (those who emphasize abstract and reflective learning) outnumber those in other learning style quadrants (Raschick, Maypole, & Day, 1998). Interestingly, students with greater pre-MSW human service work experience favored more concrete learning styles. Students whose learning styles were more similar to their field supervisors rated their field experience higher than students whose styles were not similar to those of their instructors. The authors recommended that students and field instructors formally discuss their respective learning styles and the implications for their relationship (Raschick et al., 1998).

Similar to this topic, the extent to which students reflect their field instructors' styles was explored in a study in Israel (Itzhaky & Eliahou, 1999). The researchers found that instructors tend to use what they called the personal and task-oriented styles more than their students. There was a notable preference to use the personal style both among the field instructors and among the students. The more the field instructors consider themselves to have a personal supervisory style, the more the students perceive themselves as having a personal learning style. The researchers recommended that field instructors recognize the differences between the supervisory and learning styles in relationships with students, while also realizing that students tend to see the supervisor as a model and imitate his or her style (Itzhaky & Eliahou, 1999).

Concerns about and approaches for providing social work education to students with psychiatric problems were addressed in a survey and focus group of field instructors (Gillis & Lewis, 2004). The study found that a third of the 61 participants had provided field education to students with psychiatric problems and that 13% of their students had been terminated for nonacademic reasons. Difficulties for field instructors arose from conflicting roles and responsibilities with faculty liaisons, lack of training about American With Disabilities Act (ADA) requirements, and the need for a systematic approach from the school for dealing with student suitability and psychiatric disability.

Diversity

Diversity issues are a central theme in contemporary social work practice literature and yet only two studies were found on this topic. In an exploratory study, the researchers developed and pilot tested an approach to diversity training for eleven field instructors (Armour, Bain, & Rubio, 2004). The training was offered in response to field instructors' reporting their avoidance of addressing diversity issues despite their desire to do so. They attributed this to a lack of readiness on their part. The evaluation of the training program found the participants developed some skills to enhance supervision in this area such as normalization of discomfort, awareness of retreating from exploring diversity, and permission to talk about concerns related to working with clients. They increased self-knowledge and felt empowered to address diversity issues with the agency, student, or client.

An exploratory study examined the experiences of lesbian and gay social work students in field placement (Messinger, 2004) and found the following themes: heterosexist and homophobic attitudes and behaviors, unwelcoming agency climates, absence of discussion of gay and lesbian issues in the field placement, general feelings of lack of safety or anxiety at the placement, and challenges related to disclosure of sexual orientation in the agency. Suggested supports for students included faculty support and mentoring, supportive field education staff, gay and lesbian social work professionals as mentors, educated field instructors, out gay and lesbian agency staff, education, and supportive heterosexual co-workers. In addition, institutional resources were recommended, such as resource information for lesbian and gay students, information about sexual orientation issues in placement, list of gay-friendly agencies, gay and lesbian agencies as placement sites, and resources for gay and lesbian clients.

In summary, based on the findings from these studies about student characteristics and diversity issues, some recommendations can be made that might improve field education. Schools might consider preparing students prior to the practicum with basic social work skills and strategies for maximizing field learning. The latter can include information about students' personal styles for handling stress and anxiety and about potentially significant interactional dynamics in the relationship with the field instructor such as the impact of learning and teaching styles. Schools also need to develop a systematic approach for dealing with student suitability and psychiatric disability. Further studies on diversity in field education are needed, as well as training for field instructors to deal with the impact of a range of student and client social identity characteristics. New approaches should be evaluated to identify their impact on field learning.

Models of Field Education: Individual Field Instruction

A number of researchers have examined students' perceptions of teaching activities, processes, and techniques in individual field instruction that affect their satisfaction and perception of a quality field experience (Abbott & Lyter, 1998; Choy, Leung, Tam, & Chu, 1998; Deal, 2000; Fortune & Kaye, 2002; Fortune et al., 2001; Knight, 2000, 2001; Maidment, 2000). Across studies, the majority of students reported moderately high to high satisfaction with individual field instruction and with the processes discussed in the following section. It is important to note these processes are limited to an association with satisfaction as an outcome. Fortune (Fortune et al., 2001) is the only researcher to use performance as an outcome measure, assessed by the field instructor's rating of the student on the university's evaluation form.

Supportive Relationship

Students rate highly a group of supervisor characteristics that they associate with a supportive climate: honest, likable, expert, reliable, sociable, prepared, sincere, warm, skillful, and trustworthy (Strozier, Barnett-Queen, & Bennett, 2000). Comparing first and second year student preferences, the researchers found these characteristics especially valued by first year students, although ongoing support was valued by both years. More frequent supervision and longer sessions were positively associated with students' positive evaluations of the field experience (Knight, 2001) and field instructors who received negative evaluations were those who students perceived as not engaged or supportive (Knight, 2000). Similarly the importance of tasks that support students in their learning was also found in a study in Hong Kong (Choy et al., 1998).

Learning Activities

Fortune and colleagues (2001) found three learning activities were significantly associated with students' perceptions of the quality of field instruction in the first practicum: conducting co-therapy, explanations by field instructors, and feedback on process recordings. In the second placement, the most significant learning activities were explanations from the field instructor, critiquing one's own work, making connections to theory, and observing others in professional roles. The researchers concluded that students respond positively to learning activities that provide opportunities to see and work with professional role models and that give them a conceptual framework for understanding what they are doing in their field placement. These learning activities were associated with students' perceptions; no differences were found on final evaluation of students' performance by virtue of learning activities received (Fortune et al., 2001). Another activity, completing process recordings, was investigated in Knight's (2000) study. She found the significant feature was the way in which field instructors used process recordings in teaching, rather than simply the frequency with which students were required to submit them.

In a study in New Zealand, Maidment (2000) found that students valued activities such as structured orientation to the service, access to one-on-one supervision, observation of other workers' practice, and discussion of case notes. However, there was a discrepancy between the methods students believed promoted their learning (and that field instructors rated as effective) and the degree to which these methods were reportedly used by field educators. Student responses indicated that they were most likely to experience teaching and learning activities that offer a once removed view of the students' competence, such as discussion of case notes, even though they valued more direct learning approaches.

Knight (2000) found the most influential teaching activities were reviewing and analyzing cases, helping the student understand how the agency functions, and integrating theory and practice including an awareness of the student's classroom learning. More frequent supervision and the length of the supervisory sessions were positively associated with student satisfaction. Similarly, Choy and colleagues (1998) found that students rated the educator role as most important, specifically when field instructors provided examples of application of theory to real situations.

In a study that explored how feedback that is critical can be helpful to students the researchers found that students valued the following: a positive learning environment, a balance between negative and positive comments, brainstorming solutions together, and encouraging student self-critique (Abbott & Lyter, 1998). Critical feedback was perceived negatively when delivered in a demeaning, harsh or angry way, when it did not appear to have the goal of promoting growth, and when it was offered without appropriate preparation.

Recognizing that there has been little investigation of negative behaviors or critical incidents in field education Giddings, Vodde, and Cleveland (2003) used a national random sample of social workers and asked them to recall problems with their former field instructors. Four factors emerged: (1) a lack of supervision, including lack of structure, direction, and feedback; (2) a harsh and unyielding style that was rigid, authoritarian, overly challenging or accusatory, lacked empathy and sensitivity to student needs; (3) unprofessional behavior with moderate ethical and boundary violations; and (4) extreme violations such as physical aggression, sexual harassment, and racial bias.

From the studies reviewed thus far, a constellation of field instruction factors emerges, with some supporting evidence that they are valued by students. Field instruction is valued when it includes: (1) instructor characteristics and behaviors that offer support, including providing balanced feedback on students' practice; (2) frequent field instruction sessions of duration; (3) direct learning activities such as observing and working with professional role models; (4) reflective and conceptual learning activities such as providing a conceptual framework for understanding students' practice, assistance in analyzing cases and integrating theory and practice, including concepts studied in the classroom; and (5) activities that encourage student self-critique.

Developmental or Stage Models

Developmental models of supervision in psychology propose that counselors' growth follows a series of sequential, hierarchical stages, with different supervision interventions appropriate for each stage

(Borders, 1986). Developmental models have received empirical support in psychology (Heppner & Roehlke, 1984) and there has been some theoretical interest in social work (Saari, 1989). One study was found that used a supervision checklist developed to study psychology students and was administered weekly to social work students to investigate the field instruction processes used throughout the practicum and their impact on students (Strozier, Barnett-Queen, & Bennett, 2000). A similar checklist was administered at the end of the field experience for students to rate the importance of various instructional processes. The researchers found only limited support for a developmental model of supervision. For example, as found in social work studies reviewed above, social work students value support at all developmental stages; they "want and need supervisory support at the beginning, middle and even near the end of their training" (Strozier et al., 2000, p. 36). As the practicum progressed however, students wished to take on more responsibility for their practice.

As part of a mixed method study to explore outcomes and processes of clinical social work education of 15 MSW students, Deal (2000) examined developmental themes. She found that students improved through their second year in their ability to address interpersonal processes with clients, in their receptive capacity (ability to be with and experience what the client was saying), and in a greater differentiation of personal and professional selves. However, ratings of students' process recordings were used as one measure of student performance; process recordings are generally critiqued as subject to bias of the individual writing the record.

Examination of the usefulness of different teaching activities of the field instructor based on the stage of the field experience was examined in Knight's (Knight, 2001) survey of undergraduate and graduate students at two points: one month after the beginning of the practicum and during the ending phase. She found the field relationship dynamic and evolving, with the use of a variety of skills depending on the students' stage in the learning process. Understandably, early stage activities rated as useful were those that oriented students to the field, the agency, and performance expectations. Later phase activities taught students to be self-critical and enhanced linkages between class and field learning.

Of interest in this study was the finding that students rated the quality and experience of their first year placements higher than their second year placements and rated different field instructor behaviors important for each year (Knight, 2000). In the first placement, most useful behaviors were discussing role, purpose, and taboo subjects; partializing concerns; encouraging autonomy and self-criticism; reviewing cases; and individualizing learning. In the second placement, most useful behaviors were sharing thoughts and feelings, understanding students' feelings, maintaining realistic expectations, and demonstrating awareness of classroom learning and linking those concepts to practice. Finally, a greater proportion of students expressed dissatisfaction with their field instructor at the second point of data collection leading Knight (2001) to conclude that when the student has greater familiarity with the setting, essential learning can take place, and it is ill advised to lessen the amount of supervisory time towards the end.

Two types of studies have been reviewed thus far that provide evidence towards building a model of individualized field instruction: (1) studies on students' perceptions of teaching activities, processes, and techniques that affect their satisfaction and perception of a quality field experience, and (2) studies about student preferences for educational processes at various stages of their professional development. Findings from all of these studies lead to the conclusion that students appear to value three dimensions in field instruction throughout the learning experience. First, similar to social work practice, valued field instruction emanates out of the relationship between the student and instructor. In the context of a supportive relationship, students believe they can receive and use critical feedback about their practice. Second, a range of learning activities are also valued, especially those that provide opportunities to observe practitioners and to have students' work observed. Finally, the conceptualization of practice is the third dimension identified, with analysis of student cases and the ability to self-critique. While a staged view of student development was not fully supported in these studies, there is some support for a greater emphasis on orientation in the beginning stage and greater focus on conceptual and self-assessment activities at later stages.

Models of Field Education: Group Supervision

As noted earlier, the traditional model of field instruction in social work is that of individual supervision. Given current organizational changes and the need for financial efficiencies, group supervision is increasingly recommended for field education (Jarman-Rohde et al., 1997; Tebb et al., 1996). Only two studies were found on this topic, both qualitative exploratory projects that elicited students' experience of group supervision. In the first study, 12 female masters students who were experienced case managers in child protective services received a combined approach of individual and group supervision. In exploring the students' experiences, Walter and Young (1999) found varied positive and negative responses to group supervision, in contrast to students' uniformly positive responses to individual supervision. Individual supervision was seen as helpful, especially to learn how to use a professional relationship with clients and to gain self-awareness. The respondents felt more comfortable discussing difficulties and exposing vulnerabilities in individual supervision than in group. Initially, the group supervision amplified students' anxiety and was seen as taking up valuable time. However, after the first semester, as the students gained comfort and skill, they began to value consultation with peers. Group supervision also facilitated learning to apply theory to cases.

Similar findings about group supervision emerged from a study of 18 female masters students who received group supervision as the primary modality (Bogo, Globerman, & Sussman, 2004a). Key themes were the importance of field instructors who were available and supportive, who focused on educational rather than pragmatic issues, and who provided structure for the group. Instructors' competency in working with groups was seen as crucial to facilitate learning from others, to balance students' expressions of both personal and shared experiences, and to help students process and manage group dynamics. In a further analysis of this data, Bogo and colleagues (Bogo, Globerman, & Sussman, 2004b) examined the dynamics of trust and competition in these groups and found a multifaceted process that could impede learning and professional development. Students' past histories with each other affected their ability to create a productive learning climate, which was also influenced by how each student reacted to varying levels of their peers' competence, and to their skills as group members. The field instructors' competence in facilitating group process included their ability to model effective group member behavior such as taking risks, giving constructive feedback, and communicating openly, to promote group norms, and to help students express and handle conflict openly. In summary, the few studies on group supervision revealed that this method can inhibit learning as a result of personal exposure, anxiety, and the feelings of vulnerability elicited by the group format. While students can learn from each other, they need to learn how to function as constructive members of a learning group, and field instructors need competence as group workers.

Models of Field Education: Task Supervision and Field Instruction

In agencies where there is no staff with social work degrees but relevant learning opportunities exist, a practice has developed of identifying an on-site task supervisor to address administrative issues and an off-site MSW field instructor to provide social work education. Using a focus group of four non MSW task supervisors and five MSW field instructors, the researchers found the following factors contributed to their perception of a high-quality experience (Abram, Hartung, & Wernet, 2000). When students were mature, self-confident, had experience, took initiative, were active and prepared, and had good communication skills, the approach worked well. It was important that the on-site supervisor had extensive knowledge of resources, was able to work cooperatively with the school and motivate, direct, and develop students, and that the agency was committed to student education and could accommodate the time needed for the student. Common philosophy and values, clarification of roles and division of labor, and frequent communication between the on-site and off-site instructors also contributed positively.

The studies of various models and learning activities in field education reviewed thus far provide some support for a group of core educational processes. This exploratory work contributes to a beginning empirical base for field learning. Theory building is needed to explain how and under what conditions these different models and techniques produce desired outcomes. It is timely for researchers to design studies that will test individual and group models, identify the impact of a range of educational processes on student outcome, and contrast various approaches. To contribute meaningfully to knowledge-building, these studies must use educational outcome measures other than student satisfaction.

Assessment of Student Learning and Competence

Although social work educators are committed to graduate competent practitioners, a consistent concern expressed in the field education literature over the past two decades is the lack of objective, standardized outcome measures to assess student learning and performance (Alperin, 1996; Kilpatrick et al., 1994). In two surveys of field education experts conducted ten years apart, Raskin (1983; 1994) found their top research priority was the development of methods to test for the attainment of specific skills in field instruction.

Development of Scales

Four scales to measure students' competence in various domains of social work practice are reported in the literature. For a thorough appraisal of these scales see Bogo, Regehr, Hughes, Power, and Globerman (2002); the following is a brief summary. O'Hare, Collins, and Walsh (1998) developed the Practice Skills Inventory (PSI) from a review of the psychotherapy and social work outcome research literature. A set of common therapeutic factors was used to initially generate 75 skill items which, using factor analysis, was reduced to 23 items on four factors: supportive skills, therapeutic skills, case-management skills, and insight-facilitation skills. They reported reliability and construct validity for this inventory and used it as a self-report measure to assess how frequently students use the skill. The strength of the scale derives from its inclusion of skills drawn from the empirical literature and its inclusion of sub-scales representing different dimensions of practice. Its limitation is its assessment of frequency, rather than competency, in use of skills, and that it is provided as a self-report measure and has not been tested as a method for field instructors to use in evaluation.

With a group of field instructors, Wilson (1981) developed a checklist of specific characteristics to distinguish between first year and advanced students. Twenty-six interviewing skills were selected and tested for reliability and content, concurrent, and predictive validity (Vourlekis, Bembry, Hall, & Rosenblum, 1996). The checklist was used to evaluate the quality of social work students' interviewing skills. However, the determination of quality was based on process notes of interviews, rather than actual observations of practice. The checklist does not include other dimensions of social work practice, such as relationship skills.

A third measure organized 25 interviewing skills generated by faculty members and the researchers into four subscales: interpersonal communication, assessment, intervention, and termination (Koroloff & Rhyne, 1989). In the study, both students and field instructors independently rated students' performance. The scale was able to differentiate between students at various levels of training; its limitation is that it only evaluated interviewing skills.

Bogo and colleagues (2002) reported on the reliability and validity of a measure to evaluate student field performance developed by field instructors and faculty members and used in the field practicum for over two decades. They found a consistent factor structure with internal consistency yielding seven factors: empathy and alliance, values and ethics, differential use of self, assessment, intervention planning and implementation, presentation skills, and report writing. However, there was inadequate consistency between ratings of individual students in their first and second field experience. Some predictive validity was found; the measure could differentiate between students identified as having difficulty in the first year, but not in the second year.

In summary, a number of research groups have presented their attempts at defining and measuring sets of competencies of social work students. The studies reported are "first steps" and need continuing work. Research will be strengthened through efforts to build on and refine existing scales, to replicate studies beyond one program, and to test scales using authentic data that represent observations of students' actual practice, rather than their written description of practice or their field instructors' impressions of students' practice.

Instructors' Evaluation of Student Competence

In an attempt to understand the implicit criteria field instructors use when asked to evaluate students, Bogo and colleagues (2004) experimented with a novel approach. Ten field instructors were asked to divide 20 student vignettes into categories that reflected their assessment of different levels of student competence. Instructors worked individually and in small groups to categorize and identify criteria they used in this task. Inter-rater reliability was very high between instructors for rating the 20 student vignettes and these instructors agreed on the importance of both personal/professional qualities and competencies of students at various levels.

Self-Assessment

Stressing the importance of self-directed learning and self-assessment for professionals Regehr and colleagues (Regehr, Regehr, Leeson, & Fusco, 2002) developed and tested an approach to negotiating learning priorities for students. A structured system of self-appraisal is followed by instructor and student appraisal at midterm. The respective assessments are then compared and used for defining goals for the remainder of the placement. In a study of 37 students and their instructors, the researchers found most students' ranking of learning goals moderately consistent with their instructors' ranking. However, for eight students, they found low correlations and where the correlation was under .30, three out of the four students were identified by the field director independently as experiencing problems in the field. High agreement was found in skill areas that the authors labeled as "concrete domains of practice" (p. 62), such as communication, intervention planning, and group work skills, in contrast to low agreement in areas that "deal more directly with personality styles or personal values of the students" (p. 62), such as dealing with resistance, ambivalence or conflict, functioning on a team, and adhering to social work ethics.

While not falling within the five year timeframe of this review, the work of Holden and his colleagues (Holden, Cuzzi, Rutter, Chernack, & Spitzer, 1997; Holden, Cuzzi, Rutter, Chernack, Spitzer et al., 1997) on self-efficacy as an outcome measure for field education should be noted. These researchers have, through a progressive program of research, carried out a number of studies to develop and test a self-efficacy scale to assess both social work students' and practicing social workers' confidence in performing specific tasks in their professional practice in a hospital setting. The scale has been used to evaluate outcomes of field education models on student self-efficacy (Cuzzi, Holden, Chernack, Rutter, & Rosenberg, 1997; Cuzzi, Holden, Rutter, Rosenberg, & Chernack, 1996).

Training Field Instructors

As noted throughout this review, the field instructor is crucial to a successful student learning experience, and the assumption that field instructors need and benefit from training was supported in four studies. In response to a request for training to deal more effectively with diversity issues, Armour and colleagues (2004) described and evaluated a program that participants experienced as useful for their practice, their instruction, and their work with the agency. Similarly, Cohen (1998) reported on the impact of special training on supervising group work assignments, incorporated into a mandatory twelve session seminar for new field instructors. Field instructors reported that the training was beneficial and would lead them to assign more group work for students, and use group work in their own practice and in their agencies.

Adult education principles were rated highly by field instructors in training programs. For example, the use of active learning strategies was rated highly by 88% of instructors in a training seminar of two four hour sessions (McChesney & Euster, 2000). Three active learning components were cognitive elements (talking, listening, writing, reading, reflecting), learning strategies (small groups, cooperative groups, cases, role playing, journal writing), and teaching resources (readings, homework assignments, technology, prepared education material). Small groups facilitated peer learning in this study, a finding similar to that of Barlow and colleagues (Barlow, Rogers, & Coleman, 2003) who organized small peer collaborations for experienced instructors. Following a structured seminar to develop critical reflection about their field instruction teaching practices, experienced instructors reported increased self-confidence, competence, and an enhanced repertoire of teaching and learning strategies from regular meetings with peers. All of these studies on training field instructors used participant satisfaction as the only outcome measure. In future studies, outcome measures are recommended that would link training to field instructor performance in their actual field education of students, to student perception and satisfaction, and ultimately to student learning and performance.

International Comparative Studies

Field instruction is an important required component in most schools of social work and one survey of field structures and curricula achieved a 41% response rate from 163 schools of social work representing 67 countries in 7 geographic regions (Skolnik et al., 1999). Of responding programs, 95% of bachelor and diploma programs require practicum in contrast to the requirement in all American bachelors and masters programs. An overwhelming majority of the schools (85.6%) use specific criteria to appoint field instructors. The most widely used field settings worldwide are medical hospitals (93.3%), family service agencies (92%), and psychiatric hospitals (89.6%), whereas the least used are schools (66.9%), religious organizations (62%) and day care settings for children (62%). The authors concluded that while social work is an international profession, comparative studies continue to reveal important similarities and differences in field education across national boundaries.

BARRIERS TO RESEARCH

This review of numerous studies on a range of topics in field education in the past five years indicates the presence of a group of social work educators interested in systematic investigation of key issues. While funding sources for the studies are rarely noted, the sheer volume of work suggests that investigators are managing to find resources to carry out these studies. The inauguration of a special section on Field

Education in 2004 in the Council on Social Work Education's official journal, *Journal of Social Work Education*, may also have contributed to the interest in conducting empirical studies in this area.

Since all social work programs are required to have a field practicum and personnel to offer it, there are a great number of educators engaged in this aspect of social work education. Many of the field practices and standards have evolved over time and have not been subject to empirical testing. Unfortunately, those responsible for field programs report that the challenges of administration leave little time to engage in the reflective and empirical work of building the knowledge base (Wayne, Bogo, & Raskin, 2006). When field directors join with faculty colleagues interested in understanding the educational processes and dynamics that lead to effective outcomes, programs of research can be developed and maintained.

CRITIQUE AND FUTURE DIRECTIONS

The majority of studies reviewed for this article reflect single projects on specific topics, although a few researchers have worked in a continuous way on programs of research and are contributing more in depth analysis and understanding of specific issues. See for example the work of Fortune and her colleagues on learning processes and activities (Fortune & Abramson, 1993; Fortune et al., 1985; Fortune & Kaye, 2002; Fortune et al., 2001; Fortune et al., 1995), of Holden and his colleagues on self-efficacy and rotations (Cuzzi et al., 1996; 1997; Holden et al., 1997; 1997), of Bogo and Globerman (Bogo & Globerman, 1999; Globerman & Bogo, 2002, 2003) on the organizational context of field education, and of Bogo and Regehr (Bogo et al., 2002; 2004; Regehr et al., 2002) on competency and self-assessment. Raskin has also worked with colleagues to track crucial issues in field education over more than two decades (Raskin, 1983; 1989; 1994; 1998; Wayne, Bogo, & Raskin, 2006).

Of the studies reviewed, 8 quantitative (out of 25), 7 qualitative (out of 10), and 3 mixed-method (out of 5) identified the theoretical underpinnings of their work and contributed to theory building and articulating principles for field education. In the quantitative studies most used relatively small samples. For example, of the 25 quantitative and 5 mixed-method studies, only 9 had sample sizes over 100. Only one study used a random sample; all others were samples of convenience. In seven studies both field instructors and students were included, providing different perspectives on the issue studied. However, none of the studies investigated matched pairs of student and field instructor. The great majority of the studies sampled either students or field instructors. Most samples were drawn from one school of social work; only three studies were national surveys of field directors. Only one of the studies indicated that the researchers had received approval from an institutional research ethics review board. It is strongly recommended that researchers seek and report on ethics review for their studies.

In the 10 qualitative studies the samples were all purposeful, consistent with qualitative sampling procedures. Studies sampled either field instructors or students or graduates. Only one study sampled all the participants in a field setting, but this was a study of one case. Surprisingly only 5 of the 10 studies indicated that they had obtained ethics approval from an institutional review board.

Of the 40 studies reviewed, 25 used quantitative methodology mainly survey research, 10 used qualitative methodology, and five used a mixed methods approach. The quantitative studies most often administered a survey instrument such as a questionnaire or a tool. In studies that administered a tool, only 10 reported reliability and validity of the measure and 13 did not. One study utilized secondary data analysis of existing data. Two of the studies were comparative investigations; one compared anxiety levels of traditional and non-traditional students (Zosky et al., 2003) and one compared students who were identified as having difficulties in the field with those who were not identified (Regehr et al., 2002). Four studies evaluated field instructor training.

The preferred method of data collection in the ten qualitative studies was an individual semi-structured, guided interview with two studies using focus groups. Data in all ten studies were audio-recorded and transcribed. In all but one study, data analysis procedures were described and transparent. Most studies coded the data and highlighted important themes. These studies overwhelmingly used rich description of the data as their method of data validation; in only one study was researcher bias discussed. The qualitative studies were sound methodologically and reflected trustworthiness and transparency in reporting the methodology.

There were five mixed method studies. The samples were purposeful with relatively small samples (< 100). Similar to the other studies, no matched pairs of student and field instructor were investigated. Rather, samples consisted of students or field instructors or field liaisons. A combination of methods was used, such as in depth qualitative interviews, student process recordings, and student performance ratings or both telephone and in-person interviews as well as a questionnaire, or survey followed by a focus group. Future studies could benefit from the use of these multiple perspectives.

This review of research in field education published in the last five years reveals the existence of a number of studies. Appropriate caution must be used in generalizing from the conclusions drawn due to the limits of the research designs; small samples; scales that have not established reliability and validity; reliance on survey and exploratory methods; and use of satisfaction as the sole outcome measure.

Future studies are needed that will systematically test new models and compare existing approaches to field education through the use of controlled and/or comparison studies. Studies should aim to include larger samples and matched pairs of students and field instructors. Studies originating in one school should be replicated in other locales to determine similarities and differences based on a variety of educational institutions with different student bodies and field educators. Studies would also be strengthened through establishing the reliability and validity of tools used. Furthermore, the development of a pool of instruments would increase comparability of findings between studies, assisting in the development of a tested knowledge base. Finally, education researchers are challenged to continue working on the development of a range of meaningful outcome measures to assess student learning and competence pre- and post-field experiences. Currently the majority of studies are largely reliant on student satisfaction and perception of quality field learning experiences as outcome measures. Ultimately, it is the ability of students to successfully intervene with clients that is considered an indicator of learning and progress. Since many instruments exist to assess client progress, researchers may also consider including some client change variables as outcome measures.

CONCLUSIONS

From this review, it appears that an empirically based body of knowledge about field education is emerging. Studies have investigated a wide range of topics: contextual factors regarding universities, agencies, and field instructors; student characteristics and needs; models, processes, and techniques of field education; assessment of educational outcomes; and training field instructors. Theoretically grounded general principles and processes of field instruction are articulated and receiving some support across a number of studies. Ideally, social work education programs are concerned with finding evidence to guide them in offering the most effective teaching approaches. The existing empirical work in field education provides many interesting and promising ideas for future development.

If field education is to emanate from an empirical base education, researchers will need to pursue systematic theory building about teaching and learning in the field, and develop and test models of field instruction. The aim is to articulate and disseminate field educational practices that produce meaningful outcomes in student learning and competence. Systematic and continuous programs of research are to be encouraged so that a deepening of scholarly work in this area can flourish. Success will depend on the collaboration of research groups in advancing and testing models and in schools' commitment to use resources to incorporate best practices into their programs.

NOTE

The aim of the review was to capture North American literature, though several studies within our search parameters were conducted in New Zealand, Australia, Hong Kong, and Israel and are included in this review. This review, however, does not comprehensively reflect the literature from any locale other than North America since social work and social work education journals from those regions were not systematically examined. Moreover, a considerable literature on "practice teaching" in the United Kingdom does exist but is not represented in this review as this term was not used in our search. Practice teaching is the term given to field education in the United Kingdom and sometimes in New Zealand. The final review includes 26 studies from USA, 9 studies from Canada, 1 study from Israel, 1 study from Australia, 1 study from New Zealand, and 1 study from Hong Kong, along with 1 study of schools in countries belonging to the International Association of Schools of Social Work.

The 40 articles were published in the following journals: *Journal of Social Work Education* (16), *The Clinical Supervisor* (10), *Journal of Teaching in Social Work* (9), *Health and Social Work* (2), *Social Work* (1), *International Social Work* (1), and *Social Work Education* (1).

REFERENCES

Abbott, A. A., & Lyter, S. C. (1998). The use of constructive criticism in field instruction. *The Clinical Supervisor, 17*(2), 43-57.

Abram, F. Y., Hartung, M. R., & Wernet, S. P. (2000). The non-MSW task supervisor, MSW field instructor, and the practicum student: A triad for high quality field education. *Journal of Teaching in Social Work, 20*(1/2), 171-185.

Alperin, D. E. (1996). Empirical research on student assessment in field education: What have we learned? *The Clinical Supervisor, 14*(1), 149-161.
Alperin, D. E. (1998). Factors related to student satisfaction with child welfare field placements. *Journal of Social Work Education, 34*(1), 43-54.
Armour, M. P., Bain, B., & Rubio, R. (2004). An evaluation study of diversity training for field instructors: A collaborative approach to enhancing cultural competence. *Journal of Social Work Education, 40*(1), 27-38.
Barlow, C., Rogers, G., & Coleman, H. (2003). Peer collaboration: A model for field instructor development and support. *The Clinical Supervisor, 22*(2), 173-190.
Bennett, L., & Coe, S. (1998). Social work field instructor satisfaction with faculty field liaisons. *Journal of Social Work Education, 14*(3), 345-352.
Bocage, M., Homonoff, E., & Riley, P. (1995). Measuring the impact of the current state and national fiscal crises on human service agencies and social work training. *Social Work, 40*(5), 701-705.
Bogo, M., & Globerman, J. (1999). Interorganizational relationships between schools of social work and field agencies: Testing a framework for analysis. *Journal of Social Work Education, 35*(2), 265-274.
Bogo, M., Globerman, J., & Sussman, T. (2004a). Field instructor competence in group supervision: Students' views. *Journal of Teaching in Social Work, 24*(1/2), 199-216.
Bogo, M., Globerman, J., & Sussman, T. (2004b). The field instructor as group worker: Managing trust and competition in group supervision. *Journal of Social Work Education, 40*(1), 13-26.
Bogo, M., Regehr, C., Hughes, J., Power, R., & Globerman, J. (2002). Evaluating a measure of student field performance in direct service: Testing reliability and validity of explicit criteria. *Journal of Social Work Education, 38*(3), 385-401.
Bogo, M., Regehr, C., Power, R., Hughes, J., Woodford, M., & Regehr, G. (2004). Toward new approaches for evaluating student field performance: Tapping the implicit criteria used by experienced field instructors. *Journal of Social Work Education, 40*(3), 417-426.
Borders, D. L. (1986). Facilitating supervisee growth: Implications of developmental models of counseling supervision. *Michigan Journal of Counseling and Development, 17*(2), 7-12.
Burke, S. G., Condon, S., & Wickell, B. (1999). The field liaison role in schools of social work: A break with the past. *The Clinical Supervisor, 18*(1), 203-210.
Choy, B.-K., Leung, A. Y. L., Tam, T. S. K., & Chu, C.-H. (1998). Roles and tasks of field instructors as perceived by Chinese social work students. *Journal of Teaching in Social Work, 16*(1/2), 115-132.
Cohen, C. S. (1998). Building field instructors' skills in planning and supervising group assignments. *Journal of Teaching in Social Work, 16*(1/2), 99-114.
Cohen, J. (1977). Selected constraints in the relationship between social work education and practice. *Journal of Education for Social Work, 13*(1), 3-7.
Cuzzi, L., Holden, G., Chernack, P., Rutter, S., & Rosenberg, G. (1997). Evaluating social work field instruction: Rotations versus year-long placements. *Research on Social Work Practice, 7*, 402-414.

Cuzzi, L., Holden, G., Rutter, S., Rosenberg, G., & Chernack, P. (1996). A pilot study of fieldwork rotations vs. year long placments for social work students in a public hospital. *Social Work in Health Care, 24*(1), 73-91.

Deal, K. H. (2000). The usefulness of developmental stage models for clinical social work students: An exploratory study. *The Clinical Supervisor, 19*(1), 1-19.

Donner, S. (1996). Field work crisis: Dilemmas, dangers, and opportunities. *Smith College Studies in Social Work, 66*, 317-331.

Educational Policy and Accreditation Standards. (2002). Council on Social Work Education. Alexandria, Virginia.

Euster, G. L. (1999). Gerontology field education experiences of graduate social work and gerontology certificate students. *Journal of Gerontological Social Work, 31*(3/4), 29-47.

Faria, F., Brownstein, C., & Smith, H. Y. (1988). A survey of field instructors' perceptions of the liaison role. *Journal of Social Work Education, 24*, 135-144.

Fortune, A. E., & Abramson, J. S. (1993). Predictors of satisfaction with field practicum among social work students. *The Clinical Supervisor, 11*(1), 95-110.

Fortune, A. E., Feathers, C. E., Rook, S. R., Scrimenti, R. M., Smollen, P., Stemerman, P., & Tucker, E. L. (1985). Student satisfaction with field placement. *Journal of Social Work Education, 21*(3), 92-104.

Fortune, A. E., & Kaye, L. (2002). Learning opportunities in field practica: Identifying skills and activities associated with MSW students' self-evaluation of performance and satisfaction. *The Clinical Supervisor, 21*(1), 5-28.

Fortune, A. E., McCarthy, M., & Abramson, J. S. (2001). Student learning processes in field education: Relationship of learning activities to quality of field instruction, satisfaction, and performance among MSW students. *Journal of Social Work Education, 37*(1), 111-124.

Fortune, A. E., Miller, J., Rosenblum, A. F., Sanchez, B. M., Smith, C., & Reid, W. J. (1995). Further explorations of the liaison role: A view from the field. In G. Rogers (Ed.), *Social work field education: Views and visions*. Dubuque, Iowa: Kendall/Hunt.

Frumkin, M. (1980). Social work education and the professional commitment fallacy: A practical guide to field-school relations. *Journal of Education for Social Work, 16*(2), 91-99.

Geller, C. (1994). Group supervision as a vehicle for teaching group work to students: Field instruction in a senior center. *The Clinical Supervisor, 12*(1), 199-214.

Gelman, C. R. (2004). Anxiety experienced by foundation year MSW students entering field placement: Implications for admissions, curriculum, and field education. *Journal of Social Work Education, 40*(1), 39-54.

George, A. (1982). A history of social work field instruction. In B. W. Sheafor & L. E. Jenkins (Eds.), *Quality field instruction in social work* (pp. 37-59). New York: Longman, Inc.

Giddings, M. M., Vodde, R., & Cleveland, P. (2003). Examining student-field instructor problems in practicum: Beyond student satisfaction measures. *The Clinical Supervisor, 22*(2), 191-214.

Gillis, H., & Lewis, J. S. (2004). Addressing the issue of psychiatric disability in social work interns: The need for a problem-solving framework. *Journal of Social Work Education, 40*(3), 391-402.

Globerman, J., & Bogo, M. (2002). The impact of hospital restructuring on social work field education. *Health & Social Work, 27*(1), 7-16.

Globerman, J., & Bogo, M. (2003). Changing times: Understanding social workers' motivation to be field instructors. *Social Work, 48*(1), 65-73.

Heppner, P. P., & Roehlke, H. J. (1984). Differences among supervisees at different levels of training: Implications for a developmental model of supervision. *Journal of Counseling Psychology, 31*(1), 76-90.

Holden, G., Cuzzi, L. C., Rutter, S., Chernack, P., & Spitzer, W. (1997). The hosptial social work self-efficacy scale: A replication. *Research on Social Work Practice, 7*, 490-499.

Holden, G., Cuzzi, L. C., Rutter, S., Chernack, P., Spitzer, W., & Rosenberg, G. (1997). The hospital social work self-efficacy scale: A partial replication and extension. *Health and Social Work, 22*(4), 256-263.

Itzhaky, H., & Eliahou, A. (1999). Do students reflect their field instructors? The relationship between supervisory and learning styles in social work field instruction. *The Clinical Supervisor, 18*(1), 75-84.

Jarman-Rohde, L., McFall, J., Kolar, P., & Strom, G. (1997). The changing context of social work practice: Implications and recommendations for social work educators. *Journal of Social Work Education, 33*(1), 29-46.

Kadushin, A. E. (1991). Introduction. In D. Schneck, B. Grossman & U. Glassman (Eds.), *Field education in social work: Contemporary issues and trends* (pp. 11-12). Dubuque Iowa: Kendall/Hunt.

Kilpatrick, A. C., Turner, J., & Holland, T. P. (1994). Quality control in field education: Monitoring students' performance. *Journal of teaching in Social Work, 9*(1/2), 107-120.

Knight, C. (2000). Engaging the student in the field instruction relationship: BSW and MSW students' views. *Journal of Teaching in Social Work, 20*(3/4), 173-201.

Knight, C. (2001). The process of field instruction: BSW and MSW students' views of effective field supervision. *Journal of Social Work Education, 37*(2), 357-379.

Koroloff, N. M., & Rhyne, C. (1989). Assessing student performance in field instruction. *Journal of Teaching in Social Work, 3*, 3-16.

Long, D. D., & Heydt, M. J. (2000). Qualitative analysis of a BSW field placement with a hospital-owned physician practice in a skilled nursing facility. *Health & Social Work, 25*(3), 210-218.

Maidment, J. (2000). Methods used to teach social work students in the field: A research report from New Zealand. *Social Work Education, 19*(2), 145-154.

McChesney, M.-L., & Euster, G. L. (2000). Evaluation of an active learning teaching method for field instructor training. *Journal of Teaching in Social Work, 20*(1/2), 201-215.

McFall, J. P., & Freddolino, P. P. (2000). Quality and comparability in distance field education: Lessons learned from comparing three program sites. *Journal of Social Work Education, 36*(2), 293-307.

Messinger, L. (2004). Out in the field: Gay and lesbian social work students' experiences in field placement. *Journal of Social Work Education*, *40*(2), 187-204.

O'Hare, T., Collins, P., & Walsh, T. (1998). Validation of the practice skills inventory with experienced clinical social workers. *Research on Social Work Practice*, *8*, 552-563.

Panos, P. T., Pettys, G. L., Cox, S. E., & Jones-Hart, E. (2004). Survey of international field education placements of accredited social work education programs. *Journal of Social Work Education*, *40*(3), 467-478.

Rai, G. S. (2004). International fieldwork experience: A survey of US schools. *International Social Work*, *47*(2), 213-226.

Raschick, M., Maypole, D. E., & Day, P. A. (1998). Improving field education through Kolb learning theory. *Journal of Social Work Education*, *34*(1), 31-42.

Raskin, M. (1989). Factors associated with student satisfaction in undergraduate social work field placements. In M. Raskin (Ed.), *Empirical studies in field instruction* (pp. 321-335). New York: The Haworth Press, Inc.

Raskin, M. (1994). The delphi study in field instruction revisited: Expert consensus on issues and research priorities. *Journal of Social Work Education*, *30*(1), 75-88.

Raskin, M. S. (1983). A Delphi study in field instruction: Identification of issues and research priorities by experts. *Arete*, *8*(2), 38-48.

Raskin, M. S., & Blome, W. W. (1998). The impact of managed care on field instruction. *Journal of Social Work Education*, *34*(3), 365-374.

Regehr, C., Regehr, G., Leeson, J., & Fusco, L. (2002). Setting priorities for learning in the field practicum: A comparative study of students and field instructors. *Journal of Social Work Education*, *38*(1), 55-65.

Rosenblum, A. F., & Raphael, F. B. (1983). The role and function of the faculty field liaison. *Journal of Education for Social Work*, *19*(1), 67-73.

Saari, C. (1989). The process of learning in clinical social work. *Smith College Studies in Social Work*, *60*, 35-49.

Skolnik, L., Wayne, J., & Raskin, M. S. (1999). A worldwide view of field education structures and curricula. *International Social Work*, *42*(4), 471-483.

Strozier, A. L., Barnett-Queen, T., & Bennett, C. K. (2000). Supervision: Critical process and outcome variables. *The Clinical Supervisor*, *19*(1), 21-39.

Tebb, S., Manning, D. W., & Klaumann, T. K. (1996). A renaissance of group supervision. *The Clinical Supervisor*, *14*(2), 39-51.

Tolson, E. R., & Kopp, J. (1988). The practicum: Clients, problems, interventions and influences on student practice. *Journal of Social Work Education*, *24*(2), 123-134.

Tropman, E. J. (1980). Agency constraints affecting links between practice and education. *Journal of Education for Social Work*, *13*(1), 8-14.

Unger, J. M. (2003). Supporting agency field instructors in Forgotonia: Challenges faced by rural BSW programs. *Journal of Teaching in Social Work*, *23*(1/2), 105-121.

Urdang, E. (1999). Becoming a field instructor: A key experience in professional development. *The Clinical Supervisor*, *18*(1), 85-103.

Vourlekis, B., Bembry, J., Hall, G., & Rosenblum, P. (1996). Testing the reliability and validity of an interviewing skills evaluation tool for use in practicum. *Research on Social Work Practice*, *6*, 492-503.

Walter, C. A., & Young, T. M. (1999). Combining individual and group supervision in educating for the social work profession. *The Clinical Supervisor*, *18*(2), 73-89.

Wayne, J., Bogo, M., & Raskin, M. (2006). Thinking out of the box: The need for radical change in field education. *Journal of Social Work Education*, *42*(1), 161-169.

Wilson, S. J. (1981). *Field instruction: Techniques for supervision.* New York: Macmillan.

Zosky, D. L., Unger, J. M., White, K., & Mills, S. J. (2003). Non-Traditional and traditional social work students: Perceptions of field instructors. *Journal of Teaching in Social Work*, *23*(3/4), 185-201.

doi:10.1300/J001v24n01_09

Index